THE ILLUSTRATED DIRECTORY OF

Popular
FLOWERING
PLANTS

THE ILLUSTRATED DIRECTORY OF

Popular
FLOWERING
PLANTS

PROFESSOR MARSHALL CRAIGMYLE

CHARTWELL
BOOKS, INC.

A Salamander Book

Published by
CHARTWELL BOOKS, INC.
A Division of **BOOK SALES, INC.**
114 Northfield Avenue
Edison, New Jersey 08837

©Salamander Books 2002
A member of Chrysalis Books plc

ISBN 0-7858-1621-6

All rights reserved. No part of this book may be reproduced, stored in a retrieval system or transmitted in any form or by any means, electronic, mechanical, photocopying, recording, or otherwise, without the prior permission of Salamander Books Ltd.

Designed, edited, and produced by:
Hilton/Sadler

Reproduction: Anorax Imaging, England

Printed in Slovenia

Acknowledgements

I am indebted to Samuel Dobie and Son, Seedsmen, Long Road, Paignton, Devon for allowing me to photograph their Trial Grounds.
I owe a huge debt of gratitude to the staff of Salamander Books, and to Ms Charlotte Davies in particular, for all their help.
I have to thank Ms Madeline Weston, of Norwich, for reading and correcting the proofs.
Finally, I also owe my wife a great debt of gratitude for tolerating being alone on many long winter evenings when I was in the next room on my computer, and for her constant help, advice, and encouragement.

CONTENTS

Introduction
6 – 13

SECTION ONE
Perennials
14 – 213

SECTION TWO
Shrubs
214 – 321

SECTION THREE
Annuals
322 – 357

Appendices
358 – 360

Bibliography
361

Index
362 – 368

INTRODUCTION

I suspect that I am like most gardeners in that I look for a long display of flower color when it comes to deciding which plants to include in my garden, and so for this reason I tend to avoid those plants that do not bloom for very long, unless they have some other positive attributes, such as good foliage color or interesting leaf shapes. As examples of plants with short flowering periods, Caucasian peony (*Paeonia mlokosewitschii*) and Quamash (*Camassia quamash*) are both extremely attractive specimens but they have a flowering season of less than a week. Many Irises have the same brief flowering period and so for 360 days of the year they add little in the way of visual interest to the garden. Information on the length of flowering times is therefore much needed but can be difficult to come by, which is why I decided to present my long-flowering favorites in this book.

In the pages that follow I offer a selection of plants chosen for the length of their flowering seasons, which can range from anything from several weeks to several months, or even all year around in some instances. The information is arranged in three sections: Perennials; Shrubs; and Annuals. All three categories are made up of long-flowering plants, so whatever conditions prevail in your garden, you can choose plants confident in the knowledge that they will offer a long display.

The gardening enthusiast who enjoys a blaze of flower color in summer can plant out annuals or other bedding plants, but this may result in empty, uninteresting beds over the winter months, unless the beds are planted in autumn again with hardy spring-flowering plants, such as Sweet William, Wallflowers, or Primulas. In addition to being hard work, this method of gardening also gives disappointing results in winter.

Many gardeners living busy, active lives will favor planting methods that are less labor-intensive than this. The answer could be choosing plants that are perennials and shrubs, both types of which have many evergreen members and require less work than relying on annuals. A garden with a large percentage of evergreens is not bleak and bare in winter, and if the plants are chosen primarily for their long flowering times, they can still be long-blooming in summer. All long-flowering evergreen perennials and shrubs are listed in the Appendices section (*see page 358*).

INTRODUCTION

Cobaea scandens

The Appendices section features plants that have been grouped according to shared characteristics to make choosing the right plants even easier. It lists long-flowering plants that are allergenic, those that are low-allergen, poisonous plants, and drought-tolerant plants for readers who garden in dry regions. I hope you find the right ones for your garden.

Marshall Craigmyle

INTRODUCTION

Gazania 'Daybreak' series A.G.M.

INTRODUCTION

More than 700 plants are featured in this book. Each entry is illustrated with a color picture of the plant *in situ* and the following information is given for every one:

1) Scientific name, family, and common name and category, such as biennial or shrub
2) Maximum height in imperial and metric measurements
3) Maximum spread in imperial and metric measurements
4) Aspect preferred
5) Soil type required
6) Hardiness zone (rating)
7) Propagation method(s)
8) The attributes of the plant, the nature of the flower, and the inflorescence (*see pp. 10–11*) and its flowering season
10) For shrubs, a pruning regime

The Royal Horticultural Society in the UK carries out extensive trials of all categories of plants and the accolade of the Award of Garden Merit is given to the most outstanding plants. Any plant that has the Award of Garden Merit will have the letters A.G.M. after its name.

The positive attributes and drawbacks of each plant will be given, as listed here:

Attributes
- Aromatic foliage
- Attracts bees
- Attracts butterflies
- Can be dried
- Drought-tolerant
- Evergreen
- Good cut flower
- Handsome foliage
- Low allergen
- Scented flowers

Drawbacks
- Attracts slugs
- Divide regularly
- High allergen
- Invasive
- Must deadhead
- Must not be moved
- Poisonous
- Prone to mildew
- Requires space
- Requires staking
- Seeds everywhere
- Short-lived
- Skin irritant

INTRODUCTION

LEAF AND FLOWER SHAPES

Both leaf and flower shapes can be highly variable, as you can see in the picture examples here (*right*) and in the summary chart (*below*). Plants that offer both good flower color and a long flowering season, as well as foliage that complements the blooms and maintains garden interest in the non-flowering season, are ideally what you want in a garden setting.

Gypsophila repens 'Dorothy Teacher'

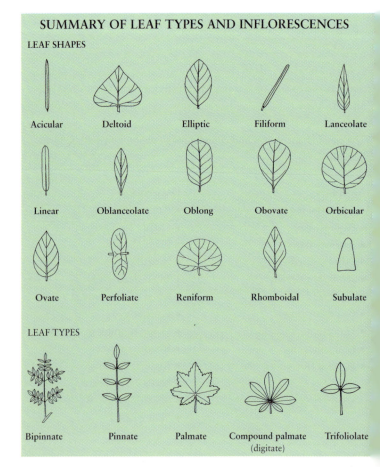

INTRODUCTION

Convolvulus tricolor 'Royal Ensign'

INFLORESCENCES

Umbel
Flattish flower head with stalks from the same point.

Panicle
Raceme that is made up of a number of smaller racemes.

Raceme
Narrow flower head with lowest buds opening first.

Spike
Similar to a raceme but the flowers are without stalks.

Cyme
Convex inflorescence with inner flowers opening first.

Corymb
Dome-shaped or flat flower head in which the outer flowers open first.

INTRODUCTION

HARDINESS ZONES

The first consideration when choosing a perennial to be grown in the garden all year round is whether it is hardy in your area. The United States Department of Agriculture (USDA) has developed a system of temperature zones as a basis for assessing which plants can be grown in different areas. The zones are based on the annual average minimum temperature in an area, and are illustrated on the maps opposite and below of North America, Australia, New Zealand, South Africa, and Europe. The maps have been divided into the USDA climatic zones, numbered from Zone 1, the coldest, with a winter minimum of -50°F (-45°C), up to Zone 11, the warmest, with a minimum of +40°F (+5°C). Every entry in the directory section of this book cites the plant's hardiness zone. To establish whether a perennial will be hardy in your garden, refer to the map of hardiness zones and find the rating for your area. Any plant with a zonal rating equal to or lower than the rating for your

Minimum winter temperature
Zone 1: Below -50° F (Below -45° C)
Zone 2: -50 to -35° F (-45 to -37° C)
Zone 3: -35 to -20° F (-37 to -29° C)
Zone 4: -20 to -10° F (-29 to -23° C)
Zone 5: -10 to -5° F (-23 to -21° C)
Zone 6: -5 to 5° F (-21 to -15° C)
Zone 7: 5 to 10° F (-15 to -12° C)
Zone 8: 10 to 20° F (-12 to -7° C)
Zone 9: 20 to 30° F (-7 to -1° C)
Zone 10: 30 to 40° F (-1 to 4° C)
Zone 11: Above +40° F (Above +5° C)

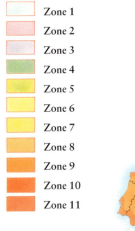

Western Europe

area will be hardy in your garden. Thus, if your area is rated Zone 7, all plants graded from Zone 1 to Zone 7 will survive and flower and plants graded Zone 8 to Zone 11 will not. However; Zone 8 plants may be grown outside provided they are given protection in the form of a deep mulch of bracken or leaves, a pane of glass, or a cloche, all of which keep the plants dry and help them substantially in surviving the winter. Zone 9 to Zone 11 plants can be grown out of doors in summer in a Zone 7 area, but will have to be lifted and kept under glass in winter or, alternatively, grown in containers and brought into a conservatory or greenhouse over winter.

Another consideration is that every garden has a number of microclimates – that is, some parts of the garden are warmer than others. It may be that the zonal rating for your area does not apply to all of your garden. So if your garden is rated Zone 7, the warmest corner, such as at the foot of a sun-facing wall, may well be Zone 8. The only way to find out is to experiment by growing Zone 8-rated plants in that site.

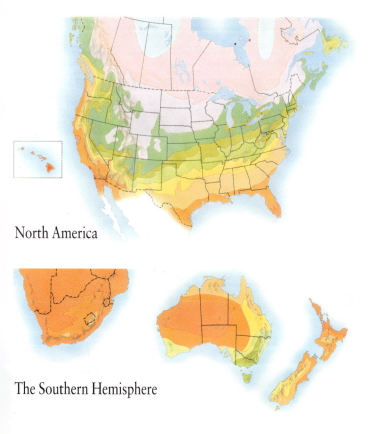

North America

The Southern Hemisphere

section one
Perennials

Perennials are non-woody plants that generally live for many years, given appropriate conditions. They may be evergreen but more commonly are herbaceous and die down to the ground in winter. Perennials are easy to cultivate, the most important requirement being good drainage. Those that are short-lived or require acid soil are highlighted in the text.

Perennials vary widely in their degree of hardiness, from being hardy in all climates to being tender and incapable of being grown as perennials in unfavorable climates. Fortunately the majority fall into the hardy category and come through winters without requiring any special treatment. Consult the Hardiness Zones section before investing in plants, to ensure you choose plants that are hardy in your particular garden.

In cold climates, tender perennials can be sustained through the winter by insulating them: cover the crown of the plant with a thick surface mulch of garden compost, cork bark, coconut shell, or newspaper. Or cover with a glass cloche.

If your garden is in Zone 7, for example, you can overwinter Zone 8 plants by protecting them in these ways; however some plants will succumb to winter damp in very wet climates and sharp drainage may also be required.

Very tender perennials have to be brought into warmth in winter; they can be grown in containers, or the plants themselves lifted and brought indoors. Many tender perennials are treated as annuals and discarded at the end of the growing season. Flowers that seed in their first season and can be bought as seedlings in early spring should be planted out when all danger of frost is past. The plants are then disposed of when they die in the autumn frosts.

It is advisable, unless seed is required, to deadhead all perennials since the plants then divert energy into building up next season's growth rather than into setting seed. Some perennials have a long flowering season only if they are deadheaded regularly, and these are indicated in the text.

ACANTHUS SPINOSUS A.G.M.

Acanthus spinosus A.G.M. (Acanthaceae)

Common name: None
Height: 5ft (1.5m)
Spread: 3ft (90cm)
Aspect: Sun or half shade
Soil: Fertile, deep, well-drained
Hardiness: Zone 6
Propagation: Seed in spring; division in spring or autumn
Flowering time: Late spring to midsummer

A clump-forming evergreen perennial. Leaves spiny, deeply-cut, dark green. Flowers in racemes, soft mauve, with purple bracts.

- Drought-tolerant
- Evergreen
- Handsome foliage
- Low allergen
- Invasive
- Prone to mildew
- Requires staking
- Seeds everywhere

Achillea 'Fanal' (Asteraceae)

Common name: None
Height: 30in (75cm)
Spread: 2ft (60cm)
Aspect: Sun
Soil: Humus-rich, fertile
Hardiness: Zone 2
Propagation: Division in spring
Flowering time: Early summer

A clump-forming hybrid, with linear, bipinnate gray-green leaves. Flowers in corymbs, bright red, fading with age, for several weeks.

- Good cut flower
- Handsome foliage
- Drought-tolerant
- Can be dried
- Prone to mildew
- Divide regularly
- High allergen

ACHILLEA (Asteraceae/Compositae)

Yarrow

A genus of only some 80 species from varied habitats in the temperate Northern Hemisphere. There are many garden hybrids. The daisy-like flowers are closely packed in tight corymbs; they lack ray petals, having only disc florets. They come in a wide range of colours and attract bees and burtterflies. The foliage is feathery (except for *A. ptarmica*) and contact with it may cause skin irritation. The flowering season is long, and the flowers are good for drying and cutting. They do best in full sun in moisture-retentive soil, but with good drainage. They are prone to powdery mildew, and may require staking. Most are well-behaved, but *AA. millefolium* and *ptarmica* are invasive. They may die out in the center, so are best lifted and divided every few years. All are drought-tolerant.

Achillea filipendulina 'Cloth of Gold' A.G.M. (Asteraceae)

Common name: Yarrow
Height: 5ft (1.5m)
Spread: 18in (45cm)
Aspect: Sun
Soil: Moist, well-drained
Hardiness: Zone 3
Propagation: Division in spring
Flowering time: Early summer to early autumn

An evergreen perennial with rosettes of light green leaves. Flowers in flat corymbs, deep yellow-gold, borne on strong stems.

- Good cut flower
- Can be dried
- Handsome foliage
- Evergreen
- Drought-tolerant
- High allergen
- Prone to mildew
- Divide regularly

Achillea 'Hoffnung' (Asteraceae)

Common name: None
Height: 30in (7cm)
Spread: 2ft (6cm)
Aspect: Sun
Soil: Humus-rich, fertile
Hardiness: Zone 6
Propagation: Division in spring
Flowering time: Several weeks in summer

A very compact, clump-forming plant, with linear, bipinnate, leaves of mid-green. Flowers in corymbs, cream, fading to sand-colored.

- Good cut flower
- Can be dried
- Attractive foliage
- Drought-tolerant
- Divide regularly
- Prone to mildew
- High allergen

Achillea 'Terracotta' (Asteraceae)

Common name: None
Height: 30in (75cm)
Spread: 2ft (60cm)
Aspect: Sun
Soil: Humus-rich, fertile
Propagation: Division in spring
Flowering time: Several weeks in summer

A compact, clump-forming perennial with ferny, bipinnate leaves. Flowers in corymbs, terracotta in color.

- Good cut flower
- Can be dried
- Handsome foliage
- Drought-tolerant
- Divide regularly
- Prone to mildew
- High allergen

Achimenes hybrida (Gesneriaceae)

Common name: Cupid's bower, Hot water plant
Height: 18in (45cm)
Spread: 1ft (30cm)
Aspect: Sun, except midday
Soil: Moist, well-drained, humus-rich, fertile
Hardiness: Zone 10
Propagation: Division in spring
Flowering time: Summer to autumn

A winter-dormant rhizomatous perennial from Central America. Leaves ovate, dark green, with red undersides, hairy, fleshy. Flowers salveri-form, borne in cymes, in pairs or singly, in a wide color range. Prone to aphids.

- Handsome foliage

Aeonium cuneatum (Crassulaceae)

Common name: None
Height: 6ft (2m)
Spread: 2ft (60cm)
Aspect: Half shade
Hardiness: Zone 9
Propagation: Seed in warmth in spring; rosette cuttings in early summer
Flowering time: Spring and early summer

A showy, evergreen, rosetted succulent. Spike-like panicles of yellow flowers.

- Handsome foliage
- Evergreen

**Ajuga reptans 'Purple Brocade'
(Lamiaceae)**

Common name: None
Height: 6in (15cm)
Spread: To 3ft (90cm)
Aspect: Half shade, no midday sun
Soil: Moist or humus-rich
Propagation: Separation of rooted stems in spring
Flowering time: Spring and early summer; again in autumn

A rhizomatous, creeping, ground-covering perennial. Leaves are spoon-shaped, mid-green; flowers clear blue.

- Evergreen
- Attracts butterflies
- Low allergen
- Handsome foliage
- Seeds everywhere

**Alcea rosea 'Chater's Double' group
(Malvaceae)**

Common name: Hollyhock
Height: 8ft (2.5m)
Spread: 2ft (60cm)
Aspect: Sun
Soil: Well-drained, fertile
Hardiness: Zone 3
Propagation: Seed, *in situ*, in summer
Flowering time: All summer

Very popular short-lived garden perennial. Leaves rounded, green, hairy. Flowers fully double in many shades. Requires staking. Hollyhock rust can be a problem: rust-proof strains are available.

- Attracts bees
- Low allergen
- Attracts slugs
- Requires staking
- Seeds everywhere
- Short-lived

Alchemilla mollis A.G.M.
(Rosaceae)

Common name: Bear's-breech
Height: 2ft (60cm)
Spread: Almost indefinite
Aspect: Any
Soil: Any
Hardiness: Zone 3
Propagation: Seed in spring
Flowering time: All summer

A very common perennial. Leaves round, lobed, toothed, softly hairy, pale green. Flowers in small, greeny-yellow cymes.

- Drought-tolerant
- Good cut flower
- Handsome foliage
- Seeds everywhere

Alonsoa warzcewiczii A.G.M.
(Scrophulariaceae)

Common name: Heartleaf maskflower
Height: 2ft (60cm)
Spread: 1ft (30cm)
Aspect: Sun
Soil: Well-drained
Hardiness: Zone 10
Propagation: Seed, in warmth, in spring or autumn
Flowering time: All summer

A red-stemmed perennial sub-shrub from Peru. Leaves ovate/lance, dark green. Flowers scarlet or white, spurred, in racemes. Best treated as an annual in cold climes.

- Good cut flower

ALSTROEMERIA (*Alstroemeriaceae*)
Alstroemeria

A genus of about 50 species of herbaceous perennials from mountains and grasslands of South America. They are tuberous-rooted, and clump up fairly rapidly; some members are invasive to a degree. The tubers are very friable and must be handled with care. Once planted about 8in (20cm) deep they should be left undisturbed. The foliage is linear/lance-shaped, green or gray-green in color, and may cause skin irritation. The flowers are 6-petaled funnels, borne in terminal 3- to 7-rayed umbels, on upright stems, and are ideal for cutting and universally handsome. The degree of hardiness varies from Zone 7 to Zone 9. A number of recently introduced hybrids are protected from being propagated without permission of the owner of the breeders' rights, and are marked PBR in the text. One such is the 'Princess' strain, which is dwarf and flowers all summer and autumn. Many of the other garden hybrids have a rather shorter flowering season. A list of hybrids not illustrated, but awarded the A.G.M. is given (*see p. 24*).

ALSTROEMERIA 'ENDLESS LOVE'

Alstroemeria aurea
(Alstroemeriaceae)

Common name: None
Height: 3ft (90cm)
Spread: 18in (45cm)
Aspect: Sun or light shade
Soil: Well-drained, moist, fertile
Hardiness: Zone 7
Propagation: Seed when ripe; division in spring or autumn
Flowering time: Summer

Tuberous. Leaves linear, mid-green. Flowers in terminal 3–7-rayed umbels, yellow-orange.

- Attracts bees
- Good cut flower
- Attracts slugs
- High allergen
- Invasive

Alstroemeria 'Endless Love' (PBR)
(Alstroemeriaceae)

Common name: None
Height: 1ft (30cm)
Spread: 18in (45cm)
Aspect: Sun or light shade
Soil: Well-drained, moist, fertile
Hardiness: Zone 7
Propagation: Division in spring or autumn

Flowering time: All summer and into autumn

Recent hybrid dwarf strain. Tuberous. Leaves linear/lance, mid-green. Flowers in terminal racemes, pink, purple spot.

- Attracts bees
- Good cut flower
- Attracts slugs
- High allergen
- Invasive

PERENNIALS

Alstroemeria ligtu **hybrids A.G.M.**
(Alstroemeriaceae)

Common name: None
Height: 3ft (90cm)
Spread: 18in (45cm)
Aspect: Sun or light shade
Soil: Moist, fertile, well-drained
Hardiness: Zone 7
Propagation: Seed when ripe; division in spring or autumn
Flowering time: All summer

Vigorous hybrids. Tuberous. Floppy unless staked. A wide range of colors from white through yellow, and orange to red.

- 🟢 Attracts bees
- 🟢 Good cut flower
- 🔴 Attracts slugs
- 🔴 High allergen
- 🔵 Invasive
- 🔴 Must not be moved

Alstroemeria **'Pink Dream' (PBR)**
(Alstroemeriaceae)

Common name: None
Height: 1ft (30cm)
Spread: 18in (45cm)
Aspect: Sun, or light shade
Soil: Well-drained, fertile, moisture-retaining
Hardiness: Zone 8
Propagation: Division in spring or autumn
Flowering time: All summer and autumn

A recent dwarf hybrid. Tuberous. Flowers flesh-colored, with a prominent pink blotch and yellow throat.

- 🟢 Attracts bees
- 🟢 Good cut flower
- 🔴 Attracts slugs
- 🔴 High allergen
- 🔴 Must not be moved

Alstroemeria 'Princess Paola'®
(Alstroemeriaceae)

Common name: None
Height: 1ft (30cm)
Spread: 18in (45cm)
Aspect: Sun or very light shade
Soil: Well-drained, moisture-retentive
Hardiness: Zone 7
Propagation: Division in spring or autumn
Flowering time: All summer and autumn

A member of the highly floriferous and extremely long-flowering 'Princess'® strain. Very choice, as are all this strain. May not be propagated without permission.

- Attracts bees
- Good cut flower
- Attracts slugs
- High allergen
- Must not be moved

Alstroemeria psittacina
(Alstroemeriaceae)

Common name: None
Height: 3ft (90cm)
Spread: 18in (45cm)
Aspect: Sun or light shade
Soil: Fertile, moisture-retentive, fertile
Hardiness: Zone 8
Propagation: Seed when ripe; division in spring or autumn
Flowering time: All summer

A species from Brazil. Stems spotted mauve. Flowers in umbels, green, overlaid dark red. Of interest, but not as spectacular as the hybrids.

- Attracts bees
- Good cut flower
- Attracts slugs
- High allergen
- Must not be moved

Alstroemeria 'Sunburst' (PBR)
(Alstroemeriaceae)

Common name: None
Height: 1ft (30cm)
Spread: 18in (45cm)
Aspect: Sun or light shade
Soil: Fertile, moisture-retentive, well-drained
Hardiness: Zone 8
Propagation: Division in spring or autumn
Flowering time: All summer, into autumn

Another very recent dwarf hybrid, with a new color break of rich plum purple. Tuberous. Very floriferous all summer and on into the autumn. Choice.

- Attracts bees
- Good cut flower
- Attracts slugs
- High allergen
- Must not be moved

Alstroemeria 'Sunny Rebecca' (PBR)
(Alstroemeriaceae)

Common name: None
Height: 1ft (30cm)
Spread: 18in (45cm)
Aspect: Sun or light shade
Soil: Fertile, moisture-retentive, well-drained
Hardiness: Zone 8
Propagation: Division in spring or autumn
Flowering time: All summer and autumn

Another very recent dwarf hybrid. Tuberous. Handsome flowers of cream, blotched red, in cymes.

- Attracts bees
- Good cut flower
- Attracts slugs
- High allergen
- Must not be moved

Other Alstroemerias awarded the A.G.M. of the Royal Horticultural Society

'Apollo'
'Coronet'
'Friendship'
'H.R.H. Princess Alexandra'
'H.R.H Princess Alice' (PBR)
'Orange Gem'
'Orange Glory'
'Princess Carmina' ®

'Princess Caroline' ®
'Princess Grace' ® (PBR)
'Princess Juliana' ®
'Princess Mira' ® (PBR)
'Solent Crest'
'Solent Rose'
'Yellow Friendship'

ALSTROEMERIA 'XANDRA'

Alstroemeria 'Sweet Love' (PBR)
(Alstroemeriaceae)

Common Name: None
Height: 1ft (30cm)
Spread: 18in (45cm)
Aspect: Sun or light shade
Soil: Well-drained, moisture-retentive, fertile
Hardiness: Zone 8
Propagation: Division in spring or autumn
Flowering time: All summer

A recent dwarf hybrid with very handsome flowers of a rich dark pink.

- Attracts bees
- Good cut flower
- Attracts slugs
- High allergen
- Must not be moved

Alstroemeria 'Xandra' (PBR)
(Alstroemeriaceae)

Common name: None
Height: 1ft (30cm)
Spread: 18in (45cm)
Aspect: Sun or light shade
Soil: Well-drained, moisture-retentive
Hardiness: Zone 8
Propagation: Division in spring or autumn, should permission have been given

Flowering time: All summer, into autumn

A recent new dwarf hybrid with flowers of a striking orange, and with a yellow throat.

- Attracts bees
- Good cut flower
- Attracts slugs
- High allergen
- Must not be moved

PERENNIALS

Althaea officinalis (Malvaceae)

Common name: Marshmallow
Height: 6ft (2m)
Spread: 30in (75cm)
Aspect: Prefers sun, but will grow in shade
Soil: Moist, fertile
Hardiness: Zone 3
Propagation: Seed, when ripe
Flowering time: Midsummer to early autumn

A tall European native plant with oval, lobed, toothed, softly hairy, mid-green leaves. Pale pink flowers open in terminal and axillarry clusters from midsummer onwards.

- Requires staking

Anchusa azurea 'Dropmore' (Boraginaceae)

Common name: Alkanet
Height: 6ft (1.8m)
Spread: 2ft (60cm)
Aspect: Full sun
Soil: Well-drained, humus-rich, fertile
Hardiness: Zone 3
Propagation: Basal cuttings in spring; root cuttings in winter
Flowering time: Early summer

An erect, clump-forming perennial. Leaves are mostly basal, lance/elliptic, stiffly hairy, mid-green. Purple-blue profuse flowers in branching panicles for several weeks.

- Good cut flower
- Attracts bees
- Low allergen
- Requires staking
- Short-lived
- Prone to mildew

Anchusa azurea 'Feltham Pride' (Boraginaceae)

Common name: Alkanet
Height: 3ft (90cm)
Spread: 2ft (60cm)
Aspect: Full sun
Soil: Humus-rich, well-drained
Hardiness: Zone 3
Propagation: Basal cuttings in spring; root cuttings in winter
Flowering time: Early summer

A compact, short-lived perennial. Leaves linear/lance-shaped, mid-green. Flowers clear blue. May be raised from seed and treated as a biennial.

- Good cut flower
- Attracts bees
- Low allergen
- Short-lived
- Prone to mildew

Anchusa azurea 'Opal'
(Boraginaceae)

Common name: Alkanet
Height: 3ft (90cm)
Spread: 2ft (60cm)
Aspect: Full sun
Soil: Humus-rich, well-drained, fertile
Hardiness: Zone 3
Propagation: Basal cuttings in spring; root cuttings in winter
Flowering time: Early summer

An upright short-lived perennial. Leaves ovate/linear, mid-green; pale blue flowers in tall branching panicles.

- Good cut flower
- Attracts bees
- Low allergen
- Requires staking
- Short-lived
- Prone to mildew

Anemone hupehensis var. *japonica* 'Prinz Heinrich' A.G.M.
(Ranunculaceae)

Common name: Dwarf Japanese anemone
Height: 3ft (90cm)
Spread: 16in (40cm)
Aspect: Sun or half shade
Soil: Humus-rich, fertile, moist
Hardiness: Zone 6
Propagation: Division in spring or autumn
Flowering time: Mid and late summer

A fibrous-rooted, suckering hybrid. Leaves basal, oval, tripalmate, deep green. Flowers in umbels, petals dark pink.

- Attracts bees
- Good cut flower
- Attracts slugs
- Invasive
- Prone to mildew
- Skin irritant

ANEMONE (Ranunculaceae)

Anemone

This is a large genus made up of some 120 species, from a diverse range of habitats in both hemispheres, and, in addition, many hybrids exist. They may be spring-, summer-, or autumn-flowering plants, and only the last group is long-flowering; they are fibrous-rooted, herbaceous, tall, and grow in open sites in the wild. Some sorts are poisonous and all are skin-irritant. They are also prone to powdery mildew and slugs damage.

Anemone x *hybrida* 'Andrea Atkinson' (Ranunculaceae)

Common name: Japanese anemone
Height: 4ft (1.2m)
Spread: Indefinite
Aspect: Sun or half shade
Soil: Moist, well-drained, humus-rich
Hardiness: Zone 6
Propagation: Division in spring or autumn
Flowering time: Late summer to autumn

A clone of a popular late-flowering perennial. Leaves tripalmate oval, mid-green. Flowers pink open saucers.

- Good cut flower
- Nice foliage
- Low allergen
- Skin irritant
- Invasive
- Must not be moved

Anemone x *hybrida* 'Honorine Jobert' A.G.M. (Ranunculaceae)

Common name: Japanese anemone
Height: 4ft (1.2m)
Spread: Indefinite
Aspect: Sun or half shade
Soil: Humus-rich, moist, well-drained
Hardiness: Zone 6
Propagation: Division in spring or autumn
Flowering time: Late summer

A vigorous, suckering hybrid. Leaves oval, tripalmate, toothed, mid-green. Flowers in umbels of up to 20, single, pure white saucers.

- Good cut flower
- Good foliage
- Low allergen
- Skin irritant
- Invasive
- Must not be moved

Anemone x *hybrida* 'Max Vogel' (Ranunculaceae)

Common name: Japanese anemone
Height: 4ft (1.2m)
Spread: Indefinite
Aspect: Sun or half shade
Soil: Humus-rich, moist, well-drained
Hardiness: Zone 6
Propagation: Division in spring or autumn
Flowering time: Late summer

Vigorous hybrid. Leaves tripalmate. Pale pink flowers in single umbels.

- Good cut flower
- Handsome foliage
- Low allergen
- Skin irritant
- Must not be moved
- Invasive

Anemone x *hybrida* 'Whirlwind'
(Ranunculaceae)

Common name: Japanese anemone
Height: 4ft (1.2m)
Spread: Indefinite
Aspect: Sun or half shade
Soil: Humus-rich, moist, well-drained
Hardiness: Zone 6
Propagation: Division in spring or autumn
Flowering time: Late summer to early autumn

A clone of Japanese anemone with umbels of semi-double white flowers with central whorled tepals.

- Good cut flower
- Handsome foliage
- Low allergen
- Skin irritant
- Invasive
- Must not be moved

Anemone multifida
(Ranunculaceae)

Common name: None
Height: 1ft (30cm)
Spread: 6in (15cm)
Aspect: Sun or half shade
Soil: Humus-rich, moist, well-drained
Hardiness: Zone 2
Propagation: Seed, when ripe
Flowering time: Late summer to early autumn

A vigorous, rhizomatous species from N. America. Leaves rounded, palmate, basal and stem. Flowers in umbels of 2–3 creamy-white saucers.

- Good cut flower
- Handsome foliage
- Attracts slugs
- Prone to mildew
- Skin irritant

ANTHEMIS (Asteraceae)
Anthemis

This is a genus made up of about 100 species from the Old World, Europe, and Eurasia in particular. They are extremely useful garden plants, being undemanding and long-flowering, and with handsome, aromatic foliage. Their main drawback is that they are generally short-lived; however, their useful garden life can be extended by shearing them over immediately after flowering in order to encourage fresh basal shoots, which will help the plant to over-winter. They do not transplant well, but benefit nevertheless from regular division in spring. The flowers are essentially daisy-like, and they may have yellow or white ray florets, and all have a yellow disc. Some types are good for cutting, and they are all drought-tolerant.

ANTHEMIS MARSCHALLIANA

Anthemis marschalliana ssp. ***biebersteiniana*** (Asteraceae)

Common name: None
Height: 18in (45cm)
Spread: 2ft (60cm)
Aspect: Full sun
Soil: Sharply-drained
Hardiness: Zone 7
Propagation: Seed or division in spring
Flowering time: Late spring to early summer

A mat-forming species originally from Turkey. Leaves obovate, bi-pinnatisect, gray, silky, aromatic. Yellow composite solitary flowers; leafy stems.

- 🟢 Aromatic foliage
- 🟢 Handsome foliage
- 🟢 Drought-tolerant
- 🔴 Attracts slugs
- 🔴 Short-lived
- 🔴 Must not be moved

Anthemis punctata ssp. ***cupaniana*** A.G.M. (Asteraceae)

Common name: Dog fennel
Height: 1ft (30cm)
Spread: 3ft (90cm)
Aspect: Full sun
Soil: Sharply-drained
Hardiness: Zone 6
Propagation: Seed, division, or basal cuttings in spring
Flowering time: Early to midsummer

A handsome evergreen from Italy, with aromatic, pinnatisect, silvery foliage. Flowers are composites, white, long-lasting.

- 🟢 Aromatic foliage
- 🟢 Drought-tolerant
- 🟢 Evergreen
- 🟢 Good cut flower
- 🟢 Handsome foliage
- 🔴 Attracts slugs
- 🔴 Must not be moved
- 🔴 Prone to mildew
- 🔴 Short-lived

Anthemis tinctoria (Asteraceae)

Common name: Ox-eye chamomile
Height: 3ft (90cm)
Spread: 3ft (90cm)
Aspect: Full sun
Soil: Sharply drained
Hardiness: Zone 6
Propagation: Seed or division in spring
Flowering time: Spring to late summer

A clump-forming perennial. Leaves basal, obovate, pinnatisect, mid-green above, downy-gray beneath. Solitary golden-yellow (or cream) flowers.

- Good cut flower
- Handsome foliage
- Drought-tolerant
- Aromatic foliage
- Short-lived
- Attracts slugs
- Prone to mildew
- Must not be moved

Anthemis tinctoria 'E.C. Buxton' (Asteraceae)

Common name: Golden marguerite, Ox-eye
Height: 28in (70cm)
Spread: 2ft (60cm)
Aspect: Full sun
Soil: Sharply-drained
Hardiness: Zone 6
Propagation: Division or basal cuttings in spring
Flowering time: From late spring

A handsome cultivar; yellow flowers.

- Aromatic foliage
- Evergreen
- Drought-tolerant
- Good cut flower
- Attracts slugs
- Prone to mildew
- Must not be moved
- Short-lived

Anthemis tinctoria 'Sauce Hollandaise' (Asteraceae)

Common name: Golden marguerite, Ox-eye
Height: 2ft (60cm)
Spread: 2ft (60cm)
Aspect: Full sun
Soil: Sharply-drained
Hardiness: Zone 6
Propagation: Division, or basal cuttings, in spring
Flowering time: Late spring to late summer

A handsome cultivar, with flowers of palest cream, bordering on white.

- Aromatic foliage
- Drought-tolerant
- Evergreen
- Attracts slugs
- Must not be moved
- Prone to mildew

Antirrhinum braun-blanquetti (Scrophulariaceae)

Common name: Snapdragon
Height: 4ft (1.2m)
Spread: 18in (45cm)
Aspect: Sun
Soil: Sharply drained, fertile
Hardiness: Zone 7
Propagation: Seed in summer, autumn, or spring
Flowering time: All summer

A glabrous perennial from the Iberian peninsula. Leaves elliptic, pointed. Flowers yellow, in spikes.

- Evergreen
- Low allergen
- Good cut flower
- Must deadhead
- Short-lived
- Prone to mildew

Antirrhinum majus 'Floral Showers' series (Scrophulariaceae)

Common name: Common snapdragon
Height: 8in (20cm)
Spread: 1ft (30cm)
Aspect: Full sun
Soil: Sharply-drained, fertile
Hardiness: Zone 7
Propagation: Seed in spring and autumn
Flowering time: All summer

A short-lived perennial, grown almost always as an annual. Leaves lance-shaped, glossy green. Flowers in a wide range of colors. Must be deadheaded regularly.

- Good cut flower
- Low allergen
- Scented flowers
- Must deadhead
- Prone to mildew
- Seeds everywhere
- Short-lived

***Antirrhinum majus* 'Sonnet' series**
(Scrophulariaceae)

Common name: Common snapdragon
Height: 18in (45cm)
Spread: 10in (25cm)
Aspect: Sun
Soil: Sharply-drained, fertile
Hardiness: Zone 7
Propagation: Seed in spring or autumn
Flowering time: All summer

A short-lived perennial, grown almost invariably as an annual. Flowers in a wide color range; must be deadheaded regularly to encourage growth of new blooms.

- Good cut flower
- Low allergen
- Must deadhead
- Prone to mildew
- Seeds everywhere
- Short-lived

Arctotis x *hybrida* (Asteraceae)

Common name: African daisy
Height: 2ft (60cm)
Spread: 1ft (30cm)
Aspect: Full sun
Soil: Moist, well-drained
Hardiness: Zone 9
Propagation: Seed in heat, in spring or autumn
Flowering time: All summer and autumn

A very handsome composite, from S. Africa. Leaves felted, often silver, elliptic, wavy-edged. Flowers solitary; colors from white through yellow, orange to pink or red.

- Handsome foliage
- High allergen
- Must deadhead

Asarina procumbens (Scrophulariaceae)

Common name: None
Height: 2in (5cm)
Spread: 2ft (60cm)
Aspect: Sun or half shade
Soil: Well-drained, gritty, fertile
Hardiness: Zone 7
Propagation: Seed, in heat, in spring
Flowering time: Long period during summer

An evergreen, trailing, brittle-stemmed plant. Leaves kidney-shaped, lobed, hairy, dark green. Flowers are snapdragon-like, cream, with yellow throats. Good wall plant.

- Evergreen
- Short-lived
- Drought-tolerant

Asclepias hallii (Asclepiadaceae)

Common name: Silkweed/milkweed
Height: 3ft (90cm)
Spread: 2ft (60cm)
Aspect: Full sun
Soil: Moist, humus-rich
Hardiness: Zone 3
Propagation: Seed or division in spring
Flowering time: Mid- and late summer

A robust, fleshy rooted perennial from western USA. Lance-shaped, deep green leaves; flowers in terminal cymes, dark pink, followed by fruits, containing silky seeds.

- Good cut flower
- Must not be moved
- Attracts bees
- Poisonous
- Can be dried
- Skin irritant

ASTER x FRIKARTII 'FLORA'S DELIGHT'

Asclepias incarnata
(Asclepiadaceae)

Common name: Swamp milkweed
Height: 4ft (1.2m)
Spread: 2ft (60cm)
Aspect: Full sun
Soil: Moist or bog
Hardiness: Zone 3
Propagation: Seed or division in spring
Flowering time: Midsummer to early autumn

A bog or water marginal perennial with ovate/ elliptic, mid-green leaves. Flowers, pinkish-purple, with paler pink horns. Fruits contain silky seeds.

- Good cut flower
- Attracts bees
- Must not be moved
- Poisonous

Asclepias tuberosa (Asclepiadaceae)

Common name: Silkweed/milkweed
Height: 3ft (90cm)
Spread: 1ft (30cm)
Aspect: Full sun
Soil: Well-drained, fertile, humus-rich
Hardiness: Zone 3
Propagation: Seed or division in spring
Flowering time: Midsummer to autumn

A strikingly handsome, perennial. Leaves lance/ovate/oblong, hairy, mid-green. Orange flowers in cymes, followed by fruits with silky seeds.

- Good cut flower
- Can be dried
- Attracts bees
- Poisonous
- Skin irritant
- Must not be moved

Aster x frikartii 'Flora's Delight'
(Asteraceae)

Common name: None
Height: 20in (50cm)
Spread: 1ft (30cm)
Aspect: Sun or part shade
Soil: Moist, fertile
Hardiness: Zone 2
Propagation: Division in spring
Flowering time: Late summer to mid-autumn.

A dense, bushy, hardy perennial. Leaves gray-green. Flowers in loose corymbs, lilac, very long-lasting.

- Attracts butterflies
- Good cut flower
- Attracts slugs
- High allergen

PERENNIALS

Aster x *frikartii* **'Monch' A.G.M.**
(Asteraceae)

Common name: None
Height: 28in (70cm)
Spread: 16in (40cm)
Aspect: Sun or half shade
Soil: Moist, fertile
Hardiness: Zone 2
Propagation: Division in spring
Flowering time: Late summer to early autumn

Hardy perennial plant. Leaves ovate/oblong, rough, deep green. Flowers very long-lasting, violet-blue in color with orange discs.

- Attracts butterflies
- Attracts slugs
- Good cut flower
- High allergen

ASTILBE x ARENDSII 'FEUER'

***Aster sedifolius* 'Nanus' (Asteraceae)**

Common name: None
Height: 18in (45cm)
Spread 18in (45cm)
Aspect: Sun or part shade
Soil: Moist, fertile
Hardiness: Zone 6
Propagation: Seed or division in spring
Flowering time: Late summer to early autumn

A compact, dwarf, hardy perennial. Flowers daisy-like, dark blue, with yellow centers, very long-lasting.

- Attracts butterflies
- Good cut flower
- Attracts slugs
- High allergen

***Astilbe* x *arendsii* 'Feuer' (Saxifragaceae)**

Common name: None
Height: 2 ft (60cm)
Spread: 18in (45cm)
Aspect: Sun or part shade
Soil: Moist or boggy
Hardiness: Zone 6
Propagation: Division in autumn or winter
Flowering time: Summer

A handsome hybrid *Astilbe*. Leaves lobed, toothed, dark green. Flowers borne in open panicles, coral-red in summer, followed by long-lasting seed heads which are excellent for drying.

- Can be dried
- Low allergen
- Handsome foliage
- Divide regularly

ASTILBE (Saxifragaceae)

A genus consisting of about a dozen species of rhizomatous perennials from North America and Southeast Asia. There are numerous garden hybrids available of complex parentage. They have handsome foliage and the flowers are borne in tapering panicles.

The flowers persist throughout the winter as seed heads, which are useful for drying, and serve to extend the season from the summer through into the autumn and winter. They do not usually require staking but they do benefit from regular division. They make excellent plants for water-retentive soils and bog gardens.

Astilbe x *arendsii* 'Irrlicht'

Common name: None
Height: 20in (50cm)
Spread: 20in (50cm)
Aspect: Sun or half shade
Soil: Moist or bog
Hardiness: Zone 6
Propagation: Division in autumn or winter
Flowering time: Late spring and early summer

A clump-forming, early-flowering hybrid plant bearing panicles of white-colored flowers.

- Handsome foliage • Divide regularly
- Can be dried
- Low allergen

Astilbe chinensis var. *davidii* 'Jo Ophurst' (Saxifragaceae)

Common name: None
Height: 4ft (1.2m)
Spread: 2ft (60cm)
Aspect: Sun or half shade
Soil: Moist or bog
Hardiness: Zone 5
Propagation: Division in autumn or winter
Flowering time: Late summer

A tallish hybrid with panicles of pink flowers. The flower heads give way to long-lasting seed heads which remain all winter and are good for drying.

- Can be dried • Divide regularly
- Low allergen
- Handsome foliage

List of other Astilbes given an Award of Garden Merit

x *arendsii* 'Brautschleir'
x *arendsii* 'Fanal'
'Bronce Elegans'
chinensis var. *pumila*
chinensis var. *taquetii* 'Superba'
x *crispa* 'Perkeo'
glaberrima var. *saxatilis*
'Rheinland'
simplicifolia
'Sprite'
'Straussenfeder'

ASTRANTIA MAJOR 'HADSPEN BLOOD'

Astrantia major (Apiaceae)

Common name: Masterwort
Height: 3ft (90cm)
Spread: 18in (45cm)
Aspect: Sun or half shade
Soil: Moist or moisture-retentive
Hardiness: Zone 6
Propagation: Seed when ripe
Flowering time: Early and midsummer

A clump-forming perennial with a basal rosette of deeply toothed, multi-lobed leaves. The flowers are white, pink, or red, backed by green-veined white bracts, in umbels, in early and midsummer, and occasionally later.

- Can be dried
- Good cut flower
- Attracts bees
- Seeds everywhere
- Attracts slugs
- Prone to mildew

Astrantia major 'Hadspen Blood' (Apiaceae)

Common name: Masterwort
Height: 3ft (90cm)
Spread: 18in (45cm)
Aspect: Sun or part shade
Soil; Moist or moisture-retentive
Hardiness: Zone 6
Propagation: Division in spring
Flowering time: Early and midsummer

A clone with flowers, and bracts, in dark red. Very handsome, and much sought-after plant. The flower heads dry on the plant, which has the effect of extending the flowering season.

- Can be dried
- Good cut flower
- Attracts bees
- Seeds everywhere
- Attracts slugs
- Prone to mildew

ASTRANTIA (Apiaceae)

Masterwort

A small genus consisting of only some 10 species found in Europe and extending across to Western Asia. There are a few clones of *A. major* in cultivation in addition. They have basal leaf rosettes, the leaves being palmate in shape. The flowers are borne in erect umbels, small, 5-petalled, and are surrounded by a ruff of attractive papery bracts, and are held in sprays well above the foliage.

Astrantias will grow in a range of different habitats, but they prefer a moist site. The flower heads are suitable for drying, which has the effect of prolonging the flowering season, and they are useful plants to include in dried-flower arrangements.

PERENNIALS 39

***Astrantia major* 'Rosensinfonie'
(Apiaceae)**

Common name: Masterwort
Height: 3ft (90cm)
Spread: 18in (45cm)
Aspect: Sun or part shade
Soil: Moist or moisture-retentive
Hardiness: Zone 6
Propagation: Division in spring
Flowering time: From early through to midsummer

A clone with flowers and bracts of rose-pink, borne in umbels. The flower heads dry on the plant, which has the effect of extending the flowering season.

- Can be dried
- Good cut flower
- Attracts bees
- Attracts slugs
- Prone to mildew
- Seeds everywhere

***Astrantia major* 'Shaggy' (= 'Margery Fish') A.G.M. (Apiaceae)**

Common name: Masterwort
Height: 3ft (90cm)
Spread: 18in (45cm)
Aspect: Sun or part shade
Soil: Moist or moisture-retentive
Hardiness: Zone 6
Propagation: Division in spring
Flowering time: From early through to midsummer

A clone with deeply-cut leaves, and white flowers and bracts, which are very long-lasting, and have green tips. The flower heads dry on the plant, thus prolonging the flowering season.

- Can be dried
- Good cut flower
- Attracts bees
- Seeds everywhere
- Attracts slugs
- Prone to mildew

***Astrantia maxima* A.G.M. (Apiaceae)**

Common name: Masterwort
Height: 2ft (60cm)
Spread: 1ft (30cm)
Aspect: Sun or part shade
Soil: Moist or moisture-retentive
Hardiness: Zone 6
Propagation: Seed or division in spring
Flowering time: Early and midsummer

Clump-forming plant. Leaves basal, deeply divided, and mid-green; flowers small, pink, and surrounded by sharply pointed bracts, in umbels. Flower heads dry on the plant, extending the season.

- Can be dried
- Good cut flower
- Attracts bees
- Attracts slugs
- Seeds everywhere
- Prone to mildew

BEGONIA (Begoniaceae)
Begonia

A huge genus of some 500 species, from subtropical and tropical regions of both hemispheres. As a consequence, the vast majority are graded Zone 10 as far as hardiness is concerned as are the innumerable hybrids in cultivation. *Begonia grandis* ssp. *evansiana*, at Zone 8, is the only hardy member of the genus, and *Begonia sutherlandii* is Zone 9.

Begonias may be tuberous- or fibrous-rooted, or rhizomatous. All have both male and female flowers on the same plant, and indeed on the same inflorescence, which is either a raceme or a cyme; female flowers have between 2 and 6 petals of equal size, whereas male flowers have between 2 and 4 petals of unequal size. The classification of the genus is complex, but 'The Plant Finder' recognizes the following categories:

Cane (C) Woody, evergreen, hybrid perennials derived mainly from Brazilian species. This category includes members grown for foliage value, and others for flowers, which appear from early spring to summer. They have bamboo-like stems. They will not tolerate direct sunlight all day long.

Rex (R) This group is grown for foliage value alone, since the flowers are inconspicuous. They are derived from crosses with *Begonia rex* as one parent. They are not included here.

Semperflorens Cultorum (S) Fibrous-rooted, compact, evergreen, hybrid perennials derived from several species; they may be grown for foliage or flowers, which appear all summer long. They do well in part-shade, and are not very tolerant of direct sunlight.

x tuberhybrida (T) Tuberous winter-dormant perennials, derived from Andean species. They may be upright or pendulous, having succulent stems, and most of them are summer-flowering. The flowering spike has one large (sometimes double) male flower and two small female ones.

Begonia grandis ssp. *evansiana* (T) (Begoniaceae)

Common name: Evans begonia
Height: 32in (80cm)
Spread: 1ft (30cm)
Aspect: Sun or part shade
Soil: Moist, moisture-retentive
Hardiness: Zone 8
Propagation: Separate tubers, in autumn
Flowering time: All summer

A hardy tuberous species. Leaves ovate, pointed, olive-green. Flowers, pink, scented in pendent cymes on tallish, branched stems.

- Drought-tolerant
- Handsome foliage
- Scented flowers
- Prone to mildew
- Seeds everywhere

BEGONIA x TUBERHYBRIDA 'NON-STOP' SERIES

Begonia x *tuberhybrida* 'Non-stop' series

Common name: Tuberous begonia
Height: 1ft (30cm)
Spread: 1ft (30cm)
Aspect: Part-shade, no midday sun
Soil: Moisture-retentive, moist
Hardiness: Zone 10
Propagation: Seed in spring; basal or side-shoot cuttings in summer
Flowering time: Throughout summer

An upright, compact series with leaves of a mid-green color, heart-shaped. Flowers solitary, double, of red, yellow, pink, white or orange. Lift tubers before first frost, and dry off.

- Handsome foliage
- Low allergen

Begonia semperflorens 'Cocktail' series A.G.M. (S) (Begoniaceae)

Common name: Wax begonia
Height: 1ft (30cm)
Spread: 1ft (30cm)
Aspect: Half shade, or protection from midday sun
Soil: Well-drained, moisture-retentive
Hardiness: Zone 10
Propagation: Division in spring
Flowering time: All summer

A very popular bedding plant, once all danger of frost is past. Leaves rounded, bright green. Flowers weather-resistant, single, in a wide range of colors, including bicolors. Lift tubers in autumn before frost and dry off.

- Handsome foliage
- Low allergen

Begonia sutherlandii A.G.M. (T) (Begoniaceae)

Common name: Sutherland begonia
Height: 6in (15cm)
Spread: 20in (50cm)
Aspect: Part-shade
Soil: Well-drained, moisture-retentive
Hardiness: Zone 9
Propagation: Seed in spring: basal or side-shoot cuttings in summer
Flowering time: All summer

A tuberous begonia from S. Africa. Leaves ovate/lance, bright green. Stems trailing. Flowers in pendent panicles, bright orange.

- Handsome foliage
- Low allergen

BIDENS FERULIFOLIA A.G.M.

Bellis perennis (Asteraceae)

Common name: Common daisy
Height: 8in (20 cm)
Spread: 8in (20cm)
Aspect: Sun or half shade
Soil: Well-drained
Hardiness: Zone 4
Propagation: Seed or division in spring
Flowering time: Late winter to late summer

A well-known evergreen perennial as a weed found in lawns. Flowers from late winter through to late summer The leaves are in rosettes, spoon-shaped, and dull green. Deadhead to avoid self-seeding. Good ground cover

- Evergreen everywhere
- Good cut flower
- Seeds
- High allergen

Bellis perennis 'Pomponette' series A.G.M. (Asteraceae)

Common name: None
Height: 8in (20cm)
Spread: 8in (20cm)
Aspect: Sun or part shade
Soil: Well-drained
Hardiness: Zone 4
Propagation: Seed or division in spring
Flowering time: Late winter to late summer

A clone in which the flower heads are fully double, and may be white, pink, or red; the petals are quilled. Leaves dull green, spoon-shaped, in basal rosettes. Evergreen. Good ground cover. Deadhead to prevent seeding.

- Evergreen
- Good cut flower
- High allergen
- Seeds everywhere

Bidens ferulifolia A.G.M. (Asteraceae)

Common name: Beggar-ticks
Height: 1ft (30cm)
Spread: Indefinite
Aspect: Full sun
Soil: Moist, well-drained
Hardiness: Zone 8
Propagation: Seed in heat in spring
Flowering time: Mid-spring to late autumn

A short-lived perennial, grown usually as an annual. Leaves tripinnate, green, the lobes lance-shaped. Flowers daisy-like, single, yellow, on spreading stems. Good in hanging baskets.

- Short-lived

PERENNIALS

Borago pygmaea (Boraginaceae)

Common name: None
Height: 2ft (60cm)
Spread: 2ft (60cm)
Aspect: Part shade
Soil: Moist
Hardiness: Zone 7
Propagation: Seed, *in situ*, in spring
Flowering time: Early summer through to early autumn

Leaves in basal rosettes, ovate, rough, green. Flowers in cymes, bell-shaped, clear blue.

- Prone to mildew
- Seeds everywhere
- Short-lived

Bracteantha 'Coco' (Asteraceae)

Common name: None
Height: 2ft (60cm)
Spread: 1ft (30cm)
Aspect: Shade
Soil: Sharply-drained, fertile
Hardiness: Zone 8
Propagation: Division in spring
Flowering time: Summer through to mid-winter

An 'everlasting' short-lived perennial plant. Leaves ovate, mid-green in color. Flowers off-white, papery. Grow in dry shade.

- Can be dried
- Short-lived
- Drought-tolerant

Buphthalmum salicifolium (Asteraceae)

Common Name: Willowleaf-oxeye
Height: 2ft (60cm)
Spread: 18in (45cm)
Aspect: Full sun
Soil: Dry, gritty, poor
Hardiness: Zone 4
Propagation: Seed or division in spring
Flowering time: All summer

A little-known garden gem. Leaves narrow, obovate, deep green. Flowers daisy-like, bright yellow, on long erect stems. Trouble-free specimen.

- Good cut flower
- High allergen

CALCEOLARIA 'SUNSET RED'

Calceolaria biflora
(Scrophulariaceae)

Common name: Slipperflower, Slipperwort
Height: 10in (25cm)
Spread: 8in (20cm)
Aspect: Sun or part shade
Soil: Acid, fertile, gritty
Hardiness: Zone 6
Propagation: Seed or division in spring
Flowering time: All summer

A rhizomatous, evergreen, mat-forming perennial plant. Leaves grow in rosettes, and are oblong in shape, toothed, and dark green. Flowers are 2-lipped, yellow, in loose racemes of up to 8.

- Evergreen
- Drought-tolerant
- Attracts slugs

Calceolaria 'Sunset Red'
(Scrophulariaceae)

Common name: None
Height: 1ft (30cm)
Spread: 1ft (30cm)
Aspect: Sun or part shade
Soil: Acid, gritty, fertile
Hardiness: Zone 9
Propagation: Seed or division in spring
Flowering time: Mid-spring through to midsummer

An evergreen, compact, bushy, perennial plant. Leaves ovate/lance-shaped, gray-green in color. Flowers pouched, red. Comes in yellow, orange, or bicolored forms. Best treated as an annual in cold areas.

- Evergreen
- Attracts slugs

PERENNIALS

CAMPANULA (Campanulaceae)
Campanula

A genus of some 300 species of annuals, biennials, and perennials from a variety of habitats in temperate zones of the Northern Hemisphere, and Turkey and south Europe in particular: their cultural needs vary therefore. They are, in general, undemanding, and bloom from late spring to late summer. The flowers may be bell- or star-shaped, or tubular. Most are well-behaved, but some (CC. *pulla*, *persicifolia*, and *takesimana* in particular) are rampant invaders, and C. *persicifolia* also seeds everywhere. Some are prone to powdery mildew, and all are slug prone.

Campanula carpatica A.G.M. (Campanulaceae)

Common name: Carpathian bellflower
Height: 8in (20cm)
Spread: 2ft (60cm)
Aspect: Sun or part shade
Soil: Moist, well-drained
Hardiness: Zone 3
Propagation: Seed in autumn
Flowering time: Several weeks in summer

A clump-forming perennial plant. Leaves are basal, ovate, toothed, mid-green in color. Flowers in summer are solitary, upturned bells, violet, or blue or white.

- Good cut flower
- Attracts slugs

Campanula carpatica 'Blue Clips' (Campanulaceaeae)

Common name: Bellflower
Height: 8in (20cm)
Spread: 2ft (60cm)
Aspect: Sun or part shade
Soil: Moist, well-drained
Hardiness: Zone 3
Propagation: Division in spring or autumn
Flowering time: Summer

A compact hybrid, very free-flowering. Will repeat-flower if deadheaded regularly. Flowers solitary, pale sky blue, for several weeks, in summer.

- Good cut flower
- Attracts slugs
- Attracts bees

CAMPANULA GLOMERATA 'SUPERBA' A.G.M.

***Campanula glomerata* 'Superba' A.G.M. (Campanulaceae)**

Common name: Clustered bellflower
Height: 2ft (60cm)
Spread: Indefinite
Aspect: Sun or half shade
Soil: Moist, well-drained, alkaline
Hardiness: Zone 3
Propagation: Seed, in spring
Flowering time: All summer

A vigorous perennial plant. Leaves are lance-shaped, toothed, dark green in color. Flowers are borne in terminal racemes, and are bell-shaped and purple-violet.

- Attracts bees
- Good cut flower
- Attracts slugs

Campanula lactiflora (Campanulaceae)

Common name: Milky bellflower
Height: 5ft (1.5m)
Spread: 2ft (60cm)
Aspect: Sun or half shade
Soil: Moist, well-drained, alkaline, fertile
Hardiness: Zone 5
Propagation: Seed in spring
Flowering time: From early summer through to early autumn

A vigorous, upright perennial plant. Leaves are ovate, toothed, mid-green in color. Flowers are borne in conical panicles, open bells, white, blue, or lavender. Will repeat-flower if deadheaded regulalrly.

- Attracts bees
- Good cut flower
- Attracts slugs
- Must not be moved
- Requires staking
- Seeds everywhere

Campanula latiloba 'Hidcote Amethyst' A.G.M. (Campanulaceae)

Common name: None
Height: 3ft (90cm)
Spread: 18in (45cm)
Aspect: Sun or part shade
Soil: Moist, well-drained, alkaline, fertile
Hardiness: Zone 3
Propagation: Division in spring or autumn
Flowering time: From mid- to late summer

A handsome clone of a Turkish species. Leaves basal, lance-shaped, toothed, green. Flowers cup-shaped, pale amethyst, in racemes.

- Attracts bees
- Good cut flower
- Attracts slugs

Campanula persicifolia alba (Campanulaceae)

Common name: Peach-leaved bellflower
Height: 3ft (90cm)
Spread: 18in (45cm)
Aspect: Sun or half shade
Soil: Moist, well-drained, alkaline, fertile
Propagation: Seed in spring; division in spring or autumn
Flowering time: From early to midsummer

A rampant, rhizomatous, evergreen *Campanula*. Leaves in basal rosettes, narrow, toothed, mid-green. Flowers in racemes, cup-shaped, white bells.

- Evergreen
- good cut flower
- Attracts bees
- Low allergen
- Attracts slugs
- Invasive
- Requires staking
- Divide regularly
- Seeds everywhere

Campanula persicifolia 'Blue Bloomers' (Campanulaceae)

Common name: Peach-leaved bellflower
Height: 3ft (90cm)
Spread: 1ft (30cm)
Aspect: Sun or part shade
Soil: Well-drained, moist, alkaline, fertile
Hardiness: Zone 3
Propagation: Division in spring or autumn
Flowering time: From early to midsummer

A handsome clone of this popular plant. Flowers in racemes, lilac-blue. Will repeat-flower if sheared over after flowering.

- Attracts bees
- Evergreen
- Good cut flower
- Low allergen
- Attracts slugs
- Divide regularly
- Invasive
- Requires staking
- Seeds everywhere

CANNA (Cannaceae)
Canna

A genus of some 50 species, but of hundreds of hybrids, which are sometimes grouped under the names, *Canna generalis* or *Canna orchiodes*. The have large paddle-shaped leaves, pinnately veined, and usually green, but may be purple; they can be handsomely striated in some clones. The asymmetric flowers are borne in racemes or panicles, and are usually paired in the leaf axils. They are brightly colored, and the flowering season is long, especially if deadheaded. Unfortunately they are not especially weather-resistant, nor are they very hardy, so in cold areas they must be given winter protection, or the rhizomes can be lifted and stored in frost-free conditions.

Cannas like full sun, good drainage, and fertile soil, but plenty of water during the growing season. They do not require to be staked except in very exposed sites. They are trouble-free, except that they are prone to attack by slugs. They are low-allergen plants, and make good cut flowers.

Canna 'Assault' (Cannaceae)

Common name: None
Height: 6ft (1.8m)
Spread: 20in (50cm)
Aspect: Full sun
Soil: Well-drained, fertile
Hardiness: Zone 8
Propagation: Division in spring
Flowering time: Midsummer to autumn

A tuberous perennial. Leaves large, paddle-shaped, purple-brown. Flowers in racemes, orange-scarlet, like gladioli.

- Good cut flower
- Attracts slugs
- Handsome foliage
- Must deadhead
- Low allergen

Canna 'Champion' (Cannaceae)

Common name: None
Height: 4ft (1.2m)
Spread: 20in (50cm)
Aspect: Sun
Soil: Well-drained, fertile
Hardiness: Zone 8
Propagation: Division in spring
Flowering time: From midsummer to mid-autumn

A half-hardy tuberous perennial plant. Leaves are large, paddle-shaped, and mid-green in color. Flowers are gladiolus-like, borne in racemes, red.

- Good cut flower
- Attracts slugs
- Handsome foliage
- Must deadhead
- Low allergen

Canna 'En Avant' (Cannaceae)

Common name: None
Height: 5ft (1.5m)
Spread: 2ft (60cm)
Aspect: Full sun
Soil: Well-drained, fertile
Hardiness: Zone 8
Propagation: Division in spring
Flowering time: Midsummer to mid-autumn

A tuberous perennial. Leaves very large, paddle-shaped, mid-green. Flowers in racemes, like gladioli, yellow, streaked brown.

- Good cut flower
- Attracts slugs
- Handsome foliage
- Must deadhead

Canna 'Fireside' (Cannaceae)

Common name: None
Height: 4ft (1.2m)
Spread: 20in (50cm)
Aspect: Full sun
Soil: Well-drained, fertile
Hardiness: Zone 8
Propagation: Division in spring
Flowering time: Midsummer to mid-autumn

A tender, tuberous perennial. Leaves large, paddle-shaped, green. Flowers in racemes, red with a yellow throat.

- Good cut flower
- Attracts slugs
- Handsome foliage
- Must deadhead
- Low allergen

Canna 'Hercule' (Cannaceae)

Common name: None
Height: 4ft (1.2m)
Spread: 2ft (60cm)
Aspect: Sun
Soil: Well-drained, fertile
Hardiness: Zone 8
Propagation: Division of tubers in spring
Flowering time: From midsummer through to mid-autumn

A tender, tuberous perennial plant. Leaves are large, paddle-shaped, and bronze in color. Flowers borne in racemes, bright red.

- Good cut flower
- Attracts slugs
- Handsome foliage
- Must deadhead
- Low allergen

Canna 'Rosemond Coles' (Cannaceae)

Common name: None
Height: 4ft (1.2m)
Spread: 20in (50cm)
Aspect: Full sun
Soil: Well-drained, fertile
Hardiness: Zone 8
Propagation: Division in spring
Flowering time: Midsummer to autumn

A tuberous perennial. Leaves large, paddle-shaped, bright green, veined cream. Flowers in racemes, like gladioli, scarlet, edged yellow.

- Good cut flower
- Attracts slugs
- Handsome foliage
- Must deadhead
- Low allergen

Canna 'Taroudant' (Cannaceae)

Common name: None
Height: 4ft (1.2m)
Spread: 2ft (60cm)
Aspect: Full sun
Soil: Well-drained, fertile
Hardiness: Zone 8
Propagation: Division of tubers in spring
Flowering time: Midsummer to mid-autumn

A tender, tuberous perennial. Leaves large, paddle-shaped, green. Flowers yellow, suffused and blotched orange, in racemes.

- Good cut flower
- Attracts slugs
- Handsome foliage
- Must deadhead
- Low allergen

Catananche caerulea (Asteraceae)

Common name: Cupid's dart
Height: 3ft (90cm)
Spread: 1ft (30cm)
Aspect: Full sun
Soil: Well-drained
Hardiness: Zone 7
Propagation: Seed or division in spring
Flowering time: Midsummer to autumn

A short-lived perennial. Leaves linear, grass-like, gray-green. Flowers, blue, with papery, silvery bracts. Must not be moved.

- Good cut flower
- Short-lived
- Can be dried
- Attracts slugs
- Drought-tolerant
- Prone to mildew
- High allergen

Catharanthus roseus **(Apocynaceae)**

Common name: None
Height: 2ft (60cm)
Spread: 2ft (60cm)
Aspect: Sun
Soil: Well-drained, fertile
Hardiness: Zone 10
Propagation: Seed in heat in spring
Flowering time: Spring to summer

A tender, evergreen perennial, usually grown as an annual in cold areas. Flowers salverform, pink, red or white in the upper leaf axils.

- Drought-tolerant
- Poisonous
- Evergreen

Celosia argentea **'Fairy Fountains'**
(Amaranthaceae)

Common mame: None
Height: 2ft (60cm)
Spread: 18in (45cm)
Aspect: Full sun
Soil: Moist, well-drained, fertile
Hardiness: Zone 9
Propagation: Seed in heat in spring
Flowering time: All summer

Tends to be grown as an annual in cold regions. Leaves lance-shaped, pale green. Inflorescence plume-like, in terminal feathery pyramidal cymes of tiny flowers, pink, cream, or red. Blooms throughout the summer period

- Can be dried
- Good cut flower

Centaurea montana (Asteraceae)

Common name: None
Height: 18in (45cm)
Spread: 2ft (60cm)
Aspect: Full sun
Soil: Well-drained
Hardiness: Zone 3
Propagation: Seed or division in spring
Flowering time: Late spring to midsummer

A rhizomatous perennial. Leaves are lance/ovate, pinnatifid, green, woolly below; flowers solitary, blue, with widely-spaced florets. Deadhead to prevent self-seeding, and to encourage longer flowering.

- Good cut flower
- Attracts bees
- Seeds everywhere
- High allergen
- Prone to mildew

Centranthus ruber (Valerianaceae)

Common name: Red valerian
Height: 3ft (90cm)
Spread: 3ft (90cm)
Aspect: Sun
Soil: Poor, well-drained, alkaline
Hardiness: Zone 7
Propagation: Seed in spring
Flowering time: Late spring to late summer

A common weed of dry, stony places. Leaves ovate, fleshy, glaucous. Flowers small, perfumed, red (or pink or white) in dense cymes. Deadhead to prevent self-seeding.

- Attracts bees
- Good cut flower
- Scented flowers
- Must not be moved
- Seeds everywhere

Chaerophyllum hirsutum 'Roseum' (Apiaceae)

Common name: None
Height: 2ft (60cm)
Spread: 18in (30cm)
Aspect: Sun or half shade
Soil: Moist, fertile
Hardiness: Zone 6
Propagation: Seed when ripe
Flowering time: Late spring

A tap-rooted, herbaceous perennial. Leaves are apple-scented, mid-green; flowers pink, in compound umbels.

- Foliage aromatic
- Good cut flower
- Attracts slugs
- Poisonous
- Must not be moved

Chelone obliqua (Scrophulariaceae)

Common name: Turtlehead
Height: 2ft (60cm)
Spread: 1ft (30cm)
Aspect: Sun or part shade
Soil: Moist, deep, fertile
Hardiness: Zone 3
Propagation: Seed or division in spring
Flowering time: Late summer to mid-autumn

A charming, unusual perennial, from the USA. Leaves lance-like/elliptic, toothed, boldly veined, and mid-green. Dark pink flowers in racemes.

- Good cut flower
- Attracts slugs
- Prone to mildew

Chrysogonum virginianum (Asteraceae)

Common name: Goldenstar
Height: 10in (25cm)
Spread: 10in (25cm)
Aspect: Sun or part shade
Soil: Moist, well-drained, humus-rich
Hardiness: Zone 5
Propagation: Seed when ripe; division in spring or autumn
Flowering time: From early spring through to late summer

A creeping, rhizomatous, evergreen perennial plant from the eastern U.S.A. Leaves ovate, hairy, green. Flowers solitary, star-shaped, 5-petaled, yellow in color.

- Evergreen

Cirsium helenioides (Asteraceae)

Common name: None
Height: 5ft (1.5m)
Spread: 2ft (60cm)
Aspect: Full sun
Soil: Moist, well-drained
Hardiness: Zone 5
Propagation: Seed in spring
Flowering time: Late spring to midsummer

A perennial plant from Eastern Europe and Russia. Leaves lanceolate, glabrous, tomentose below. Flowers from late spring through to the midsummer are purple in color and thistle-form.

- Good cut flower
- Prone to mildew

Cirsium rivulare 'Atropurpureum' (Asteraceae)

Common name: None
Height: 4ft (1.2m)
Spread: 2ft (60cm)
Aspect: Sun
Soil: Moist, well-drained
Hardiness: Zone 5
Propagation: Seed or division in spring
Flowering time: From early to midsummer

A clump-forming, spreading plant. Leaves elliptic/lance, entire/pinnatifid, dark green. Flowers on erect stems, spherical, thistle-like, crimson-purple. Deadhead to prevent self-seeding.

- Good cut flower
- Requires staking

Claytonia megarhiza (Portulacaceae)

Common name: Spring beauty
Height: 2in (5cm)
Spread: 10in (25cm)
Aspect: Full sun
Soil: Sharply-drained, humus-rich
Hardiness: Zone 4
Propagation: Seed in autumn
Flowering time: Summer

A short-lived, tap-rooted evergreen perennial from the Rocky Mountains. Leaves fleshy, spoon-shaped, deep green in color. Flowers shallow cups, borne in racemes, white or pink in color, for several weeks in summer (despite its common name).

- Evergreen
- Short-lived
- Handsome foliage

CLEMATIS (Ranunculaceae)
Old man's beard, Travellers' joy

A very diverse genus from both north and south of the equator; plants may be evergreen or deciduous, woody, or semi-woody. It has been described as the Queen of the Climbers. For the present purpose, the genus will be divided into the following categories:

Group 1
Early-flowering species These carry flowers in the winter or spring seasons, on the previous year's growth, and plants may be deciduous or evergreen. They are not particularly long-flowering.

Cc. alpina, *macropetala* **and their cultivars** These plants also flower in spring on the growth of the previous year, but they may bloom again in summer on new growth and so have an extended season.

Clematis montana **and its cultivars** These flower in the late spring on the previous year's ripened growth.

They are not particularly long-flowering, but this group requires next to no pruning or maintenance.

Group 2
Early/mid-season large-flowered cultivars These flower in the late spring or early summer on the previous year's growth, and they flower again in late summer on the current year's growth. They have a long flowering season therefore.

This group requires light pruning in late winter/early spring to remove old or dead growth.

Group 3
Late-flowering large-flowered cultivars These have flowers on the current year's shoots in summer or early autumn. They are deciduous and are not particularly long-flowering.

Late-flowering species and small-flowered cultivars These flower from summer to late autumn on the current year's growth. They are mostly deciduous.

Herbaceous cultivars and species These carry flowers on the current year's growth in summer or autumn. They are deciduous.

This group requires hard pruning, to within 18in (45cm) of the ground, in the early spring.

All *Clematis* are low allergen, but skin irritant. All should be planted deeply to minimize the risk of Clematis wilt.

Clematis 'Countess of Lovelace'
(**Ranunculaceae**)

Common name: None
Height: 10ft (3m)
Spread: 3ft (1m)
Aspect: Sun or part shade
Soil: Well-drained, fertile, humus-rich
Hardiness: Zone 6
Propagation: Division, basal cuttings, or softwood cuttings in spring
Flowering time: Early summer and again in late summer

A Group 2, large-flowered climber. Flowers in early summer are lilac-blue, double, whereas those of the second crop are single, and borne on new shoots in late summer. Prune as for Group 2.

- Low allergen
- Attracts bees
- Prone to mildew
- Skin irritant

Clematis 'Etoile Violette' A.G.M.
(**Ranunculaceae**)

Common name: None
Height: 15ft (5m)
Spread: 5ft (1.5m)
Aspect: Any
Soil: Well-drained, fertile, humus-rich
Hardiness: Zone 5
Propagation: Division, softwood cuttings, or basal cuttings in spring
Flowering time: Midsummer to late autumn

A Group 3, small-flowered, late-blooming *Clematis*. Flowers single, saucer-shaped, purple-violet, from midsummer to late autumn. Cut back to within 18in (45cm) of the ground in spring.

- Low allergen
- Attracts bees

Clematis 'Fireworks'
(**Ranunculaceae**)

Common name: None
Height: 12ft (4m)
Spread: 18in (45cm)
Aspect: Any
Soil: Well-drained, fertile, humus-rich
Hardiness: Zone 5
Propagation: Division, basal cuttings, or softwood cuttings in spring
Flowering time: Early summer and again in early autumn

A Group 2 Clematis with flowers of a purple color and with a mauve stripe.

- Attracts bees
- Low allergen
- Prone to mildew
- Skin irritant

***Clematis florida* 'Sieboldii'**
(Ranunculaceae)

Common name: None
Height: 8ft (2.5m)
Spread: 18in (45cm)
Aspect: Sun
Soil: Well-drained, fertile, humus-rich
Hardiness: Zone 7
Propagation: Division, or basal or softwood cuttings, all in spring
Flowering time: Midsummer

A Group 2, large-flowered, early/midseason climbing plant. Flowers single, creamy-white in color, with a central boss of rich purple stamens, opening from midsummer. Not a strong grower, however. Prune as for Group 2.

- Low allergen
- Attracts bees
- Prone to mildew
- Skin irritant

***Clematis* 'Minuet' A.G.M.**
(Ranunculaceae)

Common name: None
Height: 10ft (3m)
Spread: 3ft (1m)
Aspect: Any
Soil: Well-drained, fertile, humus-rich
Hardiness: Zone 6
Propagation: Division, or basal or semi-ripe cuttings, all in spring
Flowering time: Midsummer to late autumnn

A Group 3, small-flowered, late-flowering climber. Flowers are open bells, single, white, with purple veins and black anthers. Prune hard as for Group 3.

- Low allergen
- Attracts bees
- Prone to mildew
- Skin irritant

***Clematis* 'Multi Blue'**
(Ranunculaceae)

Common name: None
Height: 10ft (3m)
Spread: 3ft (1m)
Aspect: Part shade
Soil: Well-drained, fertile, humus-rich
Hardiness: Zone 6
Propagation: Division, or basal or semi-ripe cuttings, all in spring
Flowering time: Late spring and again in early autumn

A Group 2, early, large-flowered climber. Flowers are spiky, blue-purple, and double.

- Low allergen
- Attracts bees
- Prone to mildew
- Skin irritant

***Clematis* 'Nelly Moser' A.G.M.** (Ranunculaceae)

Common name: None
Height: 10ft (3m)
Spread: 3ft (1m)
Aspect: Part shade
Soil: Well-drained, fertile, humus-rich
Hardiness: Zone 5
Propagation: Division, or basal or semi-ripe cuttings, all in spring
Flowering times: Early summer and again in late summer

A Group 2, early-flowering, large-bloomed cultivar. Flowers are single, mauve-pink, with a darker central stripe, and red anthers. Flowers in early summer and again in late summer, when blooms are paler.

- Low allergen
- Prone to mildew

***Clematis* 'Sir Trevor Lawrence'** (Ranunculaceae)

Common name: None
Height: 10ft (3m)
Spread: 3ft (1m)
Aspect: Part shade
Soil: Well-drained, fertile, humus-rich
Hardiness: Zone 5
Propagation: Division, or basal or semi-ripe cuttings in spring
Flowering times: Early summer and again in late summer

A Group 3, late-flowering cultivar. Flowers are urn-shaped, red-purple in color with a red stripe. Flowers in late summer and early autumn. Prune as for Group 3.

- Low allergen
- Attracts bees
- Prone to mildew
- Skin irritant

***Clematis viticella* 'Purpurea Plena Elegans' A.G.M.** (Ranunculaceae)

Common name: None
Height: 10ft (3m)
Spread: 3ft (1m)
Aspect: Any
Soil: Well-drained, fertile, humus-rich
Hardiness: Zone 6
Propagation: Division, or basal or semi-ripe cuttings, all in spring
Flowering times: Midsummer to late autumn

A Group 3, late-flowering, small-flowered climber. Flowers are double, mauve-purple. Prune hard in spring, as for Group 3.

- Low allergen
- Attracts bees
- Prone to mildew
- Skin irritant

Clematis 'Vyvyan Pennell' A.G.M. (Ranunculaceae)

Common name: None
Height: 10ft (3m)
Spread: 3ft (1m)
Aspect: Part shade
Soil: Well-drained, fertile, humus-rich
Hardiness: Zone 6
Propagation: Division, basal, or semi-ripe cuttings in spring
Flowering time: Early spring and again in midsummer

A Group 2, early-flowering, large-flowered climbing plant. Flowers are lilac in color, double, opening in early spring, followed by mauve-blue flowers in midsummer. Prune as for group 2.

- Low allergen
- Prone to mildew

Cobaea scandens A.G.M. (Polemoniaceae)

Common name: Cup-and-saucer vine
Height: 70ft (21m)
Spread: 3ft (90cm)
Aspect: Full sun
Soil: Moist, well-drained, fertile
Hardiness: Zone 9
Propagation: Seed in heat in spring; softwood cuttings, with bottom heat, in summer
Flowering time: From summer through to autumn

A robust, upright, evergreen, semi-woody perennial climber; usually grown as an annual. Flowers scented, bell-shaped, green in color becoming purple.

- Evergreen
- Requires space

Commelina tuberosa Coelestis group (Commelinaceae)

Common name: Day flower, Widow's tears
Height: 3ft (90cm)
Spread: 18in (45cm)
Aspect: Sun or part shade
Soil: Well-drained, fertile
Hardiness: Zone 8
Propagation: Seed in heat, or division in spring
Flowering time: Late summer to mid-autumn

A clump-forming, erect, tuberous perennial. Leaves are lancelike/oblong, mid-green; vivid blue flowers in cymes.

- Drought-tolerant
- Attracts slugs
- Invasive

CONVOLVULUS ALTHAEOIDES

Convolvulus althaeoides
(Convolvulaceae)

Common name: Bindweed
Height: 1ft (30cm)
Spread: Indefinite
Aspect: Full sun
Soil: Well-drained
Hardiness: Zone 8
Propagation: Seed in heat, in spring
Flowering time: Mid to late summer

An invasive trailing perennial plant, which can be trained to grow upwards. Leaves silver-green. Flowers clear pink-colored saucers. Grow in a container sunk in the ground to prevent it spreading.

- Drought-tolerant   • Invasive

Convolvulus sabatius A.G.M.
(Convolvulaceae)

Common name: Bindweed
Height: 6in (15cm)
Spread: 2ft (60cm)
Aspect: Full sun
Soil: Well-drained
Hardiness: Zone 8
Propagation: Seed in heat, or softwood cuttings, in spring
Flowering time: Summer to early autumn

A trailing perennial. Leaves oblong/ovate, mid-green. Flowers shallow funnels, lavender blue, from the leaf axils.

- Low allergen

Convolvulus tricolor
(Convolvulaceae)

Common name: Bindweed
Height: 1ft (30cm)
Spread: 1ft (30cm)
Aspect: Sun
Soil: Well-drained
Hardiness: Zone 8
Propagation: Seed *in situ* in spring
Flowering time: Summer

A short-lived perennial plant grown almost always as an annual. Flowers are solitary, open saucers, in many colors, each lasting one day only, but in a long succession throughout the summer season.

- Low allergen   • Short-lived

Convolvulus tricolor 'Royal Ensign' (Convolvulaceae)

Common name: Dwarf glorybind
Height: 1ft (30cm)
Spread: 1ft (30cm)
Aspect: Full sun
Soil: Well-drained
Hardiness: Zone 8
Propagation: Seed *in situ* in spring
Flowering time: All summer

A bushy, short-lived perennial plant grown usually as an annual. Flowers are solitary, open shallow funnels, deep blue in color and with a yellow center, each lasting for just a single day.

- Low allergen
- Must not be moved
- Short-lived

Coreopsis grandiflora 'Early Sunrise' (Asteraceae)

Common name: Tickseed
Height: 18in (45cm)
Spread: 18in (45cm)
Aspect: Sun or part shade
Soil: Well-drained, fertile
Hardiness: Zone 7
Propagation: Division in spring
Flowering time: Late spring to late summer

A short-lived perennial with solitary flowers: ray florets golden yellow, with uneven outer edges, and disc florets dark yellow. Not for the hot dry garden. Often grown as an annual, as it will flower in its first season in the ground.

- Attracts bees
- Good cut flower
- Attracts slugs
- High allergen
- Short-lived

Coreopsis grandiflora 'Sunray' (Asteraceae)

Common name: Tickseed
Height: 30in (75cm)
Spread: 18in (45cm)
Aspect: Sun or part shade
Soil: Moist, fertile, well-drained
Hardiness: Zone 7
Propagation: Division in spring
Flowering time: Late spring to summer

A clone with semi-double flowers of deep yellow. Short-lived. Usually grown as an annual, as it will flower well in its first season. Not for the hot, dry garden.

- Good cut flower
- Attracts bees
- Short-lived
- High allergen
- Attracts slugs

Coreopsis rosea 'American Dream' (Asteraceae)

Common name: Rose coreopsis
Height: 2ft (60cm)
Spread: 18in (45cm)
Aspect: Sun or part shade
Soil: Well-drained, fertile
Hardiness: Zone 4
Propagation: Seed or division in spring
Flowering time: Summer through to early autumn

A choice clone of a North American species. Flowers solitary, single, ray florets pink in color, disc florets yellow.

- ● Attracts bees
- ● Attracts slugs
- ● High allergen
- ● Short-lived

Coreopsis verticillata 'Moonbeam' (Asteraceae)

Common name: Threadleaf coreopsis
Height: 20in (50cm)
Spread: 18in (45cm)
Aspect: Sun or part shade
Soil: Well-drained, fertile
Hardiness: Zone 6
Propagation: Division in spring
Flowering time: Late summer

A rhizomatous, perennial plant. Flowers are lemon-colored, borne in loose corymbs for several weeks during the late summer.

- ● Attracts bees
- ● High allergen
- ● Attracts slugs
- ● Short-lived

Coreopsis verticillata 'Zagreb' (Asteraceae)

Common name: Threadleaf coreopsis
Height: 1ft (30cm)
Spread: 1ft (30cm)
Aspect: Sun or half shade
Soil: Well-drained, fertile
Hardiness: Zone 6
Propagation: Division in spring
Flowering time: Several weeks in summer

A clone with flowers of golden yellow in loose corymbs. Has the virtue of being drought-tolerant.

- Attracts bees
- Drought-tolerant
- Attracts slugs
- High allergen
- Short-lived

Corydalis lutea (Papaveraceae)

Common name: Yellow corydalis
Height: 16in (40cm)
Spread: 1ft (30cm)
Aspect: Sun or half shade
Soil: Moist, fertile, well-drained
Hardiness: Zone 6
Propagation: Seed when ripe; division in autumn
Flowering time: Late spring through to early autumn

A rhizomatous, evergreen, mound-forming perennial. Leaves fern-like, light green above, glaucous below. Flowers in racemes of up to 16, spurred, golden yellow.

- Evergreen
- Handsome foliage
- Attracts slugs
- Seeds everywhere

Corydalis ochroleuca (Papaveraceae)

Common name: None
Height: 1ft (30cm)
Spread: 1ft (30cm)
Aspect: Sun or part shade
Soil: Moist, fertile, well-drained
Hardiness: Zone 5
Propagation: Seed when ripe; division in autumn
Flowering time: Late spring to summer

An evergreen, clump-forming perennial. Leaves pinnate, light green. Flowers in compact racemes, spurred, creamy-yellow in color.

- Evergreen
- Low allergen
- Handsome foliage
- Seeds everywhere
- Attracts slugs

Cosmos atrosanguineus (Asteraceae)

Common name: Chocolate cosmos
Height: 30in (75cm)
Spread: 18in (45cm)
Aspect: Full sun
Soil: Moist, well-drained, fertile
Hardiness: Zone 8
Propagation: Seed in heat, in spring
Flowering time: Midsummer through to autumn

A sprawling, tuberous perennial. Leaves pinnate/bipinnate, spoon-shaped, green. Flowers solitary, single, velvety, chocolate-scented, maroon. In winter in cold areas, bring indoors or cover.

- Attracts bees
- Good cut flower
- Handsome foliage
- Scented flowers
- Attracts slugs

Crepis incana A.G.M. (Asteraceae)

Common name: Hawk's beard, Pink dandelion
Height: 1ft (30cm)
Spread: 1ft (30cm)
Aspect: Full sun
Soil: Well-drained
Hardiness: Zone 8
Propagation: Seed when ripe
Flowering time: Summer

A perennial plant with dandelion like leaves so care must be taken not to weed it out accidentally when it is not in flower. Flowers are borne in corymbs, pink, all summer if deadheaded.

- Drought-tolerant
- Short-lived
- Seeds everywhere

Crepis rubra (Asteraceae)

Common name: Hawk's beard
Height: 16in (40cm)
Spread: 6in (15cm)
Aspect: Full sun
Soil: Well-drained
Hardiness: Zone 6
Propagation: Seed when ripe
Flowering time: Spring to summer

A short-lived perennial, with a basal rosette of leaves. Flowers solitary or in pairs, pink, on stiff stems, from spring to summer, especially if deadheaded.

- Drought-tolerant
- Seeds everywhere
- Must not be moved
- Must deadhead

CROCOSMIA (Iridaceae)

Montbretia, Cormous

A genus comprising of some six species from South Africa, but of innumerable hybrids between. The derivation of the hybrids is complex, and need not concern us here.

The hybrids are extremely useful garden plants, easy-going, tolerant of a wide range of conditions, and floriferous. They form, in time, dense clumps in which the new corms grow on top of the old. As they become densely crowded, they will stop flowering and so must be lifted and replanted regularly, but with the old corms still in place. The leaves and flowers are very popular with flower arrangers. The genus is low in allergens, and so is suitable for allergic gardeners.

Crocosmia x *crocosmiiflora* 'Jackanapes' (Iridaceae)

Common name: Cormous
Height: 2ft (60cm)
Spread: 6in (15cm)
Aspect: Sun or part shade
Soil: Moist, well-drained, humus-rich, fertile
Hardiness: Zone 7
Propagation: Division in early spring
Flowering time: From mid- through to late summer

A handsome garden hybrid plant. Leaves mid-green in color. Flowers borne on arching stems, bicolored, orange/red.

- Good cut flower
- Divide regularly
- Low allergen
- Handsome foliage

Crocosmia 'Lucifer' A.G.M.
(Iridaceae)

Common Name: Montbretia
Height: 4ft (1.2m)
Spread: 6in (15cm)
Aspect: Sun or part shade
Soil: Moist, well-drained, fertile, humus-rich
Hardiness: Zone 7
Propagation: Division in early spring
Flowering time: From mid- through to late summer

A very popular variety with gardeners, with much justification. Leaves are pleated and flowers, of an intense red color, are borne on slightly arching spikes.

- 🟢 Good cut flower
- 🔴 Divide regularly
- 🟢 Low allergen
- 🟢 Handsome foliage

Crocosmia masoniorum A.G.M.
(Iridaceae)

Common name: Montbretia, Cormous
Height: 4ft (1.2m)
Spread: 6in (15cm)
Aspect: Sun or part shade
Soil: Well-drained, fertile, humus-rich, moist
Hardiness: Zone 7
Propagation: Division in early spring
Flowering time: Midsummer

A species from South Africa. Leaves pleated; flowers upward-facing, orange-red, on arching spikes.

- 🟢 Good cut flower
- 🔴 Divide regularly
- 🟢 Low allergen
- 🟢 Handsome foliage

Crocosmia 'Severn Sunrise' (Iridaceae)

Common name: Montbretia, Cormous
Height: 32in (80cm)
Spread: 6in (15cm)
Aspect: Sun or part shade
Soil: Moist, well-drained, fertile, humus-rich
Hardiness: Zone 7
Propagation: Division in early spring
Flowering time: Mid- to late summer

A very handsome hybrid with flowers of glowing orange, with paler throats, on upright branching spikes.

- Good cut flower
- Divide regularly
- Low allergen
- Handsome foliage

Crocosmia 'Solfatare 'A.G.M. (Iridaceae)

Common name: Montbretia, Cormous
Height: 32in (80cm)
Spread: 4in (10cm)
Aspect: Sun or part shade
Soil: Moist, fertile, well-drained, humus-rich
Hardiness: Zone 8
Propagation: Division in early spring
Flowering time: Mid- to late summer

A very popular variety, dwarf, with smoky-colored leaves, but less hardy than some of the other hybrids. Flowers are apricot-yellow.

- Good cut flower
- Divide regularly
- Low allergen

Cynoglossum nervosum (Boraginaceae)

Common name: Chinese hound's tongue
Height: 32in (80cm)
Spread: 2ft (60cm)
Aspect: Sun or part shade
Soil: Moist, well-drained
Hardiness: Zone 5
Propagation: Seed or division in spring
Flowering time: Spring to summer

A hardy, clump-forming perennial. Flowers, small, azure blue, in many-flowered cymes. Not for rich soil or heavy clay.

- Must not be moved

Cypella herbertii (Iridaceae)

Common name: None
Height 2ft (60cm)
Spread: 4in (10cm)
Aspect: Full sun
Soil: Sharply-drained
Hardiness: Zone 9
Propagation: Seed in heat, when ripe
Flowering time: All summer

Bulbous perennial plant with pleated, linear leaves. Flowers have broad, mustard-colored outer tepals, and brown, purple-spotted inner ones. Tender.

• Attracts slugs

Cyrtanthus brachyscyphus (Amaryllidaceae)

Common name: Fire lily
Height: 1ft (30cm)
Spread: 4in (10cm)
Aspect: Full sun
Soil: Well-drained, fertile, humus-rich
Hardiness: Zone 9
Propagation: Seed when ripe, in heat, or by offsets, both in spring
Flowering time: Spring to summer

A deciduous, bulbous perennial. Leaves lance-shaped, bright green. Flowers red, curved tubular, in umbels. Tender.

• Low allergen

***Dactylorhiza elata* A.G.M.
(Orchidaceae)**

Common name: Marsh orchid
Height: 2ft (60cm)
Spread: 6in (15cm)
Aspect: Part shade
Soil: Moist, well-drained
Hardiness: Zone 6
Propagation: Division in spring
Flowering time: Late spring and early summer

A tuberous, deciduous, terrestrial orchid. Flowers in dense terminal umbels, purple, for a long period.

- Handsome foliage

DAHLIA (Asteraceae)
Dahlia

A genus consisting of only some 30 species, but with approximately 20,000 cultivars. The genus can be divided, for our purposes here, into two main categories of plants:

1) Tall-growing varieties suitable for borders

2) Dwarf 'bedding' varieties.

All have in common that, in warm climates, they provide color in the garden from midsummer right through to autumn, or even later with some plants. They are also excellent for cutting. They are classified according to the size of the flower as small-, medium-, and large-flowered, and according to the form of the flower into:

Single varieties
Waterlily varieties
Collerette varieties
Anemone-flowered varieties
Pompom varieties
Ball varieties
Semi-cactus varieties
Cactus varieties
Decorative varieties
Miscellaneous varieties

All Dahlias are prone to attack by slugs and snails at all stages of their life cycle, and they are also prone to powdery mildew. The tubers must be lifted and stored in a dry, frost-free area over winter, and are prone to rotting during winter storage. All are tender, and Zone 10, except *Dahlia merckii* which is Zone 9.

DAHLIA 'DAVID HOWARD' A.G.M.

Dahlia 'Bishop of Llandaff' A.G.M.
(Asteraceae)

Common name: None
Height: 4ft (1.2m)
Spread: 18in (45cm)
Aspect: Full sun
Soil: Well-drained, humus-rich, fertile
Hardiness: Zone 10
Propagation: Division in spring
Flowering time: From midsummer through to autumn

A hybrid medium-sized, 'miscellaneous' dahlia. Leaves are pinnate and black-red. Flowers peony-like, semi-double, bright red in color. Suitable for mixed borders.

- Attracts butterflies • Attracts slugs
- Good cut flower
- Handsome foliage

Dahlia 'David Howard' A.G.M.
(Asteraceae)

Common name: None
Height: 4ft (1.2m)
Spread: 18in (45cm)
Aspect: Sun
Soil: Well-drained, fertile, humus-rich
Hardiness: Zone 10
Propagation: Division in spring
Flowering time: From summer through to late autumn

A miniature, decorative dahlia. Flowers fully double. Ray florets flat, blunt-ended. Color orange, with a bright red center.

- Attracts butterflies • Attracts slugs
- Good cut flower

***Dahlia* Dwarf Border Mixed (Asteraceae)**

Height: 2ft (60cm)
Spread 1ft (30cm)
Aspect: Sun
Soil: Well-drained, fertile, humus-rich
Hardiness: Zone 10
Propagation: Seed or division in spring
Flowering time: Summer to late autumn

A common strain in seed catalogues. Flowers medium-sized, semi-double and double, miscellaneous types, in a wide range of colors. Suitable for bedding.

- Good cut flower
- Attracts slugs
- Attracts butterflies

***Dahlia merckii* (Asteraceae)**

Common name: None
Height: 6ft (1.8m)
Spread: 3ft (90cm)
Aspect: Full sun
Soil: Well-drained, fertile, humus-rich
Hardiness: Zone 9
Propagation: Seed or division in spring
Flowering time: Summer to autumn

A tuberous perennial plant from Mexico. A sprawling, ungainly, many-branched specimen bearing medium-sized single flowers of a pale pink color, with a yellow center. They can be left in the ground over winter in mild areas.

- Attracts butterflies
- Attracts slugs
- Good cut flower

Dahlia 'Moonfire' (Asteraceae)

Common name: None
Height: 3ft (90cm)
Spread: 18in (45cm)
Aspect: Full sun
Soil: Good, well-drained, fertile, humus-rich
Hardiness: Zone 10
Propagation: Division in spring
Flowering time: Summer to late autumn

A very handsome, medium-sized, single-flowered clone. Petals are yellow-colored, with dark red basal regions, and a central yellow disc.

- Attracts butterflies
- Attracts slugs
- Good cut flower

Dianthus barbatus (Caryophyllaceae)

Common name: Sweet William
Height: 28in (70cm)
Spread: 1ft (30cm)
Aspect: Full sun
Soil: Well-drained
Hardiness: Zone 4
Propagation: Seed in heat in spring
Flowering time: Late spring through to early summer

A very popular, short-lived perennial plant, grown invariably as a biennial. Flowers are borne in dense, flat terminal clusters, single, fragrant, petals bearded, in a wide range of colors. Deadhead regularly to prolong the flowering season.

- Scented flowers
- High allergen
- Must deadhead

***Dianthus chinensis* 'Carpet' series (Caryophyllaceae)**

Common name: Chinese pink
Height: 28in (70cm)
Spread: 9in (23cm)
Aspect: Sun
Soil: Well-drained
Hardiness: Zone 7
Propagation: Seed in heat in spring
Flowering time: All summer if deadheaded

A short-lived perennial plant that is grown usually as an annual or a biennial. Flowers are borne in loose terminal cymes, single, white (or red or pink).

- High allergen
- Must deadhead

***Dianthus chinensis* 'Strawberry Parfait' (Caryophyllaceae)**

Common name: None
Height: 1ft (30cm)
Spread: 9in (23cm)
Aspect: Sun
Soil: Well-drained
Hardiness: Zone 7
Propagation: Seed in heat in spring
Flowering time: All summer if deadheaded

A short-lived perennial plant, grown usually as an annual or biennial. Flowers are borne in loose terminal cymes, single, cream, with dark pink centers.

- High allergen
- Must deadhead

***Diascia* 'Eclat' (Scrophulariaceae)**

Common name: None
Height: 1ft (30cm)
Spread: 10in (25cm)
Aspect: Sun
Soil: Moist, well-drained, fertile
Hardiness: Zone 8
Propagation: Cuttings, in spring or summer
Flowering time: All summer

Flowers tubular, spurred, deep pink racemes.

- Attracts slugs
- Short-lived

DIASCIA 'ELIZABETH'

DIASCIA (Scrophulariaceae)
Twinspur

A genus comprising of some 50 annual and short-lived perennial plants from southern Africa. They are not universally hardy but some are proving to be. They like moist soil but they will not tolerate waterlogged conditions. They may be erect or prostrate and some sucker freely. Their inflorescences are terminal racemes, bearing tubular flowers of pink or salmon-pink for long periods in summer. They benefit from regular deadheading, and should be sheared over after flowering to encourage fresh growth for another season.

Diascia 'Elizabeth' (Scrophulariaceae)

Common name: None
Height: 1ft (30cm)
Spread: 10in (25cm)
Aspect: Sun
Soil: Moist, well-drained, fertile
Hardiness: Zone 8
Propagation: Cuttings taken in spring or summer
Flowering time: Throughout the summer

A compact hybrid *Diascia*. Flowers tubular in shape, spurred, two-tone pink and pale pink in color, borne in racemes.

- Attracts slugs
- Short-lived

Diascia integerrima
(Scrophulariaceae)

Common name: None
Height: 1ft (30cm)
Spread: 30in (75cm)
Aspect: Sun
Soil: Moist, well-drained, fertile
Hardiness: Zone 8
Propagation: Seed in heat when ripe; cuttings in spring or summer
Flowering time: Throughout the summer season

A creeping, suckering species from South Africa. Flowers are borne on upright, wiry stems, purplish-pink, spurred, in loose racemes.

- Attracts slugs
- Invasive

Diascia rigescens A.G.M.
(Scrophulariaceae)

Common name: None
Height: 1ft (30cm)
Spread: 16in (40cm)
Aspect: Sun
Soil: Moist, well-drained, fertile
Hardiness: Zone 8
Propagation: Seed in heat as soon as ripe; cuttings, spring or summer
Flowering time: Summer

A species with a floppy habit that requires staking. Flowers are deep pink in color, spurred, and are borne in dense racemes.

- Short-lived
- Attracts slugs
- Requires staking

Diascia 'Ruby Field' A.G.M.
(Scrophulariaceae)

Common name: None
Height: 10in (25cm)
Spread: 18in (45cm)
Aspect: Sun
Soil: Moist, well-drained, fertile
Hardiness: Zone 8
Propagation: Cuttings in spring or summer
Flowering time: Throughout the summer period

An old favorite in garden cultivation and one of the best. Flowers are tubular in shape, spurred, salmon-pink in color, and are borne in racemes.

- Attracts slugs
- Short-lived

***Dicentra* 'Pearl Drops'**
(Papaveraceae)

Common name: None
Height: 1ft (30cm)
Spread: 18in (45cm)
Aspect: Part shade
Soil: Moist, well-drained, fertile
Hardiness: Zone 5
Propagation: Division in spring
Flowering time: Mid-spring to midsummer

A quiet charmer. Ferny blue-green, glaucous foliage. Flowers pendent, white, with a hint of pink, in racemes.

- 🟢 Handsome foliage
- 🔴 Attracts slugs
- 🔴 Invasive
- 🔴 Poisonous
- 🔴 Skin irritant

***Dicentra scandens* (Papaveraceae)**

Common name: None
Height: 5ft (1.5m)
Spread: 18in (45cm)
Aspect: part shade
Soil: Moist, well-drained, fertile
Hardiness: Zone 6
Propagation: Seed when ripe, or in spring
Flowering time: Mid- to late summer

A scrambling or climbing perennial species. Flowers yellow, pendent, in long racemes on leafy, wiry stems, from midsummer. Not spectacular, but different.

- 🟢 Handsome foliage
- 🔴 Attracts slugs
- 🔴 Poisonous
- 🔴 Skin irritant

***Dicentra* 'Spring Morning'**
(Papaveraceae)

Common name: None
Height: 18in (45cm)
Spread: 18in (45cm)
Aspect: Part shade
Soil: Moist, well-drained, fertile
Hardiness: Zone 5
Propagation: Division just after the leaves die down, or in spring
Flowering time: Late summer to autumn

A rhizomatous, hardy, hybrid perennial. Leaves ferny. Flowers in arching racemes, pendent, pale pink.

- 🟢 Handsome foliage
- 🔴 Attracts slugs
- 🔴 Poisonous
- 🔴 Skin irritant

DIGITALIS (*Scrophulariaceae*)
Foxglove

A genus of about 20 biennial or short-lived perennials. They are tall, handsome architectural plants with quite a long flowering season, and are attractive to bees They are very accommodating plants, and drought-tolerant, but suffer from a number of drawbacks: they are poisonous, skin-irritant, prolific seeders, short-lived, and prone to powdery mildew. Despite these, they are very decorative, rewarding plants, and will tolerate shade.

The flowering spikes are racemes, usually one-sided, and the flowers are often beautifully marked inside, and are good for cutting. They should be deadheaded to prevent self-seeding.

Digitalis grandiflora A.G.M. (Scrophulariaceae)

Common name: Foxglove
Height: 3ft (1m)
Spread: 18in (45cm)
Aspect: Part shade
Soil: Humus-rich
Hardiness: Zone 4
Propagation: Seed in spring
Flowering time: From early to midsummer

A handsome perennial plant. Flowers are tubular, pale yellow in color, veined brown inside, well spaced out in racemes.

- Drought-tolerant
- Attracts bees
- Good cut flower
- Poisonous
- Skin irritant
- Prone to mildew
- Seeds everywhere
- Short-lived

Digitalis lanata A.G.M. (Scrophulariaceae)

Common name: Foxglove
Height: 2ft (60cm)
Spread: 1ft (30cm)
Aspect: part shade
Soil: humus-rich
Hardiness: Zone 7
Propagation: Seed in spring
Flowering time: From mid- to late summer

A perennial woodlander. Flowers pale cream/fawn in color, with violet-brown veining, and a pale cream lower lip, in dense racemes.

- Good cut flower
- Attracts bees
- Drought-tolerant
- Poisonous
- Skin irritant
- Prone to mildew
- Short-lived
- Seeds everywhere

DIGITALIS x MERTONENSIS A.G.M.

Digitalis lutea (Scrophulariaceae)

Common name: Foxglove
Height: 2ft (60cm)
Spread: 1ft (30cm)
Aspect: Part shade
Soil: Humus-rich, alkaine
Hardiness: Zone 4
Propagation: Seed in spring
Flowering time: From early to midsummer

A perennial woodlander, with glossy green leaves. Flowers are pale yellow, borne in slim racemes from the early summer onwards.

- Good cut flower
- Drought-tolerant
- Attracts bees
- Handsome foliage
- Poisonous
- Skin irritant
- Seeds everywhere
- Prone to mildew

Digitalis* x *mertonensis A.G.M. (Scrophulariaceae)

Common name: Foxglove
Height: 3ft (90cm)
Spread: 1ft (30cm)
Aspect: Part shade
Soil: Humus-rich
Hardiness: Zone 5
Propagation: Seed in spring
Flowering time: Spring to early summer

A tetraploid hybrid perennial that comes true from seed. Leaves glossy-green. Flowers pinkish, in racemes, from spring to early summer.

- Good cut flower
- Handsome foliage
- Attracts bees
- Poisonous
- Skin irritant
- Seeds everywhere
- Short-lived
- Prone to mildew

PERENNIALS

Doronicum orientale 'Finesse'
(Asteraceae)

Common name: Leopard's bane
Height: 20in (50cm)
Spread: 3ft (90cm)
Aspect: Part shade
Soil: Moist, humus-rich
Hardiness: Zone 5
Propagation: Seed in spring; division in autumn
Flowering time: From mid to late spring

A selected clone of a rhizomatous species that comes true from seed. Flowers are borne on long stems, solitary, single, yellow, with slim ray-florets.

- Good cut flower
- Attracts slugs
- Prone to mildew
- Divide regularly

Doronicum pardalianches
(Asteraceae)

Common name: Leopard's bane
Height: 3ft (90cm)
Spread: 3ft (90cm)
Aspect: Part shade
Soil: Moist, humus-rich
Hardiness: Zone 6
Propagation: Seed in spring; division in autumn
Flowering time: From late spring to midsummer

A spreading, rhizomatous woodlander. Leaves hairy, toothed, green Flowers single, yellow-colored daisies in corymbs, borne on branching stems, from late spring.

- Good cut flower
- Attracts slugs
- Prone to mildew
- Divide regularly

Eccremocarpus scaber A.G.M.
(Bignoniaceae)

Common name: Chilean gloryflower
Height: 15ft (4.5m)
Spread: 3ft (90cm)
Aspect: Full sun
Soil: Well-drained, fertile
Hardiness: Zone 9
Propagation: Seed in heat in spring
Flowering time: From late spring to autumn

An evergreen, perennial climber. Flowers tubular, orange, with red mouths, in racemes. Tender.

- Evergreen
- Handsome foliage

EPILOBIUM ANGUSTIFOLIUM 'ALBUM'

Echinacea purpurea (Asteraceae)

Common name: Coneflower
Height: 4ft (12m)
Spread: 18in (45cm)
Aspect: Full sun
Soil: Well-drained, humus-rich
Hardiness: Zone 3
Propagation: Seed in spring; division in spring or autumn
Flowering time: Midsummer to early autumn

A rhizomatous hardy perennial plant. Flowers solitary, single, ray florets reflexed, purple (or white) in color, disc florets golden-brown, from midsummer.

- 🟢 Good cut flower
- 🔴 Prone to mildew
- 🔴 Attracts slugs
- 🔴 High allergen

Echium pininiana (Boraginaceae)

Common name: Bugloss
Height: 12ft (4m)
Spread: 3ft (1m)
Aspect: Sun
Soil: Well-drained, fertile
Hardiness: Zone 9
Propagation: Seed in summer
Flowering time: Mid- and late summer

A striking, short-lived perennial from the Canary Islands. Leaves in rosettes, silver-hairy. Flowers funnel-shaped, blue, with large bracts, in huge panicle-like cyme. Not suitable for the small garden.

- 🟢 Architectural plant
- 🔴 Short-lived
- 🟢 Drought-tolerant
- 🔴 Poisonous
- 🟢 Handsome foliage
- 🔴 Skin irritant
- 🔴 Must not be moved

Epilobium angustifolium 'Album' (Onagraceae)

Common name: Willow herb
Height: 5ft (1.5m)
Spread: 3ft (1m)
Aspect: Sun or part shade
Soil: Moist, well-drained, humus-rich
Hardiness: Zone 3
Propagation: Seed when ripe
Flowering time: Midsummer to early autumn

A rhizomatous, perennial. Flowers shallow white saucers, in racemes.

- 🔴 Attracts slugs
- 🔴 Invasive
- 🔴 Seeds everywhere

PERENNIALS

Epilobium dodonaei (**Onagraceae**)

Common name: Willow herb
Height: 3ft (90cm)
Spread: 8in (20cm)
Aspect: Sun or part shade
Soil: Moist, well-drained, humus-rich
Hardiness: Zone 6
Propagation: Seed when ripe; division in spring or autumn
Flowering time: Throughout summer

Very invasive perennial. Flowers dark pink, in loose terminal racemes. Suitable for wild gardens.

- Attracts slugs
- Invasive
- Prone to mildew
- Seeds everywhere

Eremurus himalaicus (**Asphodelaceae**)

Common name: Foxtail lily
Height: 7ft (2m)
Spread: 2ft (60cm)
Aspect: Sun
Soil: Well-drained, fertile
Hardiness: Zone 3
Propagation: Seed in autumn; division after flowering
Flowering time: Late spring and early summer

A tall, architectural perennial plant. Roots spread out just below the surface, so take care if digging around the plant. Flowers are white in color, borne in dense, tall racemes. Requires cold to induce flowering.

- Drought-tolerant
- Low allergen
- Attracts slugs
- Requires staking

Eremurus robustus (Asphodelaceae)

Common name: Giant desert candle
Height: 10ft (3m)
Spread: 3ft (1m)
Aspect: Full sun
Soil: Sharply drained, fertile
Hardiness: Zone 6
Propagation: Seed in autumn; division after flowering
Flowering time: Early to midsummer

An architectural perennial plant. Roots spread just under soil surface, and plant will be killed if they are damaged. Flowers pink, in tall, dense racemes from early summer. Needs cold to induce flowering.

- Low allergen
- Attracts slugs

Erigeron aurantiacus (Asteraceae)

Common name: Daisy fleabane
Height: 1ft (30cm)
Spread: 1ft (30cm)
Aspect: Sun
Soil: Well-drained, fertile, humus-rich
Hardiness: Zone 6
Propagation: Seed or division in spring
Flowering time: All summer

A short-lived perennial. Leaves spoon-shaped, velvety, green. Flowers solitary, single, bright orange, with a central yellow boss.

- Attracts bees
- Atttracts butterflies
- Drought-tolerant
- Good cut flower
- Attracts slugs
- Divide regularly
- High allergen
- Short-lived

ERIGERON (Asteraceae)

Erigeron

A genus of more than 200 species from North America. They are accommodating, easy-going plants, requiring only sun and reasonably fertile soil. Most are reliably hardy, drought-tolerant, and can be grown in coastal gardens, particularly *Erigeron glaucus*. They attract bees and butterflies and make good cut flowers. Almost all are long-flowering; *Erigeron karvinskianus* blooms from early summer to late autumn and does not require to be deadheaded, so one could not ask for more from a plant. On the debit side, they are highly allergenic plants, benefit from regular lifting and division, and slugs are fond of their new growth.

Erigeron 'Dignity' (Asteraceae)

Common name: None
Height: 20in (50cm)
Spread: 18in (45cm)
Aspect: Sun
Soil: Well-drained, fertile, humus-rich
Hardiness: Zone 5
Propagation: Division in spring
Flowering time: From early through to midsummer

Hybrid clump-forming cultivar. Flowers solitary, ray florets violet, disc florets are yellow.

- Attracts bees
- Attracts butterflies
- Drought-tolerant
- Good cut flower
- Attracts slugs
- Divide regularly
- High allergen

Erigeron 'Four Winds' (Asteraceae)

Common name: None
Height: 20in (50cm)
Spread: 18in (45cm)
Aspect: Sun
Soil: Well-drained, fertile, humus-rich
Hardiness: Zone 5
Propagation: Division in spring
Flowering time: Early through to midsummer

A free-flowering cultivar. Flowers solitary, single, of strong pink, with yellow-colored centers.

- Attracts bees
- Attracts butterflies
- Drought-tolerant
- Good cut flower
- Attracts slugs
- Divide regularly
- High allergen

Erigeron glaucus (Asteraceae)

Common name: Beach fleabane
Height: 1ft (30cm)
Spread: 2ft (60cm)
Aspect: Sun
Soil: Well-drained, fertile, humus-rich
Hardiness: Zone 3
Propagation: Seed or division in spring
Flowering time: Late spring to midsummer

A species from coastal regions of California and Oregon. Leaves glaucus-green. Flowers solitary, semi-double, with ray florets of pale mauve, and yellow disc florets.

- Attracts bees
- Attracts butterflies
- Drought-tolerant
- Attracts slugs
- High allergen

Erigeron karvinskianus (Asteraceae)

Common name: Bonytip fleabane
Height: 1ft (30cm)
Spread: 3ft (90cm)
Aspect: Sun
Soil: Well-drained, fertile, humus-rich
Hardiness: Zone 7
Propagation: Seed or division in spring
Flowering time: From midsummer to late autumn

As long-flowering garden plants go, this is in the top flight. Flowers are single, small, white-colored, becoming pink with age. It does not require deadheading. It makes a superb wall plant and is long-lived.

- Attracts bees
- Drought-tolerant
- High allergen
- Seeds everywhere

Erigeron 'Quakeress' (Asteraceae)

Common name: None
Height: 2ft (60cm)
Spread: 18in (45cm)
Aspect: Sun
Soil: Well-drained, fertile, humus-rich
Hardiness: Zone 5
Propagation: Division in spring
Flowering time: From early to midsummer

A clump-forming perennial. Leaves gray-green in color. Flowers single, white, with a hint of pink, and yellow centers, borne in corymbs.

- Attracts bees
- Attracts butterflies
- Drought-tolerant
- Good cut flower
- Attracts slugs
- Divide regularly
- High allergen

ERIGERON 'SERENITY'

Erigeron 'Serenity' (Asteraceae)

Common name: None
Height: 30in (75cm)
Spread: 18in (45cm)
Aspect: Sun
Soil: Well-drained, fertile, humus-rich
Hardiness: Zone 5
Propagation: Division in spring
Flowering time: From early to midsummer

A lax cultivar. Flowers semi-double, violet-mauve, with yellow-colored centers, borne in corymbs from early summer onwards.

- Attracts bees
- Attracts butterflies
- Drought-tolerant
- Good cut flower
- Attracts slugs
- Divide regularly
- High allergen

Eriophyllum lanatum (Asteraceae)

Common name: Wooly eriophyllum
Height: 2ft (60cm)
Spread: 2ft (60cm)
Aspect: Sun
Soil: Sharply-drained
Hardiness: Zone 5
Propagation: Seed in autumn; division in spring
Flowering time: From late spring through to summer

A hardy, mildly invasive perennial plant. Leaves silvery-gray, white-wooly. Flowers yellow, daisy-like, with dark yellow centers, singly or in corymbs.

- Drought-tolerant
- Handsome foliage
- Attracts slugs
- High allergen
- Invasive

Erodium 'Fran's choice' (Geraniaceae)

Common name: None
Height: 8in (20cm)
Spread: 8in (20cm)
Aspect: Sun
Soil: Sharply-drained
Hardiness: Zone 7
Propagation: Division in spring
Flowering time: From early summer to autumn

A hybrid clone with pinnatisect, mid-green leaves. Flowers are pink colored, borne in short terminal umbels.

- Drought-tolerant
- Low allergen
- Seeds everywhere

ERODIUM 'MERSTHAM PINK'

Erodium manescaui (Geraniaceae)

Common name: Pyrenees heronbill
Height: 18in (45cm)
Spread: 8in (20cm)
Aspect: Sun
Soil: Sharply-drained, humus-rich
Hardiness: Zone 6
Propagation: Seed when ripe; division in spring
Flowering time: Early summer to autumn

A handsome species. Leaves pinnate, toothed, hairy, mid-green. Flowers borne in long-stemmed umbels, magenta-colored, the upper pair of petals being spotted, from early summer through to autumn.

- Drought-tolerant
- Low allergen
- Seeds everywhere

***Erodium* 'Merstham Pink'** (Geraniaceae)

Common name: None
Height: 9in (23cm)
Spread: 10in (25cm)
Aspect: Sun
Soil: Sharply-drained
Hardiness: Zone 6
Propagation: Division in spring
Flowering time: Early summer to autumn

A hybrid clone, with ferny, carrot-like foliage of dark green. Flowers in umbels, pink. Not spectacular, but very reliable. Good wall plant. Does not self-seed.

- Drought-tolerant
- Handsome foliage
- Low allergen

ERODIUM (Geraniaceae)

Erodium

A genus of some 60 species of perennials, annuals, and subshrubs, with handsome foliage and a long flowering period. They are mostly hardy, but not universally so, and are drought-tolerant. The flowers have a close resemblance to those of the *Geranium*, but have five stamens as opposed to the ten in *Geranium*. They are good coastal plants, like sun, good drainage, and will self-seed unless deadheaded.

Erodium pelargoniiflorum (Geraniaceae)

Common name: Geranium, Heronbill
Height: 1ft (30cm)
Spread: 1ft (30cm)
Aspect: Sun
Soil: Sharply drained
Hardiness: Zone 6
Propagation: Seed when ripe; division in spring
Flowering time: From early summer to early autumn

A species from Anatolia, with leaves resembling those of a Geranium. Flowers white, with upper petals marked maroon, in umbels. A little charmer.

- Low allergen
- Drought-tolerant
- Seeds everywhere

Erysimum 'Bredon' A.G.M. (Brassicaceae)

Common name: Wallflower
Height: 1ft (30cm)
Spread: 18in (45cm)
Aspect: Sun
Soil: Well-drained, fertile
Hardiness: Zone 6
Propagation: Softwood cuttings, with a heel, in spring or summer
Flowering time: From mid-spring to early summer

An evergreen, clump-forming perennial. Leaves bluish-green. Flowers bright yellow in color, opening in tall racemes from mid-spring onwards.

- Evergreen
- Handsome foliage
- Drought-tolerant
- Short-lived
- Prone to mildew
- Attracts slugs

ERYSIMUM (Brassicaceae)
Wallflower

A genus of 80 or so species of mostly evergreen annuals and perennials, but the perennials are often grown as biennials, inasmuch as they become very woody, and are short-lived; they should be trimmed over lightly after flowering to prevent legginess. The flowers have four petals in the shape of a cross. They have a long flowering season, from late spring onwards.

They like full sun and sharp drainage, and are drought-tolerant. They are prone to powdery mildew, and slugs. They come readily from seed.

ERYSIMUM LINIFOLIUM 'VARIEGATUM'

Erysimum cheiri (Brassicaceae)

Common name: Wallflower
Height: 32in (80cm)
Spread: 16in (40cm)
Aspect: Sun
Soil: well-drained, fertile
Hardiness: Zone 6
Propagation: Seed in spring
Flowering time: Spring

The well-known bedding Wallflower is technically a short-lived perennial, but is grown invariably as a biennial. Scented flowers in a wide range of colors, in short racemes for many weeks.

- Scented flowers
- Evergreen
- Drought-tolerant
- Attracts slugs
- Prone to mildew
- Short-lived

***Erysimum* 'Constant Cheer' A.G.M.** (Brassicaceae)

Common name: Wallflower
Height: 1ft (30cm)
Spread: 2ft (60cm)
Aspect: Sun
Soil: Well-drained, fertile
Hardiness: Zone 7
Propagation: Softwood cuttings with a heel in spring or autumn.
Flowering time: Mid-spring to summer

A very handsome evergreen cultivar. Leaves dark green. Flowers dusky red on opening, but becoming deep pink with time, borne in short racemes.

- Evergreen
- Drought-tolerant
- Prone to mildew
- Attracts slugs

***Erysimum linifolium* 'Variegatum'** (Brassicaceae)

Common name: Alpine wallflower
Height: 28in (70cm)
Spread: 10in (25cm)
Aspect: Sun
Soil: Well-drained, humus-rich
Hardiness: Zone 6
Propagation: Softwood cuttings, with a heel, in spring or summer
Flowering time: Mid-spring to early autumn

A woody, short-lived, perennial with linear leaves of pale green, edged in cream. Flowers lilac, in racemes.

- Drought-tolerant
- Evergreen
- Handsome foliage
- Attracts slugs
- Prone to mildew
- Short-lived

Erysimum 'Orange Flame' (Brassicaceae)

Common name: Wallflower
Height: 4in (10cm)
Spread: 18in (45cm)
Aspect: Sun
Soil: Well-drained, fertile
Hardiness: Zone 7
Propagation: Softwood cuttings with a heel in spring or autumn
Flowering time: From late spring to early autumn

An evergreen, mat-forming, creeping perennial. Leaves dark green. Flowers orange, in short, lax racemes from late spring.

- Evergreen
- Drought-tolerant
- Prone to mildew
- Attracts slugs

Erysimum 'Sprite' (Brassicaceae)

Common name: Wallflower
Height: 8in (20cm)
Spread: 18in (45cm)
Aspect: Sun
Soil: Well-drained, fertile
Hardiness: Zone 7
Propagation: Softwood cuttings with a heel in spring or autumn
Flowering time: From early through to late spring

A creeping, mat-forming, evergreen perennial plant. Flowers are pale yellow colored, borne in short racemes, throughout spring.

- Drought-tolerant
- Evergreen
- Prone to mildew
- Attracts slugs

Eucomis autumnalis (Hyacinthaceae)

Common name: Pineapple flower/lily
Height: 1ft (30cm)
Spread: 8in (20cm)
Aspect: Sun
Soil: Well-drained, fertile, dry in winter
Hardiness: Zone 8
Propagation: Offsets in spring
Flowering time: Late summer through to late autumn

A half-hardy bulbous perennial. Leaves wavy-margined, pale green. Flowers are pale greenish-white, borne in dense racemes.

- Drought-tolerant
- Good cut flower
- Handsome foliage
- Attracts slugs

EUPHORBIA POLYCHROMA

Euphorbia polychroma (Euphorbiaceae)

Common name: Spurge
Height: 16in (40cm)
Spread: 2ft (60cm)
Aspect: Sun or part shade
Soil: Well-drained, humus-rich
Hardiness: Zone 6
Propagation: Seed or division in spring
Flowering time: From mid-spring through to midsummer

A hardy herbaceous perennial. Leaves dark green in color. Flowers are inconspicuous, cyathia yellow, involucral bracts are yellow-green, borne in terminal cymes from mid-spring onwards.

- Good cut flower
- Drought-tolerant
- Must not be moved
- Poisonous
- High allergen

Eucomis bicolor (Hyacinthaceae)

Common name: Pineapple flower/lily
Height: 2ft (60cm)
Spread: 10in (25cm)
Aspect: Sun
Soil: Well-drained, fertile, and dry in winter
Hardiness: Zone 8
Propagation: Offsets in spring
Flowering time: Midsummer to late autumn

A half-hardy, bulbous perennial. Leaves wavy-edged, bright green. Flowers pale green, with purple-edged tepals, in dense racemes, topped by pineapple-like bracts.

- Drought-tolerant
- Good cut flower
- Handsome foliage
- Attracts slugs

EUPHORBIA SCHILLINGII A.G.M.

Euphorbia schillingii A.G.M.
(Euphorbiaceae)

Common name: Spurge
Height: 3ft (1m)
Spread: 1ft (30cm)
Aspect: Part shade
Soil: Moist, humus-rich
Hardiness: Zone 5
Propagation: Seed or division in spring
Flowering time: From midsummer to mid-autumn.

A hardy herbaceous perennial. Leaves dark green in color with contrasting white veins. Flowers inconspicuous, cyathia yellow, and greenish-yellow involucral bracts, in terminal cymes.

- Good cut flower
- Must not be moved
- Poisonous
- High allergen

Euphorbia sikkimensis
(Euphorbiaceae)

Common name: Spurge
Height: 4ft (1.2m)
Spread: 18in (45cm)
Aspect: Part shade
Soil: Moist, humus-rich
Hardiness: Zone 6
Propagation: Seed or division in spring
Flowering time: From mid- through to late summer

A hardy herbaceous perennial. Leaves dark green, marked red. Flowers inconspicuous. Yellow cyathia cupped by greenish-yellow-colored involucres, borne in terminal cymes.

- Good cut flower
- Must not be moved
- Poisonous
- High allergen

FRAGARIA 'LIPSTICK'

Filipendula purpurea A.G.M. (Rosaceae)

Common name: Japanese meadowsweet
Height: 4ft (1.2m)
Spread: 2ft (60cm)
Aspect: Sun or part shade
Soil: Moist, well-drained, humus-rich
Hardiness: Zone 6
Propagation: Seed or division in spring or autumn.
Flowering time: Late spring to late summer

A perennial with pinnate, toothed leaves. Flowers carmine-red, fading to pink, in dense corymbs from late spring.

- 🟢 Handsome foliage 🔴 Prone to mildew

Filipendula ulmaria (Rosaceae)

Common name: Queen of the meadow
Height: 3ft (90cm)
Spread: 2ft (60cm)
Aspect: Sun or part shade
Soil: Moist, well-drained, humus-rich
Hardiness: Zone 2
Propagation: Seed or division in spring or autumn
Flowering time: Late spring to midsummer

A hardy European perennial plant. Leaves are pinnate, strongly-veined, green, downy-white below. Flowers are creamy-white in color borne in dense branching corymbs from late spring onwards.

- 🟢 Handsome foliage 🔴 Prone to mildew

Fragaria 'Lipstick' (Rosaceae)

Common name: Strawberry
Height: 6in (15cm)
Spread: Indefinite
Aspect: Sun or part shade
Soil: Moist, well-drained, fertile
Hardiness: Zone 5
Propagation: Plantlets, from runners, at any time
Flowering time: Late spring to mid-autumn

A selected, sterile clone of the well-known stoloniferous fruiting perennial. Evergreen in mild areas. Flowers single, cerise, in cymes. Fragaria 'Pink Panda' has pink flowers.

- 🟢 Handsome foliage 🔴 Invasive
- 🔴 Prone to mildew

PERENNIALS

Gaillardia x *grandiflora* 'Burgunder' (Asteraceae)

Common name: None
Height: 2ft (60cm)
Spread: 18in (45cm)
Aspect: Sun
Soil: Sharply-drained, poor
Hardiness: Zone 4
Propagation: Softwood cuttings, in spring
Flowering time: Early summer to autumn

A short-lived clone of garden origin. Flowers large single daisies, with deep wine-red ray florets, and yellow-brown disc florets. Cut back hard in late summer to improve over-wintering.

- Drought-tolerant
- Good cut flower
- Attracts slugs
- High allergen
- Prone to mildew
- Requires staking
- Short-lived

Gaillardia x *grandiflora* 'Kobold' (Asteraceae)

Common name: None
Height: 1ft (30cm)
Spread: 18in (45cm)
Aspect: Sun
Soil: Sharply-drained, poor
Hardiness: Zone 4
Propagation: Softwood cuttings in spring
Flowering time: Mid-summer to autumn

A very compact, dwarf, short-lived hybrid clone. Flowers single, ray florets red colored, tipped with yellow, disc florets deep red-brown in color. Cut back hard in the late summer to improve the plant's chance of over-wintering successfully.

- Drought-tolerant
- Good cut flower
- Attracts slugs
- High allergen
- Prone to mildew
- Short-lived

GAILLARDIA x GRANDIFLORA 'RED PLUME'

Gaillardia x _grandiflora_ 'Red Plume' (PBR) (Asteraceae)

Common name: None
Height: 18in (45cm)
Spread: 18in (45cm)
Aspect: Sun
Soil: Sharply-drained, poor
Hardiness: Zone 4
Propagation: Softwood cuttings in spring
Flowering time: Mid-summer to autumn

A very recently introduced variety to garden cultivation. Flowers have ray florets of a deep, rich red color, and disc florets are brown-red. Cut back hard in the ate summer in order to improve the chance of over-wintering successfully.

- Attracts slugs
- Drought-tolerant
- Good cut flower
- High allergen
- Prone to mildew

***Galega* x *hartlandii* 'Alba' A.G.M.
(Papilionaceae)**

Common name: Goats-rue
Height: 5ft (1.5m)
Spread: 3ft (90cm)
Aspect: Sun or part shade
Soil: Moist
Hardiness: Zone 4
Propagation: Seed or division in spring
Flowering time: Early summer to autumn

A mildly invasive perennial plant. Flowers are borne in erect, axillary racemes, pea-like, white. Deadhead to prevent self-seeding.

- Good cut flower
- Invasive
- Must not be moved
- Requires staking
- Seeds everywhere

***Galega* 'Lady Wilson'
(Papilionaceae)**

Common name: None
Height: 5ft (1.5m)
Spread: 3ft (90cm)
Aspect: Sun or half shade
Soil: Moist
Hardiness: Zone 4
Propagation: Seed or division in spring
Flowering time: Early summer to autumn

A mildly invasive perennial. Flowers in racemes, bicolored, mauve-pink and white. Deadhead to prevent self-seeding.

- Good cut flower
- Invasive
- Must not be moved
- Requires staking
- Seeds everywhere

***Galega officinalis* (Papilionaceae)**

Common name: Common goats-rue
Height: 5ft (1.5m)
Spread: 3ft (90cm)
Aspect: Sun or part shade
Soil: Moist
Hardiness: Zone 4
Propagation: Seed or division in spring
Flowering time: Summer to autumn

A tall, vigorous perennial. Flowers white, mauve or bicolored, in racemes. Deadhead to prevent self-seeding.

- Good cut flower
- Invasive
- Must not be moved
- Requires staking
- Seeds everywhere

Galium odoratum (**Rubiaceae**)

Common name: None
Height: 18in (45cm)
Spread: Indefinite
Aspect: Sun or part shade
Soil: Moist, humus-rich
Hardiness: Zone 3
Propagation: Seed when ripe; division in spring/autumn
Flowering time: Late spring to midsummer

A rhizomatous perennial, making a useful groundcover plant. Flowers are white, star-shaped, scented, borne in umbel-like cymes.

- Scented flowers
- Invasive

Gaura lindheimeri A.G.M. (**Onagraceae**)

Common name: White gaura
Height: 5ft (1.5m)
Spread: 3ft (90cm)
Aspect: Sun
Soil: Sharply-drained
Hardiness: Zone 4
Propagation: Seed or division in spring
Flowering time: From late spring through to autumn

A hardy, short-lived perennial from Texas, but with a particularly long flowering season. Flowers are white in color, fading to pink, and are borne in loose panicles.

- Drought-tolerant
- Requires staking
- Short-lived

***Gaura lindheimeri* 'Siskyou Pink'** (**Onagraceae**)

Common name: None
Height: 5ft (1.5m)
Spread: 3ft (90cm)
Aspect: Sun
Soil: Sharply-drained,
Hardiness: Zone 4
Propagation: Division in spring
Flowering time: Late spring through to early autumn

A charming, short-lived clone for garden cultivation, with flowers colored a shade of pale to deep pink, borne in panicles.

- Drought-tolerant
- Requires staking
- Short-lived

***Gazania* 'Christopher Lloyd'**
(Asteraceae)

Common name: Treasure flower
Height: 8in (20cm)
Spread: 8in (20cm)
Aspect: Full sun
Soil: Sharply-drained
Hardiness: Zone 9
Propagation: Basal cuttings in late summer, or early autumn
Flowering time: All summer long, but opening only in sun

A selected clone of a tender, evergreen perennial. Leaves shiny-green above, white- hairy below. Flowers solitary, single, pink ray florets with a dark purple base, and a yellow-colored center.

- Drought-tolerant
- Evergreen
- Good cut flower
- High allergen
- Must deadhead

***Gazania* 'Daybreak' series A.G.M.**
(Asteraceae)

Common name: None
Height: 8in (20cm)
Spread: 8in (20cm)
Aspect: Full sun
Soil: Sharply-drained
Hardiness: Zone 9
Propagation: Seed in heat in spring
Flowering time: All summer long, but opening only in sun

A tender evergreen perennial from South Africa. Leaves glossy-green in color above, silky-white hairy below. Flowers are solitary, single, opening only in sun; white, orange, yellow or pink.

- Drought-tolerant
- Evergreen
- Good cut flower
- High allergen
- Must deadhead

GERANIUM (Geraniaceae)
Cranesbill

A genus of 300 species and innumerable hybrids. They are usually long-flowering, long-lived, easy to grow, and have handsome foliage; as a result they are indispensable. They come from a widely diverse group of habitats in the wild, and so their cultural requirements vary; for the same reason, their degree of hardiness can vary widely. What they all have in common is a dislike of boggy or waterlogged conditions.

The flowers are flat or saucer-shaped, and may be in cymes, umbels, or panicles. Most species are rather floppy in habit and some type of support is usually necessary; all should be sheared over after flowering to encourage next year's growth. All are drought-tolerant and low allergen. *Geranium thunbergii* self-seeds to a totally unacceptable degree, so it should be avoided at all costs if you are not prepared to deadhead.

About 25 have been given the accolade of an Award of Garden Merit by the Royal Horticultural Society.

Geranium 'Ann Folkard' A.G.M. (Geraniaceae)

Common name: None
Height: 2ft (60cm)
Spread 5ft (1.5m)
Aspect: Sun or part shade
Soil: Well-drained
Hardiness: Zone 7
Propagation: Division in spring
Flowering time: Midsummer through to mid-autumn

A very handsome scrambling ground-covering cultivar. Leaves are yellow at first, becoming green later. Flowers are a rich magenta color with darker colored centers.

- Drought-tolerant
- Handsome foliage
- Low allergen
- Attracts slugs
- Prone to mildew
- Requires space

***Geranium himalayense* 'Plenum'**
(Geraniaceae)

Common name: None
Height: 10in (25cm)
Spread: 18in (45cm)
Aspect: Any
Soil: Well-drained
Hardiness: Zone 4
Propagation: Seed or division in spring
Flowering time: From early summer: flowering intermittent

A double form that is more compact than the single form. Flowers are fully double, purplish-pink in color, and with dark veins.

- Drought-tolerant
- Handsome foliage
- Low allergen
- Attracts slugs
- Prone to mildew

***Geranium maderense* A.G.M.**
(Geraniaceae)

Common name: None
Height: 5ft (1.5m)
Spread: 5ft (1.5m)
Aspect: Sun
Soil: Well-drained
Hardiness: Zone 9
Propagation: Seed or division in spring
Flowering time: Late spring through to midsummer

A tender perennial plant from Madeira. Leaves lobed, toothed, bright green. Flowers flat, magenta, with pale veins, in panicles.

- Drought-tolerant
- Handsome foliage
- Low allergen
- Attracts slugs
- Prone to mildew

***Geranium* x *oxonianum* 'Rose Clair' (Geraniaceae)**

Common name: None
Height: 2ft (60cm)
Spread: 2ft (60cm)
Aspect: Sun or part shade
Soil: Well-drained
Hardiness: Zone 5
Propagation: Division in spring
Flowering time: From spring through to mid-autumn

An evergreen, clump-forming clone. Leaves lobed, toothed, mid-green. Flowers pink, fading to white, borne in loose cymes.

- Evergreen
- Low allergen
- Handsome foliage
- Drought-tolerant
- Attracts slugs
- Prone to mildew

***Geranium psilostemon* A.G.M. (Geraniaceae)**

Common name: None
Height: 4ft (1.2m)
Spread: 4ft (1.2m)
Aspect: Sun or part shade
Soil: Well-drained
Hardiness: Zone 6
Propagation: Seed or division in spring
Flowering time: From early to late summer

A hardy perennial from Armenia. Leaves are lobed, red in spring and autumn, green in summer. Flowers are large, deep magenta in color, borne in upright cymes. Excellent species.

- Drought-tolerant
- Handsome foliage
- Attracts slugs
- Prone to mildew

***Geranium pyrenaicum* 'Bill Wallis' (Geraniaceae)**

Common name: None
Height: 2ft (60cm)
Spread: 2ft (60cm)
Aspect: Sun or part shade
Soil: Well-drained
Hardiness: Zone 7
Propagation: Seed in spring
Flowering time: Spring to autumn

An evergreen hardy perennial that comes true from seed. Flowers are small, rich purple, in loose cymes.

- Evergreen
- Low allergen
- Drought-tolerant
- Handsome foliage
- Seeds everywhere
- Prone to mildew
- Attracts slugs

GERANIUM RIVERSLEIANUM 'MAVIS SIMPSON'

***Geranium riversleianum* 'Mavis Simpson'** (Geraniaceae)

Common name: None
Height: 2ft (60cm)
Spread: 3ft (90cm)
Aspect: Sun or part shade
Soil: Well-drained
Hardiness: Zone 7
Propagation: Division in spring
Flowering time: All summer

A hybrid with flowers of a pink color, with pale pink centers, borne in loose cymes. An extremely desirable addition to the garden.

- Drought-tolerant
- Handsome foliage
- Low allergen
- Attracts slugs
- Prone to mildew

***Geranium riversleianum* 'Russell Pritchard' A.G.M.** (Geraniaceae)

Common name: None
Height: 1ft (30cm)
Spread: 3ft (90cm)
Aspect: Sun or part shade
Soil: Well-drained
Hardiness: Zone 7
Propagation: Division in spring
Flowering time: All summer

A very free-flowering clone. Flowers are small, deep magenta in color, borne in loose cymes.

- Drought-tolerant
- Handsome foliage
- Low allergen
- Attracts slugs
- Prone to mildew

GERBERA JAMESONII 'PANDORA' SERIES

***Geranium sylvaticum* 'Album' (Geraniaceae)**

Common name: None
Height: 30in (75cm)
Spread: 2ft (60cm)
Aspect: Sun or part shade
Soil: Well-drained
Hardiness: Zone 4
Propagation: Division in spring
Flowering time: Spring and early summer.

A clump-forming woodland species. Flowers small, white in color, borne in dense cymes starting in spring and through to summer.

- Drought-tolerant
- Low allergen
- Handsome foliage
- Prone to mildew
- Attracts slugs

***Geranium wallichianum* 'Buxton's variety' A.G.M. (Geraniaceae)**

Common name: None
Height: 1ft (30cm)
Spread: 3ft (90cm)
Aspect: Sun or part shade
Soil: Well-drained
Hardiness: Zone 7
Propagation: Seed or division in spring
Flowering time: From midsummer through to mid-autumn

A trailing hardy perennial plant. Flowers sky blue with large, white, veined centers, in loose cymes. Can come true from seed.

- Drought-tolerant
- Handsome foliage
- Low allergen
- Attracts slugs
- Prone to mildew

***Gerbera jamesonii* 'Pandora' series (Asteraceae)**

Common name: Transvaal daisy
Height: 16in (40cm)
Spread: 18in (45cm)
Aspect: Full sun
Soil: Well-drained, fertile
Hardiness: Zone 8
Propagation: Seed in heat, or division in spring
Flowering time: Spring to summer

Cultivars have a basal rosette of leaves, and single or double flowers of red, yellow, orange, or pink.

- Good cut flower
- Handsome foliage
- Attracts slugs
- Must not be moved

PERENNIALS

Geum 'Borisii' (Rosaceae)

Common name: Avens
Height: 20in (50cm)
Spread: 1ft (30cm)
Aspect: Sun or part shade
Soil: Well-drained, fertile
Hardiness: Zone 4
Propagation: Seed or division in spring
Flowering time: Spring through to late summer

An evergreen perennial with pinnate, hairy, green leaves. Flowers brick-red, with yellow stamens, in cymes, from late spring. Will flower well only if divided every other year.

- Low allergen
- Divide regularly
- Handsome foliage
- Evergreen

Geum 'Lady Stratheden' A.G.M. (Rosaceae)

Common name: None
Height: 2ft (60cm)
Spread: 2ft (60cm)
Aspect: Sun or part shade
Soil: Well-drained, fertile
Hardiness: Zone 6
Propagation: Division in spring or autumn
Flowering time: All summer

A hybrid of *Geum chiloense*. Leaves pinnate, hairy, green. Flowers semi-double, yellow, in cymes of up to 5. Will flower well only if lifted and divided every other year.

- Handsome foliage
- Divide regularly
- Low allergen

Geum 'Mrs J. Bradshaw' (Rosaceae)

Common name: None
Height: 2ft (60cm)
Spread: 2ft (60cm)
Aspect: Sun or part shade
Soil: Well-drained, fertile
Hardiness: Zone 6
Propagation: Division in spring or autumn
Flowering time: From early to late summer

A *Geum chiloense* hybrid. Leaves pinnate, hairy green. Flowers semi-double, red, in cymes of up to 5. Will flower well only if lifted and divided every other year

- Handsome foliage
- Divide regularly
- Low allergen

GLAUCIUM GRANDIFLORUM

Geum 'Tangerine' (Rosaceae)

Common name: Avens
Height: 1ft (30cm)
Spread: 1ft (30cm)
Aspect: Sun or part shade
Soil: Well-drained, fertile
Hardiness: Zone 3
Propagation: Division in spring or autumn
Flowering time: Late spring to midsummer

A *Geum rivale* hybrid. Flowers are single, orange colored, borne in cymes, from late spring to midsummer. Will flower well only if lifted and divided every other year.

- Low allergen
- Handsome foliage
- Divide regularly

Gillenia trifoliata A.G.M. (Rosaceae)

Common name: Bowman's-root
Height: 3ft (90cm)
Spread: 2ft (60cm)
Aspect: Part shade
Soil: Acid, moist, well-drained
Hardiness: Zone 4
Propagation: Seed or division in spring or autumn
Flowering time: Late spring to late summer

A rhizomatous, perennial woodland plant. Leaves bronze-green, veined. Flowers are asymmetric, white colored, starry.

- Good cut flower
- Attracts slugs
- Requires staking

Glaucium grandiflorum (Papaveraceae)

Common name: Horned poppy
Height: 20in (50cm)
Spread: 20in (50cm)
Aspect: Full sun
Soil: Well-drained
Hardiness: Zone 7
Propagation: Seed in spring or autumn
Flowering time: Throughout summer

A short-lived perennial. Leaves silvery-green. Flowers solitary, poppy-like, dark orange, with a dark spot at the base of each petal. Blooms for most of the summer if deadheaded.

- Handsome foliage
- Must not be moved
- Poisonous

Gloriosa superba A.G.M. (Colchicaceae)

Common name: None
Height: 6ft (1.8m)
Spread: 1ft (30cm)
Aspect: Full sun
Soil: Well-drained, fertile
Hardiness: Zone 9
Propagation: Seed in heat, or separation of tubers, in spring
Flowering time: Summer to autumn

A tuberous, climbing perennial. Flowers nodding, petals reflexed, wavy-edged, red or purple, yellow-margined, or pure yellow, with long protruding stamens. Tender.

- 🔴 Poisonous
- 🔴 Skin-irritant

Gypsophila paniculata 'Rosenschleier' A.G.M. (Caryophyllaceae)

Common name: None
Height: 2ft (60cm)
Spread: 3ft (90cm)
Aspect: Full sun
Soil: Sharply-drained
Hardiness: Zone 4
Propagation: Root cuttings or grafting in late winter
Flowering time: Mid and late summer

A dense perennial. Leaves blue-green. Flowers in panicles, double, white.

- 🟢 Attracts bees
- 🔴 Must not be moved
- 🟢 Drought-tolerant
- 🔴 Short-lived
- 🟢 Good cut flower

Gypsophila repens 'Dorothy Teacher' A.G.M. (Caryophyllaceae)

Common name: Creeping gypsophila
Height: 2in (5cm)
Spread: 16in (40cm)
Aspect: Full sun
Soil: Sharply-drained
Hardiness: Zone 4
Propagation: Root cuttings or grafting in late winter
Flowering time: Throughout summer

A mat-forming perennial. Leaves blue-green. Flowers star-shaped, pale pink, borne in loose corymb-like panicles.

- 🟢 Attracts bees
- 🔴 Must not be moved
- 🟢 Drought-tolerant
- 🔴 Short-lived

HAPLOPAPPUS GLUTINOSUS

Haplopappus glutinosus
(**Asteraceae**)

Common name: None
Height: 6in (15cm)
Spread: 1ft (30cm)
Aspect: Full sun
Soil: Sharply-drained
Hardiness: Zone 9
Propagation: Seed when ripe, or in spring
Flowering time: Throughout summer

A tender, cushion-forming, evergreen perennial. Leaves sticky, dark green. Flowers solitary, single yellow.

- Drought-tolerant
- Evergreen
- Good cut flower
- Must deadhead

Hedysarum coronarium
(Papilionaceae)

Common name: Sulla sweetvetch
Height: 3ft (90cm)
Spread: 2ft (60cm)
Aspect: Sun
Soil: Sharply-drained
Hardiness: Zone 3
Propagation: Seed when ripe, or in spring

Flowering time: Throughout the spring period

A short-lived perennial plant. Flowers are small, pea-like, scented, deep red in color, and are borne in racemes on erect stems.

- Good cut flower
- Scented flowers
- Must not be moved
- Short-lived

HELIANTHUS DECAPETALUS

Helenium 'Pumilum Magnificum' (Asteraceae)

Common name: None
Height: 3ft (90cm)
Spread: 2ft (60cm)
Aspect: Sun
Soil: Moist, well-drained, humus-rich
Hardiness: Zone 5
Propagation: Division, spring or autumn
Flowering time: Summer to autumn

An erect, hardy perennial. Flowers solitary, single, daisy-like, ray florets yellow, disc florets brown.

- Attracts bees
- Good cut flower
- Skin irritant
- High allergen
- Must deadhead
- Poisonous

Helenium 'Rubinzwerg' (Asteraceae)

Common name: None
Height: 3ft (90cm)
Spread: 18in (45cm)
Aspect: Sun
Soil: Moist, well-drained, humus-rich
Hardiness: Zone 5
Propagation: Division in spring or autumn
Flowering time: Summer through to autumn

Flowers solitary, single, ray florets dark red, discs yellow. Deadheading prolongs flowering.

- Attracts bees
- Good cut flower
- Divide regularly
- High allergen
- Poisonous
- Skin irritant

Helianthus decapetalus (Asteraceae)

Common name: Thinleaf sunflower
Height: 4ft (1.2m)
Spread: Indefinite
Aspect: Sun
Soil: Moist, well-drained, humus-rich
Hardiness: Zone 5
Propagation: Division in spring or autumn
Flowering time: Summer to autumn

A highly-invasive, rhizomatous perennial plant. Leaves narrow, hairy-rough below. Flowers single, daisy-like, clear yellow, with brown centers.

- Good cut flower
- Attracts bees
- Skin irritant
- Prone to mildew
- High allergenic
- Requires staking

PERENNIALS

Helianthus 'Lemon Queen' (Asteraceae)

Common name: None
Height: 6ft (1.8m)
Spread: 4ft (1.2m)
Aspect: Sun
Soil: Good, moist, well-drained, humus-rich
Hardiness: Zone 5
Propagation: Division in spring or autumn
Flowering time: Summer to autumn

A free-flowering, rhizomatous, highly-invasive perennial. Flowers single, pale yellow, with dark yellow centers.

- Attracts bees
- Good cut flower
- High allergen
- Skin irritant
- Prone to mildew
- Requires staking

Helianthus multiflorus 'Loddon Gold' A.G.M. (Asteraceae)

Common name: None
Height: 5ft (1.5m)
Spread: 3ft (90cm)
Aspect: Sun
Soil: Moist, well-drained, humus-rich
Hardiness: Zone 5
Propagation: Division in spring or autumn
Flowering time: Late summer to mid-autumn.

A hybrid perennial sunflower. Flowers are fully double, rich yellow in color, and open from late summer onwards.

- Good cut flower
- Attracts bees
- High allergenic
- Skin irritant
- Prone to mildew
- Requires staking

Helianthus salicifolius (Asteraceae)

Common name: Willow-leaved sunflower
Height: 8ft (2.5m)
Spread: 3ft (90cm)
Aspect: Sun
Soil: Moist, humus-rich, well-drained
Hardiness: Zone 4
Propagation: Division in spring or autumn
Flowering time: Throughout autumn

Leaves reflexed, linear, green. Flowers single, pale yellow, brown centers.

- Good cut flower
- Attracts bees
- High allergenic
- Skin irritant
- Requires staking
- Prone to mildew

HELIOPSIS HELIANTHOIDES 'BRESSINGHAM DUBLOON'

Heliopsis helianthoides **'Bressingham Dubloon'** (Asteraceae)

Common name: Ox eye
Height: 3ft (90cm)
Spread 3ft (90cm)
Aspect: Sun
Soil: Moist, well-drained, humus-rich
Hardiness: Zone 4
Propagation: Division in spring or autumn

Flowering time: From midsummer through to early autumn

A plant of great value in garden cultivation. Flowers are solitary, yellow, semi-double, with dark centers, from midsummer onwards.

- Good cut flower
- Attracts bees
- Attracts slugs
- Divide regularly

Heliopsis helianthoides 'Mars' (Asteraceae)

Common name: Ox eye
Height: 5ft (1.5m)
Spread: 2ft (60cm)
Aspect: Sun
Soil: Moist, well-drained humus-rich, fertile
Hardiness: Zone 4
Propagation: Division in spring or autumn
Flowering time: Midsummer to early autumn

A tall, hardy perennial. Flowers solitary single, orange-yellow on long stems, from midsummer.

- Good cut flower
- Attracts bees
- Requires staking
- Divide regularly
- Attracts slugs

Hemerocallis 'Chicago Royal Robe' (Hemerocallidaceae)

Common name: Day-lily
Height: 2ft (60cm)
Spread: 1ft (30cm)
Aspect: Sun
Soil: Good, moist, well-drained, humus-rich
Hardiness: Zone 5
Propagation: Division in spring or autumn
Flowering time: Several weeks in midsummer

A hardy, semi-evergreen Day-lily. Flowers large, purplish-pink in color, with a yellow throat.

- Attracts bees
- Good cut flower
- Low allergen
- Attracts slugs
- Divide regularly

HEMEROCALLIS (Hemerocallidaceae)
Day-lily

A genus of only some 15 species, but some 30,000 hybrids are in cultivation. Of the species, *HH. fulva* and *lilio-asphodelus* are highly invasive weeds.

Day-lilies are clump-forming, and do best if lifted and divided every few years. They thrive in sun or light shade, and are not demanding as to soil, as long as it does not dry out. They may be evergreen, or semi-evergreen. Flowering time is summer; each flower lasts for only about 12 hours, or 16 hours in the instance of extended-flowering cultivars (some are night-flowering) but is followed by others in succession over many weeks. Some cultivars are scented. All are low-allergen and suitable for allergic gardeners. They make excellent cut flowers, and are beloved of the flower-arranger. The flower is composed of three petals and three sepals, which alternate, giving, in general, a star shape, and which are known collectively as tepals.

HEMEROCALLIS 'FRANS HALS'

Hemerocallis 'Corky' A.G.M.
(Hemerocallidaceae)

Common name: Day-lily
Height: 3ft (90cm)
Spread: 2ft (60cm)
Aspect: Sun
Soil: Moist, well-drained, humus-rich
Hardiness: Zone 5
Propagation: Division in spring or autumn
Flowering time: All summer

Free-flowering, evergreen perennial, with black stems, small, lemon-yellow flowers, borne profusely.

- Attracts bees
- Evergreen
- Low allergen
- Attracts slugs
- Divide regularly

Hemerocallis 'Frans Hals'
(Hemerocallidaceae)

Common name: Day-lily
Height: 2ft (60cm)
Spread: 2ft (60cm)
Aspect: Sun
Soil: Moist, well-drained, humus-rich
Hardiness: Zone 5
Propagation: Division in spring or autumn
Flowering time: Throughout the summer

A hardy perennial bicolored Day-lily. Flowers have rust-colored petals and creamy-colored sepals.

- Attracts bees
- Good cut flower
- Low allergen
- Attracts slugs
- Divide regularly

PERENNIALS 115

Hemerocallis 'Green Flutter' A.G.M. (Hemerocallidaceae)

Common name: Day-lily
Height: 20in (50cm)
Spread: 3ft (90cm)
Aspect: Sun
Soil: Moist, well-drained, humus-rich
Hardiness: Zone 5
Propagation: Division in spring or autumn
Flowering time: All summer

Evergreen, nocturnal-flowering. Flowers star-shaped, with yellow petals, yellow sepals with ruffled margins, and a hint of green in the throat.

- Evergreen
- Good cut flower
- Low allergen
- Attracts slugs
- Divide regularly

Hemerocallis 'Silver Veil' (Hemerocallidaceae)

Common name: Day-lily
Height 2ft (60cm)
Spread: 3ft (90cm)
Aspect: Sun
Soil: Moist, well-drained, humus-rich
Hardiness: Zone 5
Propagation: Division, in spring or autumn
Flowering time: All summer

A handsome, semi-evergreen, bicolored Day-lily. Flowers have brown-red petals, flesh pink sepals, and a bright yellow throat.

- Good cut flower
- Low allergen
- Attracts slugs
- Divide regularly

Hemerocallis 'Stafford'
(Hemerocallidaceae)

Common name: Day-lily
Height: 28in (70cm)
Spread: 3ft (90cm)
Aspect: Sun
Soil: Moist, well-drained, humus-rich
Hardiness: Zone 5
Propagation: Division in spring or autumn
Flowering time: Several weeks in midsummer

A free-flowering, evergreen perennial. Flowers in midsummer are deep scarlet, with yellow midribs and throat.

- Good cut flower
- Low allergen
- Attracts slugs
- Divide regularly

Hemerocallis 'Tutunkhamun'
(Hemerocallidaceae)

Common name: Day-lily
Height: 2ft (60cm)
Spread: 3ft (90cm)
Aspect: Sun
Soil: Moist, well-drained, humus-rich
Hardiness: Zone 5
Propagation: Division in spring or autumn
Flowering time: Midsummer

A semi-evergreen, hybrid Day-lily. Flowers have brown-colored petals with a central cream stripe, yellow sepals, and a yellow throat.

- Good cut flower
- Low allergen
- Attracts slugs
- Divide regularly

Heuchera 'Red Spangles' A.G.M.
(Saxifragaceae)

Common name: None
Height: 20in (50cm)
Spread: 10in (25cm)
Aspect: Any
Soil: Moist, well-drained, fertile
Hardiness: Zone 4
Propagation: Division, in autumn
Flowering time: All summer

Handsome, evergreen, marbled leaves. Flowers in open panicles, red. Makes a good groundcover plant.

- Evergreen
- Good cut flower
- Handsome foliage
- Low allergen
- Divide regularly

PERENNIALS

x *Heucherella alba* 'Bridget Bloom' (Saxifragaceae)

Common name: None
Height: 16in (40cm)
Spread: 1ft (30cm)
Aspect: Any
Soil: Acid to neutral, moist, well-drained
Hardiness: Zone 5
Propagation: Division, in autumn or spring
Flowering time: Late spring to autumn

An intergeneric, groundcover hybrid between *Heuchera* and *Tiarella*. Leaves evergreen, toothed, mid-green. Flowers small, pink, in panicles.

- Evergreen
- Good cut flower
- Low allergen

Hosta sieboldii A.G.M. (Hostaceae)

Common name: None
Height: 1ft (30cm)
Spread: 2ft (60cm)
Aspect: Sun or part shade
Soil: Moist, well-drained, fertile
Hardiness: Zone 5
Propagation: Division in late summer or early spring
Flowering time: Late summer and then again in early autumn

A robust hardy perennial, which has matt, olive-green leaves. Flowers are in racemes, dark violet. Minimal pruning required. Hostas usually are grown for their foliage interest.

- Handsome foliage
- Attracts slugs
- Low allergen
- Good cut flower

HYLOMECON JAPONICA

***Houttuynia cordata* 'Flore Pleno'** (Saururaceae)

Common name: None
Height: 15in (38cm)
Spread: Indefinite
Aspect: Any
Soil: Any
Hardiness: Zone 5
Propagation: Division at any time

Flowering time: Spring

An invasive hardy perennial, suitable as a groundcover plant where nothing else will grow. Flowers greenish-yellow, small, surrounded by white bracts, in spring for several weeks.

- Low allergen
- Handsome foliage
- Invasive
- Attracts slugs

Hylomecon japonica (Papaveraceae)

Common name: None
Height: 8in (20cm)
Spread: 18in (45cm)
Aspect: Part or full shade
Soil: Acid, moist, humus-rich
Hardiness: Zone 7
Propagation: Seed when ripe; division, in spring
Flowering time: Late spring to summer

A rhizomatous woodland plant. Handsome leaves. Flowers are solitary single, saucer-shaped, 4-petaled, dark yellow in color.

- Handsome foliage
- Attracts slugs
- Invasive

PERENNIALS

Hypericum cerastioides (Clusiaceae)

Common name: St John's wort
Height: 8in (20cm)
Spread: 18in (45cm)
Aspect: Sun
Soil: Sharply drained
Hardiness: Zone 7
Propagation: Division in spring or autumn
Flowering time: Spring to summer

Leaves downy, gray-green. Flowers in cymes, star-shaped, yellow. Prune by deadheading after flowering.

- Evergreen
- Low allergen
- Drought-tolerant
- Handsome foliage

Hyssopus officinalis forma *albus* (Labiatae)

Common name: Hyssop
Height: 2ft (60cm)
Spread: 3ft (90cm)
Aspect: Sun
Soil: Well-drained, fertile
Hardiness: Zone 3
Propagation: Seed in autumn
Flowering time: Midsummer to early autumn

A hardy aromatic subshrub. Flowers 2-lipped funnels white in color, in whorled spikes, opening from midsummer onwards.

- Attracts bees
- Low allergen

IMPATIENS (*Balsaminaceae*)
Impatiens

A genus of more than 800 species from a wide variety of habitats, many of these being moist in tropical and sub-tropical regions; the majority of species are therefore tender. They have succulent brittle stems and fleshy leaves, and so are not wind-tolerant. The 5-petaled flowers may be solitary, in racemes or clusters, and the seed capsules are explosive; this is important with some species, which can become highly invasive. They grow in sun or in shade in the wild. Some species have handsome foliage.

They make excellent long-flowering bedding plants, and do not require to be deadheaded; they thrive in moist, well-drained humus-rich soil, in part shade. Seedlings are very prone to damping-off, and planting out should be delayed until all danger of frost has passed.

IMPATIENS NIAMNIAMENSIS 'CONGO COCKATOO'

Impatiens 'New Guinea' hybrids (Balsaminaceae)

Common name: None
Height: 1ft (30cm)
Spread: 9in (23cm)
Aspect: Sun or part shade
Soil: Moist, well-drained, fertile
Hardiness: Zone 10
Propagation: Seed in heat in early spring
Flowering time: Throughout the summer

A race of perennials arising from crosses between several species. Foliage bronzed colored, handsome, often variegated. Flowers in many shades, or bicolored. Usually grown as annuals.

- Low allergen
- Seeds everywhere

Impatiens niamniamensis 'Congo Cockatoo' (Balsamaceae)

Common name: None
Height: 3ft (90cm)
Spread: 15in (38cm)
Aspect: Sun or part shade
Soil: Moist, well-drained, humus-rich
Hardiness: Zone 10
Propagation: Softwood cuttings in spring or early summer
Flowering time: All year round, but intermittently

A short-lived perennial. Flowers hooded, narrow, yellow and red, with hooked spurs.

- Low allergen
- Short-lived

PERENNIALS   121

Impatiens walleriana 'Accent' series A.G.M. (Balsaminaceae)

Common name: Sultan snapweed
Height: 2ft (60cm)
Spread: 2ft (60cm)
Aspect: Sun or part shade
Soil: Moist, well-drained, humus-rich
Hardiness: Zone 10
Propagation: Seed in heat in spring
Flowering time: Throughout summer

A tender perennial plant grown almost universally as an annual. Flowers are flat, in many shades, or bicolored. It does not require to be deadheaded. Deservedly highly popular in garden cultivation.

● Low allergen

Ipomoea lobata (Convolvulaceae)

Common name: None
Height: 15ft (4.5m)
Spread: 3ft (90cm)
Aspect: Full sun
Soil: Well-drained, fertile
Hardiness: Zone 8
Propagation: Seed in heat in spring
Flowering time: From summer through to autumn

A perennial climbing plant, grown usually as an annual. Stems are crimson-flushed. Flowers are borne in dense, one-sided racemes, tubular, scarlet in color, becoming orange/yellow with age.

● Prone to mildew

Iris japonica (Iridaceae)

Common name: Japanese iris
Height: 18in (45cm)
Spread: 3ft (1m)
Aspect: Sun or part shade
Soil: Moist, humus-rich
Hardiness: Zone 7
Propagation: Seed or division in spring or autumn
Flowering time: Late spring

Alone in the genus, reasonably long-flowering. Flowers frilly, white or lavender; falls have orange crests and purple patches, during spring.

- Good cut flower
- Low allergen
- Handsome foliage
- Evergreen
- Attracts slugs
- Poisonous
- Skin irritant

Kirengeshoma palmata A.G.M. (Hydrangeaceae)

Common name: None
Height: 4ft (1.2m)
Spread: 6ft (2m)
Aspect: Part shade
Soil: Moist, acidic, well-drained
Hardiness: Zone 5
Propagation: Division or seed in spring
Flowering time: Late summer and early autumn

A rhizomatous woodland perennial from Japan and Korea. Leaves ovate, pale gray-green. Flowers in threes on terminal cymes, yellow.

- Good cut flower
- Low allergen
- Attracts slugs

Knautia macedonica (Dipsacaceae)

Common name: None
Height: 32in (80cm)
Spread: 18in (45cm)
Aspect: Sun
Soil: Well-drained, fertile
Hardiness: Zone 6
Propagation: Seed or basal cuttings in spring
Flowering time: Mid- to late summer

A clump-forming hardy perennial. Flowers on tall stems, solitary, long-lasting, purple-red, with bristly involucral bracts.

- Good cut flower
- Attracts bees
- Drought-tolerant
- Requires staking

Lachenalia aloides lutea (Hyacinthaceae)

Common name: Cape cowslip
Height: 1ft (30cm)
Spread: 3in (8cm)
Aspect: Full sun
Soil: Sharply drained, dry in summer period
Hardiness: Zone 9
Propagation: Remove plantlets in late summer
Flowering time: Winter and spring

A tender South African bulbous species. Leaves spotted; flowers pendent, tubular, yellow, in racemes, during winter and early spring. Trouble free in the garden.

- Handsome foliage

Lathyrus latifolius A.G.M. (Papilionaceae)

Common name: Everlasting pea
Height: 6ft (2m)
Spread: 2ft (1m)
Aspect: Sun or light shade
Soil: Well-drained, humus-rich, fertile
Hardiness: Zone 5
Propagation: Seed, after soaking, in early spring
Flowering time: Summer to autumn

A hardy, deciduous, perennial climber. Leaves blue-green. Flowers pea-like, pink or purple, from summer to early autumn. Seeds poisonous.

- Low allergen
- Drought-tolerant
- Good cut flower
- Seeds everywhere
- Attracts slugs
- Poisonous

Lathyrus vernus (Papilionaceae)

Common name: Spring vetchling
Height: 18in (45cm)
Spread: 18in (45cm)
Aspect: Sun or half shade
Soil: Well-drained, humus-rich, fertile
Hardiness: Zone 4
Propagation: Seed, after soaking, in spring
Flowering time: Spring

A dwarf herbaceous plant. Flowers pea-like, blue-purple, in one-sided racemes, for many weeks if deadheaded. Attractive brown seed pods.

- Drought-tolerant
- Low allergen
- Attracts slugs
- Must not be moved
- Poisonous

Laurentia axillaris **'Blue Stars'**
(Campanulaceae)

Common name: None
Height: 1ft (30cm)
Spread: 1ft (30cm)
Aspect: Full sun
Soil: Well-drained, fertile
Hardiness: Zone 9
Propagation: Seed in heat in spring; softwood cuttings in summer
Flowering time: Spring to autumn

A tender perennial, grown usually as an annual. Flowers small, star-shaped, solitary, long-tubed, dark blue, abundant. Good in baskets and as a bedding plant.

- Skin irritant

Lavatera thuringiaca **'Ice Cool'**
(Campanulaceae)

Common name: Mallow
Height: 5ft (1.5m)
Spread: 5ft (1.5m)
Aspect: Sun
Soil: Well-drained, fertile
Hardiness: Zone 8
Propagation: Softwood cuttings in spring
Flowering time: Throughout the summer

A half-hardy herbaceous perennial plant. Flowers are large, open saucers, white in color, borne in loose racemes, during the summer period.

- Drought-tolerant
- Short-lived
- Good cut flower

LEUCANTHEMUM x SUPERBUM 'BEAUTE NIVELLOISE'

Leucanthemum x *superbum* 'Beaute Nivelloise' (Asteraceae)

Common name: None
Height: 3ft (1m)
Spread: 2ft (60cm)
Aspect: Sun or part shade
Soil: Moist, well-drained, fertile
Hardiness: Zone 5
Propagation: Division in spring or autumn
Flowering time: All summer

A hardy perennial. Leaves glossy-green. Flowers single, solitary, white, with irregularly disposed squinny ray florets, and yellow disc florets.

- Good cut flower
- Handsome foliage
- Requires staking
- Attracts slugs
- Skin irritant

Leucanthemum x *superbum* 'Phyllis Smith' (Asteraceae)

Common name: None
Height: 3ft (90cm)
Spread: 2ft (60cm)
Aspect: Sun or half shade
Soil: Moist, well-drained
Hardiness: Zone 5
Propagation: Division in spring or autumn
Flowering time: Early to late summer

A hardy perennial. Leaves glossy-green. Flowers solitary, single, white, with narrow, twisted and intertwined ray florets, and a yellow disc.

- Good cut flower
- Handsome foliage
- High allergen
- Attracts slugs
- Skin irritant

Leucanthemum x *superbum* 'Sonnenschein' (Asteraceae)

Common name: None
Height: 3ft (90cm)
Spread: 2ft (60cm)
Aspect: Sun or part shade
Soil: Moist, well-drained
Hardiness: Zone 5
Propagation: Division in spring or autumn
Flowering time: Early to late summer

A hardy perennial plant. Leaves glossy-green. Flowers solitary, single, pale cream, with yellow centers, throughout summer.

- Good cut flower
- Handsome foliage
- Requires staking
- Attracts slugs
- Skin irritant
- High allergen

***Leucanthemum* x *superbum* 'Wirral Supreme' A.G.M. (Asteraceae)**

Common name: None
Height: 3ft (1m)
Spread: 2ft (60cm)
Aspect: Sun or part shade
Soil: Moist, well-drained
Hardiness: Zone 5
Propagation: Division in spring or autumn
Flowering time: Throughout summer

A hardy perennial. Leaves glossy-green. Flowers solitary, semi-double, white, with yellow-colored centers.

- Good cut flower
- Handsome foliage
- Requires staking
- Attracts slugs
- Skin irritant
- High allergen

***Lewisia cotyledon* Ashwood strain (Portulacaceae)**

Common name: None
Height: 1ft (30cm)
Spread: 16in (40cm)
Aspect: Part shade, dry in winter
Soil: Acidic, sharply drained, humus-rich.
Hardiness: Zone 6
Propagation: Seed in autumn; division in early summer
Flowering time: Spring to summer

Leaves fleshy, in rosettes. Flowers in panicles or cymes, open funnels, in a wide range of colors, over long periods from spring. No winter wet.

- Evergreen
- Handsome foliage
- Attracts slugs

***Libertia formosa* (Iridaceae)**

Common name: None
Height: 3ft (90cm)
Spread: 2ft (60cm)
Aspect: Sun
Soil: Moist, well-drained, humus-rich, fertile
Hardiness: Zone 8
Propagation: Seed when ripe; division in spring
Flowering time: Late spring to midsummer

A rhizomatous, half-hardy, evergreen perennial. Leaves upright, stiff. Flowers in clustered panicles, white in color, opening in a long succession from late spring.

- Evergreen
- Good cut flower

Limonium sinuatum (Plumbaginaceae)

Common name: Notch-leaf sea-lavender
Height: 16in (40cm)
Spread: 2ft (60cm)
Aspect: Sun
Soil: Sharply-drained
Hardiness: Zone 9
Propagation: Seed or division in spring
Flowering time: Early through to late summer

A tender perennial usually grown as an annual in cold areas. Flowers on stiff stems, in panicles, in many colors, tiny funnel-shaped, enclosed in differently colored calyces.

- ● Can be dried
- ● Drought-tolerant
- ● Good cut flower
- ● Prone to mildew

Linaria purpurea (Scrophulariaceae)

Common name: Purple toadflax
Height: 3ft (90cm)
Spread: 1ft (30cm)
Aspect: Sun
Soil: Sharply-drained
Hardiness: Zone 6
Propagation: Seed or division in spring
Flowering time: Early summer through to autumn

An erect, hardy perennial. Flowers 2-lipped, snapdragon-like, pink, purple or violet in color, with curved spurs, borne in dense, slender racemes.

- ● Drought-tolerant
- ● Good cut flower
- ● Prone to mildew
- ● Seeds everywhere

***Linaria purpurea* 'Winifred's Delight'** (Scrophulariaceae)

Common name: None
Height: 1ft (30cm)
Spread: 1ft (30cm)
Aspect: Sun
Soil: Sharply-drained
Hardiness: Zone 6
Propagation: Seed or division in spring
Flowering time: Early summer through to autumn

A hardy perennial. Flowers in slender, dense racemes, snapdragon-like, with curved spurs, creamy-yellow.

- ● Drought-tolerant
- ● Good cut flower
- ● Prone to mildew
- ● Seeds everywhere

***Linum* Gemmell's hybrid A.G.M.**
(Linaceae)

Common name: None
Height: 6in (15cm)
Spread: 8in (20cm)
Aspect: Sun
Soil: Sharply-drained, humus-rich
Hardiness: Zone 6
Propagation: Stem-tip cuttings in early summer

Flowering time: Long periods in summer

A semi-evergreen, rounded, perennial plant. Leaves grayish. Flowers broad funnels, bright yellow in color, in terminal cymes, borne profusely throughout summer.

● Drought-tolerant   ● Attracts slugs

Linum narbonense (Linaceae)

Common name: Narbonne flax
Height: 2ft (60cm)
Spread: 18in (45cm)
Aspect: Sun
Soil: Sharply-drained
Hardiness: Zone 7
Propagation: Seed, in spring or autumn
Flowering time: Early to midsummer

A short-lived perennial. Flowers rich blue saucers with white eyes, in few-flowered terminal cymes, borne continuously.

- Drought-tolerant
- Attracts slugs
- Must not be moved
- Short-lived

Linum perenne (Linaceae)

Common name: Perennial flax
Height: 2ft (60cm)
Spread: 1ft (30cm)
Aspect: Sun
Soil: Sharply-drained, humus-rich
Hardiness: Zone 5
Propagation: Seed, in spring or autumn
Flowering time: Early to late summer

A lax, straggly species. Leaves glaucous blue-green. Flowers blue, fading to pale blue over the day, cup-shaped, in terminal panicles, borne continuously throughout summer.

- Drought-tolerant
- Handsome foliage
- Attracts slugs
- Must not be moved

Liriope muscari A.G.M. (Convallariaceae)

Common name: Lilyturf
Height: 1ft (30cm)
Spread: 18in (45cm)
Aspect: Full or part shade
Soil: Acid, well drained, humus-rich
Hardiness: Zone 6
Propagation: Seed or division in spring
Flowering time: Early to late autumn

An evergreen hardy perennial. Flowers small, ovoid, bright violet-mauve, in dense spikes, on purple-green stems throughout autumn.

- Evergreen
- Low allergen
- Drought-tolerant
- Good cut flower
- Attracts slugs

LOBELIA ERINUS PENDULA

Lobelia erinus (Campanulaceae)

Common name: Edging lobelia
Height: 8in (20cm)
Spread: 6in (15cm)
Aspect: Sun
Soil: Moist, well-drained, fertile
Hardiness: Zone 9
Propagation: Seed as soon as ripe
Flowering time: Ssummer to autumn

A tender perennial, grown as an annual in cold climates. Flowers 2-lipped, tubular, white, pink, red or purple, with yellow or white eyes, in loose racemes.

- Attracts slugs
- Short-lived
- Skin irritant

Lobelia erinus pendula (Campanulaceae)

Common name: None
Height: 8in (23cm)
Spread: 6in (15cm)
Aspect: Sun
Soil: Moist, well-drained, fertile
Hardiness: Zone 9
Propagation: Seed as soon as ripe
Flowering time: Summer to autumn

A tender perennial plant, grown as an annual in cold climates. Flowers 2-lipped, tubular, white, pink, red, or purple in color, with yellow- or white-colored eyes, borne in loose racemes from summer through to autumn.

- Skin irritant
- Slugs like
- Short-lived

Lobelia x *gerardii* 'Vedrariensis' (Campanulaceae)

Common name: None
Height: 4ft (1.2m)
Spread: 1ft (30cm)
Aspect: Sun or part shade
Soil: Moist, humus-rich
Hardiness: Zone 7
Propagation: Division in spring
Flowering time: Throughout the summer

A rhizomatous hardy perennial. Leaves in basal rosette. Flowers 2-lipped, tubular, purple, in many-flowered racemes.

- Good cut flower
- Low allergen
- Attracts slugs
- Short-lived
- Skin irritant

Lobelia 'Kompliment Scharlach' A.G.M. (Campanulaceae)

Common name: None
Height: 3ft (90cm)
Spread: 1ft (30cm)
Aspect: Sun or half shade
Soil: Moist, deep, humus-rich
Hardiness: Zone 7
Propagation: Division in spring
Flowering time: Summer to autumn

A clump-forming, short-lived, hardy perennial plant. Flower sare tubular, scarlet in color, borne in loose racemes, from summer into the autumn.

- Good cut flower
- Skin irritant
- Short-lived
- Attracts slugs

Lobelia tupa (Campanulaceae)

Common name: None
Height: 3ft (90cm)
Spread: 1ft (30cm)
Aspect: Sun
Soil: Moist, deep, humus-rich
Hardiness: Zone 8
Propagation: Seed when ripe; division in spring
Flowering time: Summer to mid-autumn

A half-hardy perennial plant. Leaves downy, gray-green. Flowers narrow tubular, brick red with purple-red calyces, in racemes, from late summer.

- Good cut flower
- Handsome foliage
- Skin irritant
- Short-lived
- Attracts slugs

LOTUS CORNICULATUS

***Lobularia maritima* 'Easter Bonnet' series (Brassicaceae)**

Common name: None
Height: 1ft (30cm)
Spread: 1ft (30cm)
Aspect: Full sun
Soil: Well-drained, fertile
Hardiness: Zone 8
Propagation: Seed *in situ* in late spring
Flowering time: All summer

A short-lived perennial, grown usually as an annual. Leaves gray-green. Flowers white or pink, scented, in corymb-like racemes. Shear over to promote a second flush of flowers.

- Scented flowers
- Short-lived

***Lotus corniculatus* (Papilionaceae)**

Common name: Bird's foot trefoil
Height: 1ft (30cm)
Spread: 18in (45cm)
Aspect: Sun
Soil: Well-drained, fertile
Hardiness: Zone 5
Propagation: Seed in autumn or spring
Flowering time: Spring to early summer

A spreading, short-lived, hardy perennial plant. Leaves blue-green. Flowers pea-like, clear yellow in color, borne in umbel-like racemes, opening from spring onwards.

- Drought-tolerant
- Handsome foliage
- Short-lived
- Invasive
- Seeds everywhere

PERENNIALS

LYCHNIS CORONARIA

Lychnis coronaria **(Caryophyllaceae)**

Common name: Rose campion
Height: 32in (80cm)
Spread: 18in (45cm)
Aspect: Sun
Soil: Sharply-drained, fertile
Hardiness: Zone 4
Propagation: Seed or division in spring

Flowering time: Throughout summer

A short-lived hardy perennial plant. Leaves woolly silver-gray. Flowers single, scarlet, in small racemes. Deadheading prolongs flowering.

- Drought tolerant
- Good cut flower
- Handsome foliage
- Attracts slugs
- Must deadhead
- Seeds everywhere

Lychnis coronaria 'Oculata' group (Caryophyllaceae)

Common name: None
Height: 32in (80cm)
Spread: 18in (45cm)
Aspect: Sun
Soil: Sharply-drained, fertile
Hardiness: Zone 4
Propagation: Seed or division in spring
Flowering time: Long period in summer

A short-lived hardy perennial plant. Leaves silver-gray. Flowers single salvers, white, with a pink eye, opening in summer.

- Drought-tolerant
- Good cut flower
- Handsome foliage
- Attracts slugs
- Must deadhead
- Seeds everywhere

Lychnis flos-jovis 'Hort's Variety' (Caryophyllaceae)

Common name: Flower-of-love
Height: 1ft (30cm)
Spread: 18in (45cm)
Aspect: Sun
Soil: Sharply-drained, fertile
Hardiness: Zone 5
Propagation: Division in spring
Flowering time: Early through to late summer

A hardy perennial. Leaves are gray-green. Flowers single, rose-pink in color, borne in loosely-rounded cymes throughout summer.

- Drought-tolerant
- Handsome foliage
- Attracts slugs

Lysimachia punctata **(Primulaceae)**

Common name: Yellow loosestrife
Height: 3ft (90cm)
Spread: 2ft (60cm)
Aspect: Any
Soil: Any
Hardiness: Zone 5
Propagation: Division in spring
Flowering time: From mid- through to late summer

An invasive, rhizomatous, hardy perennial. Flowers are cup-shaped, yellow in color, borne in whorls from the leaf axils, opening from midsummer onwards.

- Good cut flower
- Low allergen
- Invasive
- Attracts slugs

Lythrum salicaria **(Lythraceae)**

Common name: Purple loosestrife
Height: 4ft (1.2m)
Spread: 18in (45cm)
Aspect: Sun
Soil: Wet, or bog, fertile
Hardiness: Zone 3
Propagation: Seed in heat, or division in spring
Flowering time: Midsummer to early autumn

A clump-forming hardy, marginal aquatic. Flowers star-shaped, bright red, in spiky racemes. Deadhead to prevent self-seeding.

- Attracts bees
- Low allergen
- Requires staking
- Attracts slugs

***Lythrum salicaria* 'Robert'** **(Lythraceae)**

Common name: Pink loosestrife
Height: 4ft (1.2m)
Spread: 18in (45cm)
Aspect: Sun
Soil: Bog or wet
Hardiness: Zone 3
Propagation: Division in spring
Flowering time: Midsummer to early autumn

A selected clone, with bright pink starry flowers in spiky racemes. Marginal aquatic or bog plant. Deadhead to prevent self-seeding.

- Good cut flower
- Low allergen
- Attracts bees
- Seeds everywhere
- Attracts slugs
- Requires staking

MALVA SYLVESTRIS 'PRIMLEY BLUE'

Malva moschata (Malvaceae)

Common name: Musk mallow
Height: 3ft (90cm)
Spread: 2ft (60cm)
Aspect: Sun
Soil: Well-drained, moist, fertile
Hardiness: Zone 3
Propagation: Seed or basal cuttings in spring
Flowering time: From early summer through to autumn

A short-lived, woody perennial plant. Foliage aromatic. Flowers saucer-shaped, pale pink or white in color, borne in axillary clusters. Deadhead to prevent self-seeding

- 🟢 Attracts bees
- 🔴 Attracts slugs
- 🔴 Requires staking
- 🔴 Seeds everywhere

Malva sylvestris 'Primley Blue' (Malvaceae)

Common name: None
Height: 8in (20cm)
Spread: 2ft (60cm)
Aspect: Sun
Soil: Moist, well-drained, fertile
Hardiness: Zone 5
Propagation: Basal cuttings taken in spring
Flowering time: From late spring through to mid-autumn

A floppy, hairy, woody, short-lived hardy perennial plant. Flowers are pale blue in color, with dark-blue veining, borne in axillary clusters.

- 🟢 Attracts bees
- 🔴 Seeds everywhere
- 🔴 Short-lived

PERENNIALS

Malva sylvestris 'Zebrina' (Malvaceae)

Common name: None
Height: 5ft (1.5m)
Spread: 3ft (90cm)
Aspect: Sun
Soil: Moist, well-drained, fertile
Hardiness: Zone 5
Propagation: Basal cuttings in spring
Flowering time: Late spring to mid-autumn

A wide-spreading, woody perennial. Flowers in axillary clusters, open funnel-shaped, deep blue-purple, and with darker veins. Very prone to rust.

- Attracts bees
- Requires staking
- Short-lived

Malvastrum lateritium (Malvaceae)

Common name: False mallow
Height: 9in (22cm)
Spread: Indefinite
Aspect: Sun
Soil: Well-drained
Hardiness: Zone 8
Propagation: Seed in spring; softwood cuttings in early summer
Flowering time: From late spring to summer

A prostrate, half-hardy perennial. Flowers solitary, peach-colored, yellow-centered cups, from late spring. Can be invasive given the right conditions.

- Drought-tolerant
- Invasive

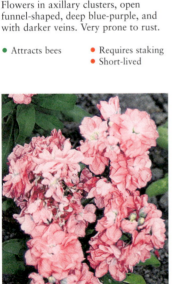

Matthiola incana 'Brompton' series (Brassicaceae)

Common name: Common stock
Height: 18in (45cm)
Spread: 9in (23cm)
Aspect: Full sun
Soil: Moist, well-drained, fertile
Hardiness: Zone 6
Propagation: Seed in heat in early spring
Flowering time: Spring to late summer

A perennial plant, grown almost always as a biennial. Leaves gray-green in color. Flowers scented, borne in upright panicles, single or double, in a range of colors.

- Handsome foliage
- Good cut flower
- Scented flowers

MECONOPSIS CAMBRICA

Matthiola incana 'Ten Week' series
(Brassicaceae)

Common name: None
Height: 1ft (30cm)
Spread: 10in (25cm)
Aspect: Full sun
Soil: Moist, well-drained, fertile
Hardiness: Zone 6
Propagation: Seed in heat in early spring
Flowering time: Spring to late summer

A perennial grown usually as an annual. Foliage gray-green. Flowers scented, single or double, in a range of colors, in panicles, from late spring.

- Good cut flower
- Handsome foliage

Matthiola white perennial
(Brassicaceae)

Common name: None
Height: 18in (45cm)
Spread: 1ft (30cm)
Aspect: Sun
Soil: Moist, well-drained, fertile
Hardiness: Zone 7
Propagation: Seed in spring or autumn
Flowering time: Summer and autumn

A short-lived, woody perennial plant. Leaves gray-green. Flowers scented, double, white in color, borne in terminal spikes.

- Good cut flower
- Handsome foliage
- Scented flowers
- Short-lived

Meconopsis cambrica
(Papaveraceae)

Common name: Welsh-poppy
Height: 18in (45cm)
Spread: 1ft (30cm)
Aspect: Any
Soil: Any
Hardiness: Zone 6
Propagation: Seed when ripe
Flowering time: Spring to autumn

A grow-anywhere, tap-rooted perennial plant. Leaves are ferny. Flowers single, solitary, yellow in color, cup-shaped, borne on tall stems.

- Handsome foliage
- Attracts slugs
- Must not be moved
- Prone to mildew
- Seeds everywhere

MECONOPSIS CAMBRICA var. AURANTIACA 'FLORE PLENO'

***Meconopsis cambrica* var. *aurantiaca* 'Flore Pleno'**
(Papaveraceae)

Common name: Orange Welsh-poppy
Height: 18in (45cm)
Spread: 1ft (30cm)
Aspect: Any
Soil: Any
Hardiness: Zone 6
Propagation: Seed when ripe
Flowering time: Spring to autumn

A double orange form of the Welsh poppy, which is reputed not to self-seed to the same degree as the single form. Flower open on tallish stems from spring onwards.

- Handsome foliage
- Attracts slugs
- Must not be moved
- Prone to mildew
- Seeds everywhere

Mertensia simplicissima
(Boraginaceae)

Common name: None
Height: 3ft (90cm)
Spread: 1ft (30cm)
Aspect: Part shade
Soil: Sharply-drained
Hardiness: Zone 6
Propagation: Division in spring; seed in autumn
Flowering time: Early autumn

A hardy, prostrate perennial. Leaves in rosettes, glaucous blue-green. Flowers tubular, turquoise blue, in terminal cymes on prostrate stems.

- Handsome foliage
- Attracts slugs

Microseris ringens (Asteraceae)

Common name: None
Height: 2ft (60cm)
Spread: 1ft (30cm)
Aspect: Sun
Soil: Well-drained, humus-rich
Hardiness: Zone 8
Propagation: Seed in spring or autumn
Flowering time: Early summer

A half-hardy perennial. Leaves hairy, rough, green. Flowers single yellow daisies, in flat-topped racemes, in early summer, and again in autumn if deadheaded.

- Good cut flower
- High allergen

MIMULUS (Scrophulariaceae)
Monkey-flower

A genus of some 150 species found in damp and sandy areas, so attention has to be paid to their cultural needs. They have snapdragon-like, 2-lipped, 5-lobed flowers, spotted or bicolored; these are borne from spring to autumn on upright stems. They are low-allergen plants, prone to powdery mildew when young, and attract slugs and snails.
(*See also under Shrubs.*)

Mimulus 'Andean Nymph' A.G.M. (Scrophulariaceae)

Common name: Monkey-flower
Height: 8in (20cm)
Spread: 1ft (30cm)
Aspect: Sun or part shade
Soil: Humus-rich, fertile
Hardiness: Zone 6
Propagation: Division in spring; softwood cuttings in early summer
Flowering time: Throughout the summer period

A rhizomatous, hardy perennial plant. Flowers are attractive, trumpet-shaped, white, with cream-colored throats spotted with pink, borne on leafy racemes.

- Low allergen
- Attracts slugs
- Prone to mildew
- Short-lived

Mimulus cardinalis A.G.M. (Scrophulariaceae)

Common name: Monkey-flower
Height: 3ft (90cm)
Spread: 2ft (60cm)
Aspect: Sun or part shade
Soil: Humus-rich, fertile, well-drained.
Hardiness: Zone 7
Propagation: Seed in autumn or spring; division in spring
Flowering time: Throughout summer

A creeping perennial with downy-green leaves. Flowers solitary, axillary, tubular, scarlet, wide-lipped, throughout summer.

- Handsome foliage
- Low allergen
- Short-lived
- Prone to mildew
- Attracts slugs

Mimulus lewisii A.G.M. (Scrophulariaceae)

Common name: Monkey-flower
Height: 2ft (60cm)
Spread: 18in (45cm)
Aspect: Full sun
Spoil: Well-drained, humus-rich
Hardiness: Zone 5
Propagation: Division in spring
Flowering time: Throughout the summer period

A hardy perennial plant. Flowers axillary, solitary, tubular, deep rose-pink, with cream-colored throats, opening in summer.

- Low allergen
- Attracts slugs
- Prone to mildew
- Short-lived

Mimulus luteus (Scrophulariaceae)

Common name: Golden monkey-flower
Height: 1ft (30cm)
Spread: 2ft (60cm)
Aspect: Sun or half shade
Soil: Bog or marginal aquatic
Hardiness: Zone 7
Propagation: Seed or division in spring
Flowering time: Late spring through to midsummer

A vigorous, verging on invasive, hardy perennial. Flowers two per axil, yellow, with red-spotted throats and lobes, borne freely.

- Low allergen
- Attracts slugs
- Prone to mildew
- Seeds everywhere
- Short-lived

MIRABILIS JALAPA

Mimulus moschatus (**Scrophulariaceae**)

Common name: None
Height: 1ft (30cm)
Spread: 1ft (30cm)
Aspect: Sun or part shade
Soil: Wet or marginal aquatic
Hardiness: Zone 7
Propagation: Seed or division in spring

Flowering time: Summer through to autumn

A creeping, marginal aquatic perennial. Flowers pale yellow, spotted and blotched dark brown. Scented of musk.

- Low allergen
- Scented flowers
- Attracts slugs
- Prone to mildew
- Short-lived

Mirabilis jalapa (**Nyctaginaceae**)

Common name: Common four-o'clock
Height: 2ft (60cm)
Spread: 2ft (60cm)
Aspect: Sun, no winter wet
Soil: Well-drained, fertile
Hardiness: Zone 8
Propagation: Seed in warmth, or division in spring
Flowering time: From early through to late summer

A tuberous, half-hardy perennial plant. Flowers, from early summer onwards, scented, in several colors, unusually often present on the plant at the same time, lasting only from late afternoon to night.

- Scented flowers
- Attracts slugs

PERENNIALS

MONARDA (Lamiaceae)

Bergamot

A small genus of only about 15 species, but large numbers of hybrids are in cultivation. The flowers are 2-lipped, sage-like, with colorful bracts, and are borne in terminal whorls from midsummer to early autumn. The flowers attract bees. The foliage is aromatic. They do well in sun or partial shade, and like soil that is moist, well-drained, and humus-rich. They dislike winter wet. They are mildew prone, but some cultivars are resistant. They are also prone to slug damage.

Monarda 'Cambridge Scarlet' A.G.M. (Lamiaceae)

Common name: Bergamot
Height: 3ft (1m)
Spread: 18in (45cm)
Aspect: Sun or part shade
Soil: Moist, humus-rich, well-drained
Hardiness: Zone 4
Propagation: Division or basal cuttings in spring
Flowering time: From midsummer to early autumn

A hardy, rhizomatous perennial plant. Leaves aromatic and flowers tubular, sage-like, 2-lipped, scarlet in color, borne in terminal whorls, opening from midsummer onwards.

- Good cut flower
- Attracts bees
- Low allergen
- Requires staking
- Prone to mildew
- Attracts slugs

Monarda 'Croftway Pink' A.G.M. (Lamiaceae)

Common name: Bergamot
Height: 3ft (90cm)
Spread: 18in (45cm)
Aspect: Sun or part shade
Soil: Moist, well-drained, humus-rich
Hardiness: Zone 4
Propagation: Division or basal cuttings in spring
Flowering time: Midsummer to early autumn

A rhizomatous hardy perennial plant. Leaves aromatic. Flowers 2-lipped, sage-like, tubular, pink in color, borne in terminal whorls, from midsummer onwards.

- Good cut flower
- Attracts bees
- Low allergen
- Requires staking
- Prone to mildew
- Attracts slugs

Monarda didyma (Lamiaceae)

Common name: Bee-balm
Height: 3ft (90cm)
Spread: 18in (45cm)
Aspect: Sun or part shade
Soil: Moist, well-drained, fertile
Hardiness: Zone 4
Propagation: Division or basal cuttings in spring
Flowering time: From mid- through to late summer

A hardy perennial plant. Leaves aromatic. Flowers open on long stems, each bearing 2 whorls of pink, 2-lipped, sage-like, tubular blooms. Deadhead regularly to prolong the flowering season.

- Attracts bees
- Good cut flower
- Low allergen
- Attracts slugs
- Prone to mildew
- Requires staking

Monarda 'Loddon Crown' A.G.M. (Lamiaceae)

Common name: Bergamot
Height: 3ft (90cm)
Spread: 18in (45cm)
Aspect: Sun or part shade
Soil: Moist, well-drained, humus-rich
Hardiness: Zone 4
Propagation: Division or basal cuttings in spring
Flowering time: Midsummer to early autumn

A hardy perennial with aromatic foliage. Flowers 2-lipped, sage-like, tubular, dark red-purple, with brown bracts, in terminal whorls, from midsummer.

- Good cut flower
- Attracts bees
- Low allergen
- Requires staking
- Attracts slugs
- Prone to mildew

Nemesia denticulata A.G.M. (Scrophulariaceae)

Common name: None
Height: 16in (40cm)
Spread: 8in (20cm)
Aspect: Sun
Soil: Acidic, moist, well-drained, fertile
Hardiness: Zone 8
Propagation: Seed in heat in spring or autumn
Flowering time: Throughout the summer period

A neat, compact, half-hardy perennial plant. Flowers are scented, a smoky-pink color, with an attractive yellow eye, opening throught summer.

- Scented flowers

Nepeta longipes (Lamiaceae)

Common name: None
Height: 2ft (60cm)
Spread: 18in (45cm)
Aspect: Sun or part shade
Soil: Well-drained
Hardiness: Zone 5
Propagation: Division in spring or autumn
Flowering time: Many weeks during the summer period

A hardy perennial plant. Leaves are aromatic, toothed, gray-green in color. Flowers open during summer on tallish upright stems, lilac-blue in color, borne in close-formed whorls.

- Attracts bees
- Drought-tolerant
- Low allergen
- Attracts slugs
- Prone to mildew

NEPETA (Lamiaceae)
Nepeta

A genus of some 250 species, from a wide range of habitats, from hot and dry to cool and moist. The flowers are tubular, 2-lipped, in white and blue, sometimes yellow; they are borne in cymes, for long periods in the case of the plants featured here. The foliage may be aromatic, and cats love to make a bed of it. The plant also attracts bees.

Nepeta varies in its requirements, so see details of the individual plants. They are prone to powdery mildew and slug damage.

Nepeta 'Six Hills Giant' (Lamiaceae)

Common name: None
Height: 3ft (90cm)
Spread: 2ft (60cm)
Aspect: Sun or part shade
Soil: Well-drained
Hardiness: Zone 3
Propagation: Division in spring or autumn
Flowering time: Throughout the summer period

A tall hardy perennial plant. Leaves aromatic, hairy, gray-green. Flowers abundant, lavender-blue in color, borne in spiky, whorled cymes throughout summer.

- Attracts bees
- Drought-tolerant
- Low allergen
- Attracts slugs
- Prone to mildew
- Requires staking

Nepeta subsessilis (Lamiaceae)

Common name: None
Height: 3ft (90cm)
Spread: 1ft (30cm)
Aspect: Sun or part shade
Soil: Well-drained
Hardiness: Zone 7
Propagation: Division spring or autumn
Flowering time: Midsummer to early autumn

A clump-forming perennial plant. Leaves aromatic, toothed, deep green. Flowers bright blue in color, borne in whorled cymes.

- Attracts bees
- Drought-tolerant
- Low allergen
- Attracts slugs
- Prone to mildew
- Requires staking

Nepeta tuberosa (Lamiaceae)

Common name: None
Height: 3ft (90cm)
Spread: 1ft (30cm)
Aspect: Sun or part shade
Soil: Well-drained
Hardiness: Zone 8
Propagation: Seed in autumn; division spring or autumn
Flowering time: Several weeks in summer

A tender, tuberous perennial plant. Leaves green in color, aromatic. Flowers violet-purple, borne in spikes during summer.

- Attracts bees
- Drought-tolerant
- Low allergen
- Attracts slugs
- Prone to mildew
- Requires staking

Nerine bowdenii A.G.M. (Amaryllidaceae)

Common name: Cape colony nerine
Height: 18in (45cm)
Spread: 4in (10cm)
Aspect: Sun
Soil: Well-drained, fertile
Hardiness: Zone 8
Propagation: Seed in heat when ripe; division after flowering
Flowering time: Autumn

A half-hardy, bulbous perennial. Leaves strap-like, green. Flowers very weather-resistant, scented, pink, funnel-shaped, with recurved tepals, in open umbels of up to 7.

- Drought-tolerant
- Good cut flower
- Attracts slugs
- Poisonous

NICOTIANA (Solanaceae)

Nicotiana

A genus of more than 60 species of plants from usually moist sites in tropical areas of the world. The flowers are tubular or trumpet-shaped, may be scented, and are borne in panicles or racemes over long periods during the summer period, and perhaps into autumn. The flowers open during the evening or at night, but they may also open during the day if they are grown in a shady site.

Nicotiana likes moist, but well-drained soil, and grows in sun or part shade. Plants may require to be staked. Perennial species can be over-wintered outside in warm areas. (*See also under Annuals.*)

NICOTIANA x SANDERAE 'HAVANA APPLEBLOSSOM'

Nicotiana x *sanderae* '**Havana Appleblossom**' (**Solanaceae**)

Common name: None
Height: 15in (38cm)
Spread: 1ft (30cm)
Aspect: Sun or part shade
Soil: Moist, well-drained, fertile
Hardiness: Zone 7
Propagation: Seed in heat in spring
Flowering time: Early to late summer

An upright, dwarf, short-lived perennial plant, grown usually as an annual. Flowers are open salvers of white or pale pink, borne in attractive panicles.

- Scented flowers
- Short-lived
- Skin irritant

NICOTIANA 'ROULETTE' SERIES

Nicotiana 'Roulette' series (Solanaceae)

Common name: None
Height: 10in (25cm)
Spread: 9in (23cm)
Aspect: Sun or part shade
Soil: Moist, well-drained, fertile
Hardiness: Zone 8
Propagation: Seed in heat in spring
Flowering time: Throughout the summer period

An upright, short-lived perennial plant, grown usually as an annual. Flowers open salvers, in a range of colors, and bicolored, in panicles.

- Scented flowers
- Short-lived
- Skin irritant

Nicotiana sylvestris A.G.M. (Solanaceae)

Common name: None
Height: 5ft (1.5m)
Spread: 2ft (60cm)
Aspect: Part shade
Soil: Moist, well-drained
Hardiness: Zone 8
Propagation: Seed in heat in spring
Flowering time: Throughout the summer period

A robust, short-lived perennial. Flowers nodding, perfumed, long trumpets, white, in densely-packed panicles; closed in full sun.

- Scented flowers
- Short-lived
- Skin irritant

Nierembergia repens (Solanaceae)

Commom name: White cupflower
Height: 4in (10cm)
Spread: 18in (45cm)
Aspect: Full sun
Soil: Moist, well-drained
Hardiness: Zone 8
Propagation: Seed or division in spring
Flowering time: Throughout the summer period

A prostrate perennial plant. Flowers open, upward-facing cups, white, with yellow-colored centers, opening over a long period during summer.

- Attracts slugs

Nierembergia scoparia 'Mont Blanc'
(Solanaceae)

Common name: Cupflower
Height: 8in (20cm)
Spread: 8in (20cm)
Aspect: Full sun
Soil: Moist, well-drained
Hardiness: Zone 8
Propagation: Stem-tip cuttings during summer
Flowering time: From midsummer through to early autumn

A shrubby perennial plant. Flowers cup-shaped, opening white, with yellow throats, from summer through to autumn.

• Attracts slugs

Nolana paradoxa 'Blue Bird'
(Solanaceae)

Common name: None
Height: 10in (25cm)
Spread: 2ft (60cm)
Aspect: Full sun
Soil: Any fertile
Hardiness: Zone 9
Propagation: Seed in heat in early spring, or *in situ* in late spring
Flowering time: Summer

A tender perennial plant, grown as an annual in cold areas. Leaves in a basal rosette, green. Flowers blue, solitary, cups, with white eyes, and bright yellow throats, in summer for many weeks. Flowers open only if positioned in full sun.

OENOTHERA (*Onagraceae*)

Oenothera

A genus of some 150 species of perennials, biennials, and annuals. They grow invariably on well-drained soils, such as mountain slopes and deserts. While many are nocturnal-flowering, not all are. The individual flowers last only one day or night, but flowers are borne in a long succession over many weeks during the summer season. Yellow is the predominant color in the genus, but some are pink, others white. The flowers may be perfumed in some types. Some are tap-rooted and therefore do not survive transplantation; many are also short-lived.

Oenothera fruticosa (**Onagraceae**)

Common name: Common sundrops
Height: 3ft (90cm)
Spread: 1ft (30cm)
Aspect: Full sun
Soil: Sharply-drained
Hardiness: Zone 4
Propagation: Division in early spring
Flowering time: From late spring to late summer

A short-lived perennial plant. Flowers are diurnal, cup-shaped, dark yellow in color, and borne in racemes of up to 10.

- Attract bees
- Drought-tolerant
- Good cut flower everywhere
- Attracts slugs
- Must not be moved
- Seeds
- Short-lived

Oenothera glazioviana (**Onagraceae**)

Common name: None
Height: 5ft (1.5m)
Spread: 2ft (60cm)
Aspect: Sun
Soil: Sharply-drained
Hardiness: Zone 3
Propagation: Seed in spring
Flowering time: Mid- and late summer

A short-lived perennial. Leaves in a basal rosette. Flowers large, bowl-shaped, yellow, nocturnal, in racemes.

- Attracts bees
- Drought-tolerant
- Good cut flower
- Attracts slugs
- Must not be moved
- Seeds everywhere
- Short-lived

Oenothera macrocarpa A.G.M.
(Onagraceae)

Common name: None
Height: 6in (15cm)
Spread: 2ft (60cm)
Aspect: Sun
Soil: Sharply-drained
Hardiness: Zone 5
Propagation: Seed in spring
Flowering time: Late spring to early autumn

A prostrate, herbaceous perennial. Flowers are large, solitary, golden yellow in color, opening in the daytime, from late spring and into the autumn.

- Attracts bees
- Drought-tolerant
- Attracts slugs
- Must not be moved

Oenothera speciosa 'Siskyou'
(Onagraceae)

Common name: Showy evening primrose
Height: 1ft (30cm)
Spread: 1ft (30cm)
Aspect: Full sun
Soil: Sharply-drained
Hardiness: Zone 5
Propagation: Division in spring
Flowering time: Early summer to autumn

A low-growing, hardy perennial. Very choice clone. Flowers pink, with yellow centers. May be invasive.

- Attracts bees
- Drought-tolerant
- Attracts slugs
- Must not be moved
- Short-lived

Omphalodes cappadocica 'Starry Eyes' (Boraginaceae)

Common name: None
Height: 1ft (30cm)
Spread: 18in (45cm)
Aspect: Part shade
Soil: Moist, humus-rich
Hardiness: Zone 6
Propagation: Division in spring
Flowering time: Early spring

An evergreen, woodland perennial. Flowers small, blue, with a white eye, and a central white stripe on each petal, in loose racemes. *Omphalodes* 'Cherry Ingram' is very similar, with unmarked blue flowers.

- Evergreen
- Low allergen
- Attracts slugs

Origanum 'Buckland' (Lamiaceae)

Common name: Marjoram
Height: 8in (20cm)
Spread: 6in (15cm)
Aspect: Sun
Soil: Well-drained, fertile
Hardiness: Zone 7
Propagation: Division or basal cuttings in spring
Flowering time: Throughout the summer

An upright, bushy, perennial. Leaves hairy, aromatic, gray-green. Flowers tubular, pink in color, borne in whorls, surrounded by pink bracts, which last for many weeks during the summer season.

- Attracts bees
- Drought-tolerant

Origanum laevigatum 'Herrenhausen' A.G.M. (Lamiaceae)

Common name: None
Height: 18in (45cm)
Spread: 18in (45cm)
Aspect: Sun
Soil: Well-drained, fertile
Hardiness: Zone 8
Propagation: Division or basal cuttings in spring
Flowering time: Late spring to autumn

An evergreen, half-hardy perennial. Leaves aromatic, purple-green. Flowers deep pink, tubular, in dense panicle-like whorls, and surrounded by purple-red bracts.

- Attracts bees
- Drought-tolerant
- Evergreen

Osteospermum jucundum var. *compactum* A.G.M. (Asteraceae)

Common name: None
Height: 8in (20cm)
Spread: 3ft (90cm)
Aspect: Full sun
Soil: Well-drained, humus-rich
Hardiness: Zone 7
Propagation: Seed in heat, in spring
Flowering time: Early summer to autumn

A hardy, prostrate, evergreen perennial plant. Flowers single, solitary, with mauve ray florets and yellow disc florets from early summer.

- Evergreen
- Good cut flower
- High allergen
- Must deadhead

Pandorea jasminoides 'Rosea' (Bignoniaceae)

Common name: Bower plant
Height: 18ft (6m)
Spread: 3ft (90cm)
Aspect: Full sun
Soil: Moist, well-drained, fertile
Hardiness: Zone 9
Propagation: Layer in spring; greenwood cuttings with bottom heat in summer
Flowering time: Spring to summer

A tender evergreen climber. Flowers tubular, pink, with darker pink throats, in small panicles, from spring to summer. Prune annually after flowering if flowering on the previous year's growth; otherwise, in spring.

● Evergreen

Papaver croceum (Papaveraceae)

Common name: Icelandic poppy
Height: 1ft (30cm)
Spread: 6in (15cm)
Aspect: Full sun
Soil: Deep, well-drained
Hardiness: Zone 2
Propagation: Seed in spring
Flowering time: Summer

A short-lived hardy perennial plant, grown usually as a biennial. Leaves blue-green, hairy. Flowers scented, solitary, bowl-shaped, in a wide range of colors, borne on short stems for many weeks during the summer season.

● Scented flowers   ● Prone to mildew
● Handsome foliage ● Short-lived
● Low allergen   ● Seeds everywhere

Papaver 'Fireball' (Papaveraceae)

Common name: Poppy
Height: 1ft (30cm)
Spread: Indefinite
Aspect: Full sun
Soil: Well-drained, fertile
Hardiness: Zone 7
Propagation: Seed or division in spring
Flowering time: Late spring to midsummer

A hardy, invasive perennial. Flowers solitary, semi-double, hemispherical, orange-red in color, on shortish stems from late spring onwards.

● Good cut flower   ● Invasive
● Low allergen

Papaver spicatum (Papaveraceae)

Common name: Poppy
Height: 2ft (60cm)
Spread: 6in (15cm)
Aspect: Sun
Soil: Well-drained, fertile
Hardiness: Zone 8
Propagation: Seed, in spring
Flowering time: Several weeks in summer

A perennial plant with pale green leaves in a basal rosette. Flowers in a slender raceme, pale orange colored, outward-facing.

- Low allergen
- Must not be moved

Passiflora caerulea A.G.M. (Passifloraceae)

Common name: Passion-flower
Height: 30ft (9m)
Spread: 3ft (90cm)
Aspect: Sun or part shade
Soil: Moist, well-drained, fertile
Hardiness: Zone 7
Propagation: Layer in spring or autumn; semi-ripe cuttings in summer
Flowering time: Summer to autumn

Flowers flat, white, with coronas zoned in purple, blue, and white; edible fruits. Prune in early spring. Hardy.

- Evergreen
- Low allergen
- Invasive
- Requires space

Passiflora quadrangularis A.G.M. (Passifloraceae)

Common name: Passion-flower
Height: 50ft (15m)
Spread: 3ft (90cm)
Aspect: Sun or part shade
Soil: Moist, well-drained, fertile
Hardiness: Zone 10
Propagation: Layer in spring or autumn; semi-ripe cuttings in summer
Flowering time: Summer to autumn

A tuberous, vigorous climbing plant. Flowers scented, pendent, red, with large coronas of purple-colored filaments, banded red; followed by edible fruits. Prune for shape and size as and when needed.

- Evergreen
- Low allergen
- Scented flowers
- Requires space

PELARGONIUM (Geraniaceae)
Pelargonium

A genus of about 230 species, but the many thousands of commercial cultivars are derived from only a handful of species. They are mostly of South African origin, and all are Zone 9 or 10 (with the single exception of *P. endlicherianum*, which is Zone 7). They flower all year round in warm climates, but only over the summer in cool countries, unless they are given protection from the winter cold in a warm greenhouse or conservatory. There are three major groups of flowering pelargoniums:

Zonal pelargoniums This, the largest group, comprises evergreen perennials, many with variegated foliage, and can be divided further into six subclasses, depending on flower shape and size, but for the purpose of this book can be regarded as belonging to two main groups: a) those raised from seed for bedding out, are single-flowered, and come true from seed, and b) large-flowered cultivars raised from cuttings and which can be bedded out but which also make excellent house or conservatory plants during the winter in cold counties. The blooms of double-flowered cultivars of this group, in particular, can be spoiled by rain.

Regal pelargoniums This group is also evergreen, but may be perennial or shrubby.

Ivy-leaved pelargoniums These are evergreen, trailing perennials, and make excellent specimens for hanging baskets.

Contact with the foliage of pelargoniums may cause, or exacerbate, skin problems, and the plants are highly allergenic. Routine deadheading is important in keeping pelargoniums flowering continuously.

There are specialist nurseries, societies, and books devoted to the pelargonium, and the reader who requires further in-depth information should consult these.

Pelargonium endlicherianum (Geraniaceae)

Common name: None
Height: 10in (25cm)
Spread: 6in (15cm)
Aspect: Full sun, no winter wet
Soil: Sharply-drained
Hardiness: Zone 7
Propagation: Seed in heat in spring
Flowering time: Many weeks in summer

The only hardy *Pelargonium*. Leaves basal, crenate, dark green. Flowers deep pink in color, veined purple, in tall scapes, opening in summer. Dislikes winter wet.

- High allergen
- Must deadhead
- Skin irritant

Pelargonium peltatum (Geraniaceae)

Common name: None
Height: 8in (20cm)
Spread: 3ft (90cm)
Aspect: Sun, no winter wet
Soil: Well-drained, fertile
Hardiness: Zone 10
Propagation: Seed in heat, or softwood cuttings in spring
Flowering time: All summer

An evergreen, prostrate, or trailing, tender perennial. Leaves stiff, lobed, pointed, green. Flowers single or double, in shades of pink, red, white, orange, reddish-black, or purple.

- Evergreen
- High allergen
- Must deadhead
- Skin irritant

Pelargonium regale hybridus (Geraniaceae)

Common name: None
Height: 1ft (30cm)
Spread: 10in (25cm)
Aspect: Part shade, no winter wet
Soil: Well-drained, fertile
Hardiness: Zone 9
Propagation: Seed in heat, or softwood cuttings, in spring
Flowering time: All summer

Leaves rounded, mid-green. Flowers single, rarely double, in clusters, in red, pink, purple, white, orange, or reddish-black, or bicolored. Likes half shade.

- Evergreen
- High allergen
- Must deadhead
- Skin irritant

Pelargonium tricolor (= 'Splendide') (Geraniaceae)

Common name: None
Height: 1ft (30cm)
Spread: 8in (20cm)
Aspect: Sun
Soil: Moist, well-drained
Hardiness: Zone 9
Propagation: Softwood cuttings in spring to autumn
Flowering time: Summer

A tender perennial. Leaves hairy, deeply-cut, gray-green. Flowers with red upper petals, with a black base, and white lower petals.

- Evergreen
- High allergen
- Must deadhead
- Skin irritant

PELARGONIUM ZONALE HYBRIDUS

Pelargonium zonale hybridus (= **cultorum**) (Geraniaceae)

Common name: None
Height: 2ft (60cm)
Spread: 1ft (30cm)
Aspect: Sun or part shade; no winter wet
Soil: Moist, well-drained
Hardiness: Zone 9
Propagation: Softwood cuttings in spring, summer, or autumn

Flowering time: Throughout the summer

Bushy evergreen perennials. Leaves rounded, hairy, green or zoned bronze/maroon. Flowers single or double, red, pink, purple, white, or orange. Deadhead regularly.

- Evergreen
- High allergen
- Must deadhead
- Skin irritant

PERENNIALS

PENSTEMON (Scrophulariaceae)
Penstemon

A genus of about 250 species, but many hundreds more hybrids. They can be evergreen or deciduous. They are mostly half-hardy, but some are hardy. The foxglove-like flowers may be tubular, bell-shaped, or funnel-shaped, and are borne in panicles or racemes from early summer to mid-autumn.

Penstemons like sun or part shade, and a soil which is well-drained, and not over fertile; they do not flower well or overwinter well, if overfed. They should be given a shear over after flowering, and a dry mulch over winter in cold regions. They are prone to slug damage and powdery mildew. (*See also under Shrubs.*)

Penstemon 'Flamingo' (Scrophulariaceae)

Common name: None
Height: 3ft (90cm)
Spread: 1ft (30cm)
Aspect: Sun or half shade
Soil: Well-drained
Hardiness: Zone 7
Propagation: Division in spring

Flowering time: Early summer to mid-autumn

A hybrid semi-evergreen perennial. Flowers tubular, white with pink margins, in racemes.

- Low allergen
- Attracts slugs
- Must deadhead
- Prone to mildew

Penstemon heterophyllus 'Blue Springs' (Scrophulariaceae)

Common name: Chaparral penstemon
Height: 20in (50cm)
Spread: 20in (50cm)
Aspect: Sun or part shade
Soil: Well-drained
Hardiness: Zone 8
Propagation: Division in spring
Flowering time: Several weeks in summer

An evergreen plant. Leaves bluish-green. Flowers tubular, blue in color, with lilac lobes, in racemes, opening in summer.

- Evergreen
- Handsome foliage
- Low allergen
- Attracts slugs
- Must deadhead
- Prone to mildew

Penstemon 'Osprey' A.G.M. (Scrophulariaceae)

Common name: None
Height: 3ft (90cm)
Spread: 18in (45cm)
Aspect: Sun or part shade
Soil: Well-drained, fertile
Hardiness: Zone 7
Propagation: Division in spring
Flowering time: Early summer to autumn

A tall hybrid. Flowers tubular, rose-carmine, with a white-colored throat, borne in racemes.

- Low allergen
- Attracts slugs
- Must deadhead
- Prone to mildew
- Requires staking

Penstemon 'Rosy Blush' (Scrophulariaceae)

Common name: None
Height: 3ft (90cm)
Spread: 18in (45cm)
Aspect: Sun or part shade
Soil: Well-drained, fertile
Hardiness: Zone 8
Propagation: Division in spring
Flowering time: Early to late summer

A hybrid perennial plant. Flowers tubular or bell-shaped, pink, with a white interior, and violet mouth, in one-sided racemes.

- Low allergen
- Attracts slugs
- Must deadhead
- Prone to mildew

Penstemon 'Sour Grapes' (Scrophulariaceae)

Common name: None
Height: 2ft (60cm)
Spread: 18in (45cm)
Aspect: Sun or part shade
Soil: Well-drained, fertile
Hardiness: Zone 6
Propagation: Division in spring
Flowering time: Summer through to autumn

A half-hardy perennial plant. Flowers tubular, or bell-shaped, dull lilac-blue in color, with white throats, opening in one-sided racemes from summer onwards.

- 🟢 Low allergen
- 🔴 Attracts slugs
- 🔴 Must deadhead
- 🔴 Prone to mildew

Persicaria affinis 'Superba' A.G.M. (Polygonaceae)

Common name: None
Height: 10in (25cm)
Spread: Indefinite
Aspect: Sun or part shade
Soil: Moist
Hardiness: Zone 3
Propagation: Division in spring or autumn
Flowering time: Summer to autumn

A vigorous, ground-covering perennial. Flowers cup-shaped, pale pink, in spikes. Flowers remain brown into the winter. Foliage bronze in winter.

- 🟢 Evergreen
- 🔴 Poisonous
- 🔴 Skin irritant
- 🔴 High allergen
- 🔴 Invasive

Persicaria amplexicaulis 'Firetail' A.G.M. (Polygonaceae)

Common name: Bistort
Height: 4ft (1.2m)
Spread: 4ft (1.2m)
Aspect: Sun or part shade
Soil: Moist
Hardiness: Zone 5
Propagation: Division in spring or autumn
Flowering time: Midsummer to early autumn

A robust perennial. Flowers bell-shaped, bright red, in narrow spikes.

- 🟢 Evergreen
- 🔴 Poisonous
- 🔴 Skin irritant
- 🔴 High allergen

PETREA VOLUBILIS

***Persicaria bistorta* 'Superba'
A.G.M. (Polygonaceae)**

Common name: Bistort
Height: 3ft (90cm)
Spread: 3ft (90cm)
Aspect: Sun or part shade
Soil: Any
Hardiness: Zone 4
Propagation: Division in spring or autumn
Flowering time: Summer

A semi-evergreen. Flowers bell-shaped, pink, in dense cylindrical spikes.

- Poisonous
- Skin irritant
- High allergen

***Petrea volubilis* (Verbenaceae)**

Common name: None
Height: 40ft (12m)
Spread: 5ft (1.5m)
Aspect: Full sun
Soil: Moist, well-drained, fertile
Hardiness: Zone 10
Propagation: Semi-ripe cuttings with bottom heat in summer
Flowering time: Late winter to summer

A semi-evergreen climbing plant. Flowers salverform, amethyst blue in color, borne in arching panicles, from late winter. Prune for size and shape when flowering has finished.

- Requires space

PERENNIALS 163

Petunia x *hybrida* 'Prism Sunshine' series (Solanaceae)

Common name: Garden petunia
Height: 10in (25cm)
Spread: 15in (38cm)
Aspect: Full sun
Soil: Well-drained
Hardiness: Zone 7
Propagation: Softwood cuttings in spring
Flowering time: Late spring to late autumn

A free-flowering perennial plant, grown invariably as an annual. Flowers large, yellow colored, veined, and fade-resistant.

- Low allergen
- Attracts slugs
- Must deadhead

Petunia x *hybrida* 'Summer Morn' series (Solanaceae)

Common name: Garden petunia
Height: 1ft (30cm)
Spread: 18in (45cm)
Aspect: Sun
Soil: Well-drained
Hardiness: Zone 7
Propagation: Softwood cuttings in spring
Flowering time: Spring to late autumn

A compact, free-flowering perennial, grown as an annual. Flowers large, in a range of colors, self-colored, or throated in a paler color. Deadheading prolongs flowering.

- Low allergen
- Attracts slugs
- Must deadhead

Petunia x *hybrida* 'Surfinia' series (Solanaceae)

Common name: Garden petunia
Height: 16in (40cm)
Spread: 3ft (90cm)
Aspect: Full sun
Soil: Well-drained
Hardiness: Zone 7
Propagation: Softwood cuttings in spring
Flowering time: Spring to late autumn

A grandiflora petunia, of trailing habit, ideal for hanging baskets. Perennial, but invariably grown as an annual. Flowers large, in shades of blue, lavender, pink, or magenta.

- Low allergen
- Attracts slugs
- Must deadhead

***Petunia* x *hybrida* 'Ultra' series (Solanaceae)**

Common name: Garden petunia
Height: 1ft (30cm)
Spread: 3ft (90cm)
Aspect: Full sun
Soil: Well-drained
Hardiness: Zone 7
Propagation: Seed in heat in spring
Flowering time: Late spring to autumn

A grandiflora petunia. Perennial, but almost always grown as an annual. Flowers large, in very many colors, with central white stars. Weather-resistant.

● Low allergen   ● Attracts slugs
                  ● Must deadhead

***Phlox* 'Chattahoochee' A.G.M. (Polemoniaceae)**

Common name: None
Height: 6in (15cm)
Spread: 1ft (30cm)
Aspect: Half shade
Soil: Moist, well-drained, humus-rich, fertile
Hardiness: Zone 4
Propagation: Softwood cuttings of blind shoots, in spring
Flowering time: Summer to autumn

A short-lived, prostrate perennial. Flowers salveriform, lavender-blue, with a red eye, in cymes.

● Low allergen   ● Attracts slugs
                  ● Prone to mildew
                  ● Short-lived

Phuopsis stylosa (**Rubiaceae**)

Common name: None
Height: 6in (15cm)
Spread: 3ft (90cm)
Aspect: Sun or part shade
Soil: Moist, sharply-drained, fertile
Hardiness: Zone 7
Propagation: Seed in autumn; division spring or autumn
Flowering time: All summer

A mat-forming, sprawling perennial. Leaves musk-scented. Flowers scented, small, pink, in dense globular heads. Shear over after flowering to keep compact.

- Scented flowers
- Seeds everywhere

Podranea ricasoliana (**Bignoniaceae**)

Common name: None
Height: 15ft (4.5m)
Spread: 3ft (90cm)
Aspect: Part shade
Soil: Moist, well-drained, fertile
Hardiness: Zone 9
Propagation: Seed in heat, or layer, in spring
Flowering time: Winter through to following summer

An evergreen climbing plant. Flowers in panicles of up to 12, pink in color. Prune just after flowering has finished by cutting back to within 3 or 4 buds of the permanent framework. Tender.

- Evergreen
- Requires space

POTENTILLA (Rosaceae)
Cinquefoil

A genus of more than 500 species of annuals, biennials, perennials, and shrubs, from the Northern Hemisphere, but only the last two groups are included here. The flowers are saucer- or cup-shaped, have 5 petals, and may be star-shaped or circular in outline, single or double. They are borne singly, in cymes or in panicles, over a long period from spring to autumn. The leaves are not unlike those of the strawberry.

Cinquefoils like to be planted where they will receive full sun. Drainage should be good or sharp. Fertility should be low, else the plants will make foliage at the expense of flowers.

They benefit from being cut hard back in autumn. They attract bees, are low-allergen plants, and are good for cutting.

Potentilla aurea (Rosaceae)

Common name: Cinquefoil
Height: 4in (10cm)
Spread: 8in (20cm)
Aspect: Sun
Soil: Well-drained
Hardiness: Zone 5
Propagation: Division in spring
Flowering time: Late spring through to summer

A mat-forming, hardy perennial plant. Leaves glossy-green, silver-margined. Flowers flat, deep yellow in color, borne in cymes.

- Attracts bees
- Handsome foliage
- Low allergen

Potentilla 'Flamenco' (Rosaceae)

Common name: Cinquefoil
Height: 18in (45cm)
Spread: 2ft (60cm)
Aspect: Sun
Soil: Well-drained
Hardiness: Zone 5
Propagation: Division in spring
Flowering time: Late spring to midsummer

A clump-forming hardy perennial. Leaves palmate, mid-green. Flowers single, saucer-shaped, scarlet with black centers, in panicles from late spring onwards.

- Attracts bees
- Low allergen

***Potentilla* 'Gloire de Nancy'** (Rosaceae)

Common name: Cinquefoil
Height: 18in (45cm)
Spread: 2ft (60cm)
Aspect: Sun
Soil: Well-drained
Hardiness: Zone 5
Propagation: Division in spring or autumn
Flowering time: Early to late summer

A clump-forming hardy perennial plant. Flowers double, orange-red, in racemes, from early summer onwards.

- Attracts bees
- Low allergen

***Potentilla nepalensis* 'Miss Willmott' A.G.M.** (Rosaceae)

Common name: Nepal cinquefoil
Height: 18in (45cm)
Spread: 2ft (60cm)
Aspect: Sun
Soil: Well-drained
Hardiness: Zone 5
Propagation: Division in spring or autumn
Flowering time: All summer

Hardy; clumpforming. Flowers flat, cherry-red, with dark pink centers, in loose cymes.

- Attracts bees
- Low allergen

***Potentilla recta* 'Alba'** (Rosaceae)

Common name: Cinquefoil
Height: 2ft (60cm)
Spread: 18in (45cm)
Aspect: Sun
Soil: Well-drained
Hardiness: Zone 5
Propagation: Division in spring or autumn
Flowering time: Early through to late summer

An upright, clump-forming perennial plant. Flowers saucer-shaped, white in color, borne in flat cymes, opening from early summer.

- Attracts bees
- Low allergen

***Potentilla* 'William Rollison' A.G.M.
(Rosaceae)**

Common name: None
Height: 18in (45cm)
Spread: 2ft (60cm)
Aspect: Sun
Soil: Well-drained
Hardiness: Zone 5
Propagation: Division in spring or autumn
Flowering time: Early through to late summer

A hardy, clump-forming perennial plant. Flowers flat, semi-double, orange-red in color, borne in cymes.

- Attracts bees
- Low allergen

Pratia pedunculata
(Campanulaceae)

Common name: None
Height: 1in (2.5cm)
Spread: Indefinite
Aspect: Shade
Soil: Well-drained, humus-rich
Hardiness: Zone 7
Propagation: Division at any time of the year

Flowering time: Long periods in summer

A creeping, mat-forming perennial plant. Flowers almost stemless, small, star-shaped, deep blue in color.

- Attracts slugs
- Invasive

Primula obconica (**Primulaceae**)

Common name: None
Height: 16in (40cm)
Spread: 10in (25cm)
Aspect: Light shade
Hardiness: Zone 8
Propagation: Surface-sown seed in heat in early spring
Flowering time: Winter to spring

A rosetted, evergreen perennial plant, grown commonly as an annual. Flowers salverform, white, pink, lilac, or red in color, borne in whorls, opening from winter through to the spring.

- Evergreen
- Handsome foliage
- Poisonous
- Skin irritant
- Attracts slugs

Pulmonaria rubra 'Bowles Red' (**Boraginaceae**)

Common name: None
Height: 16in (45cm)
Spread: 3ft (90cm)
Aspect: Shade, part or full
Soil: Moist, humus-rich, fertile
Hardiness: Zone 5
Propagation: Division after flowering, or in autumn
Flowering time: Winter to mid-spring

A rhizomatous, creeping perennial. Leaves have pale green spots. Flowers funnel-shaped, coral-red, in cymes.

- Attracts bees
- Low allergen
- Handsome foliage
- Attracts slugs
- Prone to mildew
- Seeds everywhere

Pulmonaria saccharata
(**Boraginaceae**)

Common name: Bethlehem sage
Height: 1ft (30cm)
Spread: 2ft (60cm)
Aspect: Part or full shade
Soil: Moist, humus-rich, fertile
Hardiness: Zone 3
Propagation: Seed when ripe; division in late spring or autumn
Flowering time: Late winter through to late spring

A rhizomatous, evergreen perennial. Leaves green, spotted white. Flowers funnel-shaped, red, or white, in cymes.

- Handsome foliage
- Attracts slugs
- Low allergen
- Prone to mildew

Ratibida pinnata (**Asteraceae**)

Common name: Mexican hat
Height: 4ft (1.2m)
Spread: 18in (45cm)
Aspect: Sun
Soil: Sharply drained
Hardiness: Zone 3
Propagation: Seed or division in spring
Flowering time: Summer to autumn

A tall, upright perennial. Leaves bluish-green. Flowers daisy-like, ray florets yellow, disc florets brown, on a proud cone, from summer onwards. Often grown as an annual.

- Drought-resistant
- High allergen
- Good cut flower
- Handsome foliage

Rehmannia elata **(Scrophulariaceae)**

Common name: Beverly-bells rehmannia
Height: 4ft (1.2m)
Spread: 20in (50cm)
Aspect: Sun; no winter wet
Soil: Well-drained, humus-rich, fertile
Hardiness: Zone 9
Propagation: Seed in warmth, or separate runners, in early spring
Flowering time: Summer through to autumn

A tender perennial, grown as a biennial in cold areas. Flowers tubular, semi-pendent, pink, with spotted throats, borne in racemes. *Rehmannia glutinosa* A.G.M. is very similar.

- Drought-tolerant
- Attracts slugs
- Short-lived

Rhodochiton atrosanguineus **(Scrophulariaceae)**

Common name: None
Height: 10ft (3m)
Spread: 1ft (30cm)
Aspect: Full sun
Soil: Moist, well-drained, fertile
Hardiness: Zone 9
Propagation: Seed in heat when ripe, or in spring
Flowering time: Summer through to autumn

A tender climber. Leaves heart-shaped, green, veined/marbled with red. Flowers pendent, solitary, tubular, black, or deep purple in color, with long-tubed corollas.

- Handsome foliage

Rhodohypoxis baurii var. *confecta* (Hypoxidaceae)

Common name: None
Height: 4in (10cm)
Spread: 4in (10cm)
Aspect: Sun; no winter wet
Soil: Sharply-drained, humus-rich
Hardiness: Zone 8
Propagation: Seed, in heat when ripe; offsets in autumn
Flowering time: Throughout the summer

A cormous perennial. Leaves grayish-green. Flowers solitary, flat, pink. Dislikes winter wet and in such areas grow *R. milloides*.

- Drought-tolerant
- Handsome foliage

Roscoea purpurea (Zingiberaceae)

Common name: None
Height: 3ft (90cm)
Spread: 3ft (90cm)
Aspect: Part shade
Soil: Moist, well-drained, humus-rich, fertile
Hardiness: Zone 6
Propagation: Seed when ripe; division in spring
Flowering time: Long period in late summer and early autumn

A tuberous, herbaceous perennial which does not reappear till midsummer, so mark the position well. Flowers hooded, purple in color.

- Low allergen
- Attracts slugs
- Requires staking

RUDBECKIA (Asteraceae)

Rudbeckia

A genus of only some 20 species of annuals and perennials. The flowers are daisy-like, solitary, usually single, with yellow or orange ray florets, and brown or black disc florests in a cone. They are borne on long stems for a long period from summer to autumn. They like sun or part shade, and a soil that is moist and does not dry out. Some perennial species, such as *R. hirta*, are often grown as annuals. Slugs are fond of the genus.

RUDBECKIA FULGIDA var. SULLIVANTII 'GOLDSTURM' A.G.M.

Rudbeckia fulgida var. *sullivantii* 'Goldsturm' A.G.M. (Asteraceae)

Common name. Showy coneflower
Height: 2ft (60cm)
Spread: 18in (45cm)
Aspect: Sun or part shade
Soil: Well-drained, humus-rich, fertile
Hardiness: Zone 4
Propagation: Division in spring or autumn
Flowering time: Late summer to mid-autumn

A rhizomatous, hardy perennial plant. Flowers solitary, single, yellow-colored daisies, each with a raised, black center, opening from late summer onwards.

- Attracts bees
- Good cut flower
- Attracts slugs
- High allergen

Rudbeckia 'Herbstonne' (Asteraceae)

Common name: None
Height: 6ft (1.8m)
Spread: 4ft (1.2m)
Aspect: Sun or part shade
Soil: Well-drained, humus-rich, fertile
Hardiness: Zone 3
Propagation: Division in spring or autumn
Flowering time: Late summer to late autumn

A tall, invasive hardy rhizomatous perennial. Flowers single, solitary, yellow daisies, with prominent dark centers. Superb cut flower.

- Attracts bees
- Good cut flower
- High allergen
- Requires space
- Requires staking

Rudbeckia hirta 'Rustic Dwarf' strain (Asteraceae)

Common name: Black-eyed Susan
Height: 2ft (60cm)
Spread: 18in (45cm)
Aspect: Sun or part shade
Soil: Well-drained, humus-rich, fertile
Hardiness: Zone 4
Propagation: Seed in early spring
Flowering time: Summer to late autumn

A dwarf strain of an erect, short-lived perennial, grown as an annual in cold climates. Flowers single, solitary, yellow daisies, with dark central boss.

- Attracts bees
- Good cut flower
- Attracts slugs
- Short-lived

RUDBECKIA LACINIATA 'GOLDQUELLE' A.G.M.

Rudbeckia laciniata 'Goldquelle' A.G.M. (Asteraceae)

Common name: None
Height: 3ft (90cm)
Spread: 18in (45cm)
Aspect: Sun or part shade
Soil: Well-drained, humus-rich
Hardiness: Zone 3
Propagation: Division in spring or autumn

Flowering time: Summer through to autumn

A rhizomatous, compact, hardy perennial plant. Flowers solitary, double, lemon-yellow in color, becoming yellow with age, and green centers.

- Attracts bees
- Good cut flower
- Attracts slugs
- High allergen

PERENNIALS 175

Rudbeckia maxima (Asteraceae)

Common name: Great coneflower
Height: 5ft (1.5m)
Spread: 3ft (90cm)
Aspect: Sun or part shade
Soil: Well-drained, humus-rich, fertile
Hardiness: Zone 7
Propagation: Seed or division in spring
Flowering time: Late summer to mid-autumn

A hardy perennial plant. Flowers solitary, single, yellow-colored daisies, with prominent dark central cones, from late summer.

- Attracts bees
- Good cut flower
- High allergen
- Requires staking

Rudbeckia subtomentosa (Asteraceae)

Common name: Sweet coneflower
Height: 28in (70cm)
Spread: 2ft (60cm)
Aspect: Sun or part shade
Soil: Well-drained, humus-rich, fertile
Hardiness: Zone 5
Propagation: Seed or division in spring
Flowering time: Late summer to mid-autumn

A hardy perennial plant. Flowers solitary, single, yellow daisies, with dark brown centers.

- Attracts bees
- Good cut flower
- High allergen

Saintpaulia ionantha (Gesneriaceae)

Common name: None
Height: 4in (10cm)
Spread: 8in (20cm)
Aspect: Sun, but not in summer
Soil: Sharply-drained
Hardiness: Zone 10
Propagation: Seed in heat, when ripe, or in spring
Flowering time: All year – provided there are 12 hours of daylight or fluorescent light and with temperature not below 65°F (18°C)

A tender perennial plant. Leaves in rosettes, gray-green in color. Flowers blue, borne in cymes.

- Handsome foliage
- Prone to mildew

SALVIA (Lamiaceae)
Salvia

A genus consisting of about 900 species of plants from the temperate and tropical regions of the world, and a wide range of habitats. They may be annual, biennial, or perennial; they include species that are subshrubs, evergreen, or deciduous, fully hardy or tender. The foliage is handsome and may also be aromatic. The flowers are 2-lipped: the upper petal is a hood, and the lower is forked. Calyces and bracts may be colored. The flowers are borne in axillary whorls or panicles, on tall stems, over long periods in summer and autumn.

Cultivation requirements vary, but in general, salvias like moist, humus-rich, well-drained, fertile soil and a position in the garden where they receive part shade. Those species with woolly or hairy leaves require full sun and sharp drainage, and protection from winter wet and cold, drying winds. Salvias are low-allergen, but prone to slug damage. The tall varieties require to be staked.

Salvia africana-lutea (**Lamiaceae**)

Common name: None
Height: 3ft (90cm)
Spread: 3ft (90cm)
Aspect: Sun
Soil: Moist, well-drained, humus-rich
Hardiness: Zone 9
Propagation: Basal or softwood cuttings, in spring

Flowering time: Summer to late autumn

A tender, evergreen subshrub. Foliage aromatic. Flowers red-brown, with purple-tinted calyces, in dense terminal racemes.

- Attracts bees
- Attracts slugs
- Low allergen

Salvia coccinea (Lamiaceae)

Common name: None
Height: 30in (75cm)
Spread: 1ft (30cm)
Aspect: Sun
Soil: Moist, well-drained, humus-rich, fertile
Hardiness: Zone 8
Propagation: Seed in heat in spring
Flowering time: Summer through to autumn

A short-lived perennial plant. Flowers 2-lipped, cherry-red, borne in terminal spikes from summer to autumn.

- Attracts bees
- Low allergen
- Attracts slugs
- Short-lived

Salvia farinacea 'Snowball' (Lamiaceae)

Common name: None
Height: 2ft (60cm)
Spread: 1ft (30cm)
Aspect: Sun
Soil: Moist, well-drained, fertile, humus-rich
Hardiness: Zone 9
Propagation: Seed, in heat, in spring
Flowering time: Summer to autumn

A tender perennial, grown usually as an annual. Flowers white, in whorls on tall, slim, dense spikes.

- Attracts bees
- Low allergen
- Attracts slugs

Salvia farinacea 'Victoria' A.G.M. (Lamiaceae)

Common name: Sage
Height: 2ft (60cm)
Spread: 1ft (30cm)
Aspect: Sun
Soil: Moist, well-drained, humus-rich, fertile
Hardiness: Zone 9
Propagation: Seed, in heat, in spring
Flowering time: Summer to autumn

A tender, densely branched perennial, grown usually as an annual. Flowers 2-lipped, deep blue, in tall, slim, dense spikes, from summer to autumn. Good bedding plant.

- Attracts bees
- Low allergen
- Attracts slugs

***Salvia involucrata* 'Bethellii'**
(Lamiaceae)

Common name: Sage
Height: 5ft (1.5m)
Spread: 3ft (90cm)
Aspect: Sun
Soil: Moist, well-drained, humus-rich, fertile
Hardiness: Zone 9
Propagation: Basal or semi-ripe cuttings taken in spring
Flowering time: Summer through to autumn

A tall, tender perennial plant. Flowers 2-lipped, purple-red in color, with pink bracts, borne in dense terminal racemes, from summer.

- Attracts bees
- Low allergen
- Attracts slugs

Salvia microphylla var. ***neurepia***
(Lamiaceae)

Common name: Sage
Height: 4ft (1.2m)
Spread: 4ft (1.2m)
Aspect: Sun
Soil: Moist, well-drained, humus-rich, fertile
Hardiness: Zone 9
Propagation: Basal or softwood cuttings in spring
Flowering time: Summer to autumn

A tender perennial. Flowers 2-lipped, cherry-red and pink, whorled or paired, from late summer.

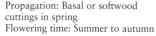

- Attracts bees like
- Low allergen
- Attracts slugs

***Salvia nemorosa* 'Pusztaflamme'**
A.G.M. (Lamiaceae)

Common name: None
Height: 3ft (90cm)
Spread: 2ft (60cm)
Aspect: Sun
Soil: Moist, well-drained, humus-rich, fertile
Hardiness: Zone 5
Propagation: Basal or softwood cuttings, in spring
Flowering time: Summer through to autumn

An upright, hardy perennial plant. Flowers 2-lipped, purple, borne in dense terminal racemes.

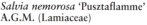

- Attracts bees
- Low allergen
- Attracts slugs

Salvia patens A.G.M. (Lamiaceae)

Common name: Gentian salvia
Height: 2ft (60cm)
Spread: 18in (45cm)
Aspect: Sun
Soil: Moist, well-drained, humus-rich, fertile
Hardiness: Zone 8
Propagation: Seed or division in spring
Flowering time: Midsummer through to mid-autumn

A half-hardy, tuberous perennial plant. Flowers 2-lipped, deep blue, borne in sparse racemes from midsummer through autumn.

- Attracts bees
- Attracts slugs
- Low allergen

Salvia pratensis Haematodes Group A.G.M. (Lamiaceae)

Common name: Sage
Height: 3ft (1m)
Spread: 1ft (30cm)
Aspect: Sun
Soil: Moist, well-drained, humus-rich, fertile
Hardiness: Zone 3
Propagation: Seed in spring
Flowering time: Early to midsummer

A short-lived, much-branched, hardy perennial. Flowers 2-lipped, bluish-violet, in panicles, from early to midsummer.

- Attracts bees
- Attracts slugs
- Low allergen
- Short-lived

Salvia sclarea var. *turkestanica* (Lamiaceae)

Common name: Sage
Height: 3ft (1m)
Spread: 1ft (30cm)
Aspect: Sun
Soil: Moist, or wet, humus-rich, fertile
Hardiness: Zone 5
Propagation: Softwood cuttings in spring; semi-ripe cuttings in late summer
Flowering time: From spring through to summer

An unpleasant-smelling hardy perennial. Flowers 2-lipped, white, edged with pink, in terminal panicles.

- Attracts bees
- Attracts slugs
- Low allergen

Salvia splendens 'Scarlet King' A.G.M. (Lamiaceae)

Common name: Scarlet sage
Height: 10in (25cm)
Spread 1ft (30cm)
Aspect: Sun
Soil: Moist, well-drained, humus-rich, fertile
Hardiness: Zone 10
Propagation: Seed in heat early spring
Flowering time: Summer and again in autumn

A well-known and much-liked perennial in garden cultivation when it is grown as an annual bedding plant. Foliage dark green. Flowers scarlet in color, borne in dense spikes.

- Attracts bees
- Low allergen
- Attracts slugs

Salvia splendens 'Sizzler' series (Lamiaceae)

Common name: Scarlet sage
Height: 16in (40cm)
Spread: 14in (35cm)
Aspect: Sun, but not midday
Soil: Moist, well-drained, humus-rich, fertile
Hardiness: Zone 10
Propagation: Seed in heat in early spring
Flowering time: Summer to autumn

A perennial grown invariably as an annual. This strain has flowers in a wide range of pastel colors, in dense terminal spikes.

- Attracts bees
- Low allergen
- Attracts slugs

Salvia uliginosa **A.G.M.**
(Lamiaceae)

Common name: Sage
Height: 5ft (1.5m)
Spread: 3ft (1m)
Aspect: Sun
Soil: Moist or wet, humus-rich
Hardiness: Zone 9
Propagation: Basal or softwood cuttings in spring

Flowering time: Summer through to mid-autumn

An attractive, swamp-living, tender perennial plant. Flowers 2-lipped, clear blue in color, borne in terminal racemes, from late summer through to mid-autumn.

- Attracts bees
- Low allergen
- Attracts slugs

Sandersonia aurantiaca
(Colchicaceae)

Common name: None
Height: 30in (75cm)
Spread: 4in (10cm)
Aspect: Sun, no winter wet
Soil: Humus-rich, well-drained, fertile
Hardiness: Zone 9
Propagation: Seed when ripe; division in autumn or spring
Flowering time: Summer

A tuberous perennial from South Africa. Leaves alternate, lance-shaped, mid-green. Flowers urn-shaped, pendent, orange, on down-turned stems. Lift and store tubers in frost-free conditions in cold regions.

- Requires staking

Scabiosa caucasica 'Clive Greaves' A.G.M. (Dipsacaceae)

Common name: Scabious
Height: 2ft (60cm)
Spread: 2ft (60cm)
Aspect: Sun
Soil: Well-drained, fertile
Hardiness: Zone 4
Propagation: Seed when ripe, or in spring; division in spring
Flowering time: Summer

A clump-forming hardy perennial. Flowers solitary, domed, lavender, double, on long stems, all summer.

- Good cut flower
- Must not be moved
- Attracts butterflies
- Must deadhead
- Low allergen

Scabiosa columbaria var. *ochroleuca* (Dipsacaceae)

Common name: Small scabious
Height: 30in (75cm)
Spread: 3ft (90cm)
Aspect: Sun
Soil: Well-drained, fertile
Hardiness: Zone 6
Propagation: Seed when ripe or in spring, division in spring
Flowering time: Summer to Autumn

A hardy perennial, with ferny gray foliage. Flowers solitary, semi-double, lemon-yellow, on long stems.

- Handsome foliage
- Must not be moved
- Good cut flower
- Low allergen

Scabiosa 'Irish Perpetual-flowering' (Dipsacaceae)

Common name: Scabious
Height: 1ft (30cm)
Spread: 18in (45cm)
Aspect: Sun
Soil: Well-drained, fertile
Hardiness: Zone 5
Propagation: Seed in spring
Flowering time: Long periods in summer

A hardy perennial plant. Flowers solitary, double, pink in color, borne on long stems.

- Good cut flower
- Must not be moved
- Low allergen

SCHIZOSTYLIS COCCINEA 'SUNRISE' A.G.M.

Schizostylis coccinea (Iridaceae)

Common name: Kaffir lily
Height: 2ft (60cm)
Spread: Indefinite
Aspect: Sun
Soil: Moist or wet, well-drained, fertile
Hardiness: Zone 6
Propagation: Division or seed in spring
Flowering time: Autumn and early winter

A spreading, evergreen perennial. Flowers gladiolus-like, open, cup-shaped, scarlet, in spikes in autumn and early winter; will flower longer given cold greenhouse conditions.

- Low allergen
- Good cut flower
- Divide regularly
- Requires staking

Schizostylis coccinea var. *alba* (Iridaceae)

Common name: White Kaffir lily
Height: 2ft (60cm)
Spread: Indefinite
Aspect: Sun
Soil: Moist or wet, well-drained, fertile
Hardiness: Zone 6
Propagation: Division in spring
Flowering time: Autumn and early winter

An evergreen, spreading perennial. Flowers gladiolus-like, open, cup-shaped, white, in spikes, in autumn and early winter; will flower longer given cold greenhouse conditions.

- Low allergen
- Good cut flower
- Divide regularly
- Requires staking

Schizostylis coccinea 'Sunrise' A.G.M. (Iridaceae)

Common name: Kaffir lily
Height: 2ft (60cm)
Spread: Indefinite
Aspect: Sun
Soil: Moist or wet, fertile
Hardiness: Zone 6
Propagation: Division in spring
Flowering time: Autumn to winter

A vigorous, evergreen perennial. Flowers gladiolus-like, open cups, pink, in spikes, from autumn to winter. Will flower longer into the winter given cold greenhouse conditions.

- Evergreen
- Good cut flower
- Low allergen
- Divide regularly
- Requires staking

PERENNIALS

SENECIO (Asteraceae)

Senecio

A large and very diversified genus of more than 1,000 species of annuals, perennials, and shrubs, from an extremely wide range of habitats, and so cultural requirements vary widely; some are very drought-tolerant, for example, while others prefer moist soil. All like full sun. The flowers are daisy-like, and may be solitary or in corymbs. They have a long flowering season. All parts are poisonous, and they are high allergen. They are attractive to bees, and make good cut flowers.

Senecio doronicum (**Asteraceae**)

Common name: None
Height: 16in (40cm)
Spread: 1ft (30cm)
Aspect: Full sun
Soil: Sharply-drained, fertile
Hardiness: Zone 5
Propagation: Division in spring

Flowering time: Early and midsummer

A hardy perennial. Foliage gray-green, ferny. Flowers single, yellow daisies, in loose corymbs.

- Attracts bees
- Drought-tolerant
- Handsome foliage
- High allergen
- Poisonous

SIDALCEA 'CROFTWAY RED'

Senecio smithii **(Asteraceae)**

Common name: None
Height: 4ft (1.2m)
Spread: 2ft (60cm)
Aspect: Sun or part shade
Soil: Moist, or wet
Hardiness: Zone 7
Propagation: Division in spring
Flowering time: Early to late summer

A robust, hardy perennial. Leaves glossy gray-green. Flowers white, with yellow centers, in large corymbs. A useful bog or aquatic marginal plant.

- Attracts bees
- Good cut flower
- Handsome foliage
- High allergen
- Poisonous

Serratula seoanei **(Asteraceae)**

Common name: None
Height: 1ft (30cm)
Spread: 8in (20cm)
Aspect: Sun
Soil: Well-drained
Hardiness: Zone 7
Propagation: Seed in spring or autumn
Flowering time: Autumn through to winter

A dwarf perennial that flowers when little else in the garden does. Flowers long-lasting, solitary, or in few-flowered panicles, thistle-like, purple-pink in color.

- Drought-tolerant

Sidalcea **'Croftway Red'** **(Malvaceae)**

Common name: Checkerbloom
Height: 4ft (1.2m)
Spread: 18in (45cm)
Aspect: Sun
Soil: Acidic, moist, well-drained, fertile
Hardiness: Zone 6
Propagation: Division in spring or autumn
Flowering time: Early and midsummer

An upright perennial. Flowers rich red-pink, borne in racemes, from early summer onwards.

- Good cut flower
- Attracts bees
- Low allergen
- Requires staking
- Attracts slugs

PERENNIALS

***Sidalcea* 'Party Girl' (Malvaceae)**

Common name: Prairie mallow
Height: 4ft (1.2m)
Spread: 18in (4 cm)
Aspect: Sun
Soil: Acidic, moist, well-drained, fertile
Hardiness: Zone 6
Propagation: Division in spring or autumn

Flowering time: Early through to midsummer

An upright perennial plant. Flowers saucer-shaped, deep pink in color, borne in racemes, from early summer onwards.

- Good cut flower
- Attracts bees
- Low allergen
- Requires staking
- Attracts slugs

***Sidalcea* 'William Smith' A.G.M.
(Malvaceae)**

Common name: Checkerbloom
Height: 4ft (1.2m)
Spread: 18in (45cm)
Aspect: Sun
Soil: Acidic, moist, well-drained, fertile
Hardiness: Zone 6
Propagation: Division in spring or autumn
Flowering time: Early and midsummer

An upright perennial. Flowers deep pink, in upright racemes, from early summer

- Good cut flower
- Attracts bees
- Low allergen
- Requires staking
- Attracts slugs

Sinningia speciosa (Gesneriaceae)

Common name: Gloxinia
Height: 1ft (30cm)
Spread: 1ft (30cm)
Aspect: Sun; dry all winter
Soil: Moist, well-drained, humus-rich, not alkaline
Hardiness: Zone 10
Propagation: Surface-sown seed in heat, or division of tuber in spring
Flowering time: Summer

A temperamental, tuberous perennial. Leaves dark green, hairy. Flowers solitary, or clustered, tubular- or bell-shaped, white, red, or violet in color, opening for many weeks during the summer season.

- Handsome foliage

SOLANUM (Solanaceae)

Solanum

A genus consisting of about 1,500 species, one of which is the potato (*S. tuberosum*), and another the eggplant (*S. melongena*). The flowers are 5-petaled, shallow cups in white, blue, or purple. Flowers are borne singly or in corymbs or cymes, from spring to autumn, followed by fruits. Most are tender, some are half-hardy. They can be evergreen or deciduous.

They like full sun, and soil that is moist, but well-drained or even sharply-drained. All parts are poisonous, and especially the fruits of some species. (See also under Shrubs.)

Solanum crispum 'Glasnevin' A.G.M. (Solanaceae)

Common name: None
Height: 20ft (6m)
Spread: 3ft (90cm)
Aspect: Sun
Soil: Moist, well-drained, fertile, alkaline
Hardiness: Zone 8
Propagation: Semi-ripe cuttings with bottom heat, in summer
Flowering time: Summer to autumn

An evergreen, or semi-evergreen climber. Flowers fragrant, deep purple-blue, in terminal corymbs.

- Scented flowers
- Poisonous
- Requires space

Solanum laxum 'Album' A.G.M. (Solanaceae)

Common name: Potato vine
Height: 20ft (6m)
Spread: 3ft (1m)
Aspect: Sun
Soil: Alkaline, moist, well-drained, fertile
Hardiness: Zone 9
Propagation: Semi-ripe cuttings with bottom heat in summer
Flowering time: Summer and autumn

An evergreen climber. Leaves glossy-green. Flowers fragrant, white, in terminal and axillary clusters. Requires space, not for the small garden.

- Evergreen
- Poisonous
- Scented flowers

Sphaeralcea fendleri (Malvaceae)

Common name: None
Height: 32in (80cm)
Spread: 2ft (60cm)
Aspect: Sun
Soil: Sharply-drained
Hardiness: Zone 8
Propagation: Seed in spring; softwood cuttings in summer
Flowering time: Early summer to mid-autumn

A woody, sprawling subshrub. Leaves gray-green. Flowers pale pink in color, borne in axillary panicles from early summer onwards.

- Drought-tolerant
- Short-lived
- Handsome foliage

Sphaeralcea munroana (Malvaceae)

Common name: None
Height: 32in (80cm)
Spread: 3ft (90cm)
Aspect: Sun
Soil: Sharply-drained
Hardiness: Zone 8
Propagation: Seed in spring; softwood cuttings in summer
Flowering time: Midsummer to mid-autumn

A sprawling perennia plantl. Leaves gray-green in color. Flowers deep pink, borne in axillary panicles, opening from midsummer.

- Drought-tolerant
- Handsome foliage

Stachys byzantina (**Lamiaceae**)

Common name: Lamb's-ears, Wooly betony
Height: 18in (45cm)
Spread: 2ft (60cm)
Aspect: Sun
Soil: Well-drained, fertile
Hardiness: Zone 5
Propagation: Seed, or division in spring
Flowering time: Early summer to autumn

A mat-forming perennial. Leaves whitish and wooly. Flowers 2-lipped, pink-purple, in wooly spikes.

- Attracts bees
- Attracts slugs
- Drought-tolerant
- Divide regularly
- Good cut flower
- Prone to mildew
- Handsome foliage
- Low allergen

Stachys macrantha '**Superba**' (**Lamiaceae**)

Common name: None
Height: 2ft (60cm)
Spread: 1ft (30cm)
Aspect: Sun or part shade
Soil: Well-drained, fertile
Hardiness: Zone 5
Propagation: Seed or division in spring
Flowering time: Early summer through to autumn

An upright perennial plant. Flowers 2-lipped, hooded, purple in color, borne in dense spikes starting in early summer for a long period.

- Attracts bees
- Attracts slugs
- Good cut flower
- Prone to mildew
- Low allergen
- Requires staking

Stachys officinalis '**Rosea Superba**' (**Lamiaceae**)

Common name: Common betony
Height: 2ft (60cm)
Spread: 1ft (30cm)
Aspect: Sun or part shade
Soil: Well-drained, fertile
Hardiness: Zone 5
Propagation: Division in spring
Flowering time: Early summer through to autumn

A dwarf perennial with basal leaf rosettes. Flowers 2-lipped, rose-pink, in upright, dense spikes.

- Attracts bees
- Attracts slugs
- Drought-tolerant
- Prone to mildew
- Good cut flower

Stokesia laevis (**Asteraceae**)

Common name: Stokes' Aster
Height: 2ft (60cm)
Spread: 18in (45cm)
Aspect: Sun
Soil: Acidic, moist, well-drained, fertile
Hardiness: Zone 5
Propagation: Division in spring; seed in autumn
Flowering time: Midsummer through to early autumn

An evergreen, rosette-forming perennial plant. Flowers solitary, long-lasting, with fringed, blue-colored ray florets, with darker basal regions, and blue disc florets, opening from midsummer onwards.

- Evergreen
- Good cut flower
- Requires staking
- High allergen

Streptocarpus hybridus
(Gesneriaceae)

Common name: None
Height: 1ft (30cm)
Spread: 18in (45cm)
Aspect: Part shade
Soil: Moist, humus-rich, well-drained; just damp in winter
Hardiness: Zone 10
Propagation: Division or leaf cuttings in spring/summer
Flowering time: Spring to autumn; all year in warm areas

Leaves hairy, wrinkled, veined. Flowers tubular, in a wide range of colors, borne in cymes.

- Handsome foliage

Streptocarpus 'Crystal Ice'
(Gesneriaceae)

Common name: None
Height: 1ft (30cm)
Spread: 1ft (30cm)
Aspect: Part shade
Soil: Moist, well-drained, humus-rich; just damp in winter
Hardiness: Zone 10
Propagation: Division or leaf cuttings in spring/summer
Flowering time: Throughout the year in warm areas

Leaves in rosettes, hairy, veined. Flowers tubular, white, with lilac-colored throats, borne in cymes.

- Handsome foliage

Streptocarpus saxorum
(Gesneriaceae)

Common name: Cape primrose
Height 6in (15cm)
Spread: 2ft (60cm)
Aspect: Part shade
Soil: Moist, humus-rich, well-drained: just damp in winter
Hardiness: Zone 10
Propagation: Seed or division in spring
Flowering time: Spring and early summer

A prostrate perennial plant. Leaves hairy, gray-green. Flowers pale lilac with white throats, singly or paired, in spring and early summer.

- Handsome foliage

Stylophorum diphyllum (Papaveraceae)

Common name: Celandine poppy
Height: 1ft (30cm)
Spread: 1ft (30cm)
Aspect: Part or full shade
Soil: Moist, humus-rich, fertile
Hardiness: Zone 7
Propagation: Division in spring; seed in autumn
Flowering time: Spring and again summer

A perennial woodlander. Leaves pinnatisect, in basal rosette. Flowers poppy-like, yellow, in terminal umbels, opening in spring and again in summer.

- Handsome foliage   • Seeds everywhere

Symphytum x *uplandicum* (Boraginaceae)

Common name: None
Height: 6ft (1.8m)
Spread: 4ft (1.2m)
Aspect: Sun or part shade
Soil: Moist, fertile
Hardiness: Zone 5
Propagation: Seed or division in spring; division in autumn

Flowering time: Late spring through to late summer

A large much-branched, rhizomatous, invasive perennial. Flowers purple-blue from pinkish buds, in cymes.

- Low allergen
- Invasive
- Poisonous
- Requires space
- Skin irritant

Tanacetum parthenium 'Aureum' (Asteraceae)

Common name: Feverfew
Height: 2ft (60cm)
Spread: 1ft (30cm)
Aspect: Sun
Soil: Sharply drained
Hardiness: Zone 6
Propagation: Seed or division in spring
Flowering time: Summer

An aromatic herb, and prolific self-seeder. Foliage golden yellow. Flowers small, single, daisies, white with yellow centers, borne in corymbs.

- Handsome foliage
- Good cut flower
- Drought tolerant
- Must deadhead
- Seeds everywhere
- Short-lived
- High allergen

Tanacetum parthenium 'Rowallane' (Asteraceae)

Common name: Feverfew
Height: 2ft (60cm)
Spread: 1ft (30cm)
Aspect: Sun
Soil: Sharply drained
Hardiness: Zone 6
Propagation: Seed or division in spring
Flowering time: Throughout the summer

An aromatic perennial. Flowers fully double, white pompom-like, in dense corymbs, for several weeks in summer, and again later if deadheaded.

- Good cut flower
- Drought tolerant
- Seeds everywhere
- Skin irritant
- Must deadhead

Tellima grandiflora (**Saxifragaceae**)

Common name: Alaska fringe-cup
Height: 30in (75cm)
Spread: 1ft (30cm)
Aspect: Sun or part shade
Soil: Good, moist or dry, humus-rich
Hardiness: Zone 6
Propagation: Seed or division in spring

Flowering time: From late spring through to midsummer

A rosette-forming woodland perennial plant. Flowers greenish-white in color, borne in terminal racemes, from late spring onwards.

- Low allergen
- Good cut flower
- Seeds everywhere
- Attracts slugs

Thalicrum kiusianum (**Ranunculaceae**)

Common name: None
Height: 4in (10cm)
Spread: 1ft (30cm)
Aspect: Part shade
Soil: Acid, moist, humus-rich
Hardiness: Zone 8
Propagation: Seed when ripe; seed or division in spring
Flowering time: Summer

A compact, mat-forming rhizomatous perennial. Leaves ferny. Flowers mauve-pink, in few-flowered corymbs on short stems.

- Handsome foliage
- Low allergen
- Prone to mildew
- Attracts slugs

Thunbergia alata (**Acanthaceae**)

Common name: Clockvine
Height: 8ft (2.5m)
Spread: 2ft (60cm)
Aspect: Sun
Soil: Moist, well-drained, fertile
Hardiness: Zone 10
Propagation: Seed in heat, or layer, in spring; greenwood cuttings in early summer
Flowering time: From summer through to autumn

An evergreen, perennial climber, grown often as an annual. Flowers single salvers, orange or yellow, with chocolate-colored centers.

- Evergreen

Tiarella wherryi A.G.M. (**Saxifragaceae**)

Common name: None
Height: 8in (20cm)
Spread: 6in (15cm)
Aspect: Part or full shade
Soil: Moist, humus-rich
Hardiness: Zone 6
Propagation: Seed when ripe; seed or division in spring
Flowering time: Late spring through to early summer

Slow-growing, compact, woodland perennial plant. Flowers white in color, tinged with pink, borne in racemes from late spring.

- Low allergen
- Attracts slugs

***Tradescantia* x *andersoniana* 'Isis'**
A.G.M. (Commelinaceae)

Common name: None
Height: 2ft (60cm)
Spread: 2ft (60cm)
Aspect: Sun or part shade
Soil: Moist, fertile
Hardiness: Zone 5
Propagation: Division in spring or autumn
Flowering time: Summer to autumn

A clump-forming perennial. Flowers 3-petaled, flat, dark blue in color, borne in paired terminal cymes.

- Low allergen
- Divide regularly
- Skin irritant

***Tradescantia* x *andersoniana*
'Osprey' A.G.M. (Commelinaceae)**

Common name: None
Height: 2ft (60cm)
Spread: 2ft (60cm)
Aspect: Sun or part shade
Soil: Moist, fertile
Hardiness: Zone 5
Propagation: Division in spring or autumn
Flowering time: Early summer through to autumn

A clump-forming perennial plant. Flowers 3-petaled, flat, white in color, borne in paired terminal cymes.

- Low allergen
- Divide regularly
- Skin irritant

TROPAEOLUM (Tropaeolaceae)
Nasturtium

A genus of just under 100 species of mostly tuberous perennials and climbing, trailing, or bushy annuals. Nasturtiums have edible leaves and come from cool mountain regions of the world. The flowers are trumpet-shaped, with five clawed petals, borne singly over long periods in summer and autumn.

Nasturtiums prefer a position in full sun and moist, but well-drained soil. They can self-seed freely and are prone to attack from slugs and blackfly. The climbing varieties require support, or they will scramble up through other plants.

Tropaeolum polyphyllum (Tropaeolaceae)

Common name: Wreath nasturtium
Height: 4in (10cm)
Spread: Indefinite
Aspect: Sun
Soil: Good, well-drained, humus-rich
Hardiness: Zone 8
Propagation: Division in early spring; stem or basal cuttings in summer
Flowering time: Throughout the summer

A tuberous, trailing herbaceous perennial plant. Leaves glaucous, blue-green. Flowers yellow in color, opening over a long period during the summer season. Can travel underground for long distances before re-emerging.

● Handsome foliage   ● Attracts slugs

Tropaeolum speciosum A.G.M. (Tropaeolaceae)

Common name: Vermilion nasturtium
Height: 10ft (3m)
Spread: Indefinite
Aspect: Sun, roots in cool shade
Soil: Acid, moist, humus-rich,
Hardiness: Zone 8
Propagation: Division in early spring
Flowering time: Summer to autumn

A frail perennial climber. Leaves 5- and 7-palmate, green. Flowers bright red, spurred, with clawed petals. Never reappears where it was planted, but several feet away, so tread carefully.

- Handsome foliage • Invasive

Tropaeolum tuberosum 'Ken Aslet' A.G.M. (Tropaeolaceae)

Common name: None
Height: 12ft (4m)
Spread: 3ft (1m)
Aspect: Sun
Soil: Moist, well-drained
Hardiness: Zone 8
Propagation: Division in spring
Flowering time: Midsummer through to autumn

A tuberous perennial climbing plant. Flowers long-spurred, cup-shaped, orange, with brown-colored veins, and red sepals.

- Attracts slugs

Tulbaghia cepacea (Alliaceae)

Common name: None
Height: 2ft (60cm)
Spread: 8in (20cm)
Aspect: Sun
Soil: Well-drained, humus-rich, fertile
Hardiness: Zone 8
Propagation: Seed when ripe; seed or division in spring
Flowering time: Late spring through to autumn

A rhizomatous perennial plant. Leaves aromatic, gray-green in color. Flowers tubular, night-scented, soft pink, borne in umbels for a long period from late spring onwards.

- Handsome foliage
- Scented flowers
- Drought-tolerant
- Aromatic foliage

Tulbaghia violacea (Alliaceae)

Common name: None
Height: 2ft (60cm)
Sprtead: 1ft (30cm)
Aspect: Sun
Soil: Well-drained, humus-rich, fertile
Hardiness: Zone 7
Propagation: Seed when ripe; seed or division in spring
Flowering time: Summer to autumn

Rhizomatous perennial from South Africa. Leaves narrow, linear, grayish-green. Flowers in terminal umbels, scented, from summer onwards.

- Scented flowers
- Drought-tolerant

VERBASCUM (Scrophulariaceae)
Mullein

A genus of more than 300 species of biennials, annuals, perennials, and subshrubs, of which only the last two groups are covered here. They grow in woodland or on dry stony slopes, and are drought-tolerant. The leaves are often white-woolly, and in basal rosettes. The flowers are borne, usually, in upright spikes or racemes; the individual flowers are outward-facing, and short-lived, but followed by others over a long period during the summer and autumn.

Mulleins do best in full sun and sharp drainage; the soil should be poor, else they grow tall and require to be staked. They are short-lived, but worthwhile nevertheless. They are attractive to bees but are prone to mildew.

Verbascum chaixii 'Album' (Scrophulariaceae)

Common name: Mullein
Height: 3ft (90cm)
Spread: 2ft (60cm)
Aspect: Sun
Soil: Sharply drained, poor
Hardiness: Zone 5
Propagation: Seed or division in spring
Flowering time: Mid- through to late summer

An upright, rosetted perennial plant. Leaves gray-hairy. Flowers saucer-shaped, white, with mauve-colored centers, borne in slender panicles, from mid- to late summer.

- Good cut flower
- Drought-tolerant
- Attracts bees
- Handsome foliage
- Requires staking
- Seeds everywhere
- Prone to mildew

Verbascum dumulosum A.G.M.
(Scrophulariaceae)

Common name: Mullein
Height: 1ft (30cm)
Spread: 18in (45cm)
Aspect: Sun
Soil: Sharply drained, poor
Hardiness: Zone 8
Propagation: Seed or division in spring
Flowering time: Throughout the summer

A rosette-forming, short-lived perennial plant. Flowers saucer-shaped, yellow in color, in closely set clusters on branched spikes.

- Evergreen
- Drought-tolerant
- Attracts bees
- Prone to mildew
- Short-lived

Verbascum 'Helen Johnson' A.G.M.
(Scrophulariaceae)

Common name: Mullein
Height: 3ft (90cm)
Spread: 18in (45cm)
Aspect: Sun
Soil: Poor, sharply-drained
Hardiness: Zone 7
Propagation: Division in spring; root cuttings in winter
Flowering time: Early to late summer

An evergreen perennial. Leaves downy, gray-green. Flowers pinkish-brown saucers, in erect, branched spikes.

- Attracts bees
- Drought-tolerant
- Evergreen
- Handsome foliage
- Prone to mildew
- Seeds everywhere

Verbascum 'Jackie'
(Scrophulariaceae)

Common name: Mullein
Height: 3ft (90cm)
Spread: 18in (45cm)
Aspect: Sun
Soil: Poor, sharply drained
Hardiness: Zone 6
Propagation: Division in spring; root cuttings in winter
Flowering time: Summer

A rosette-forming perennial. Leaves downy, gray-green. Flowers saucer-shaped, buff pink in color, with a purple eye, borne in erect spikes.

- Attracts bees
- Handsome foliage
- Drought-tolerant
- Prone to mildew

Verbascum phoeniceum
(Scrophulariaceae)

Common name: Mullein
Height: 4ft (1.2m)
Spread: 18in (45cm)
Aspect: Sun
Soil: Sharply drained, poor
Hardiness: Zone 6
Propagation: Seed or division in late spring
Flowering time: Late spring to early summer

An evergreen, rosette-forming biennial or short-lived perennial plant. Flowers saucer-shaped, white, purple or pink in color, borne in slim racemes, opening from late spring through to early summer.

- Attracts bees
- Drought-tolerant
- Prone to mildew
- Seeds everywhere
- Short-lived

Verbena bonariensis (Verbenaceae)

Common name: None
Height: 6ft (1.8m)
Spread: 30in (75cm)
Aspect: Sun
Soil: Well-drained, fertile
Hardiness: Zone 8
Propagation: Seed or division in spring
Flowering time: Midsummer to early autumn

A clump-forming perennial plant. Flowers lilac in color, salverform, borne in cymes. Particularly loved by butterflies.

- Attracts butterflies
- Drought-tolerant
- Prone to mildew
- Seeds everywhere

VERBENA (Verbenaceae)
Verbena

A genus consisting of approximately 250 species of subshrubs, annuals, and perennials; many of the last group are grown widely as annuals.

They grow in both tropical and temperate zones of the world, and in moist or dry but open, sunny sites. The flowers are salveriform, borne in cymes, panicles, or racemes; flowers open over a long period in summer.

Verbenas prefer humus-rich, well-drained soil, and a position in full sun. They are very attractive to butterflies, but they are also prone to attack by slugs, and powdery mildew.

Verbena hastata (Verbenaceae)

Common name: None
Height: 4ft (1.2m)
Spread: 2ft (60cm)
Aspect: Sun
Soil: Well-drained, fertile
Hardiness: Zone 3
Propagation: Seed or division in spring
Flowering time: From early summer through to autumn

An upright perennial plant. Flowers white, pink-purple, or violet-blue in color, borne in stiff, erect panicles from early summer for a long time until autumn.

- Attracts butterflies
- Attracts slugs
- Good cut flower
- Prone to mildew

Verbena x *hybrida* 'Imagination' (Verbenaceae)

Common name: None
Height: 18in (45cm)
Spread: 20in (50cm)
Aspect: Sun
Soil: Well-drained, fertile
Hardiness: Zone 9
Propagation: Division in spring; stem-tip cuttings in late summer
Flowering time: Summer and autumn

A sprawling perennial, grown almost invariably as an annual. Flowers salver-form, blue, in corymb-like panicles, in summer and autumn. Good in hanging baskets.

- Attracts butterflies
- Attracts slugs
- Prone to mildew

Verbena x ***hybrida*** 'Loveliness' (Verbenaceae)

Common name: None
Height: 18in (45cm)
Spread: 20in (50cm)
Aspect: Sun
Soil: Humus-rich, well-drained
Hardiness: Zone 9
Propagation: Division in spring; stem-tip cuttings in late summer
Flowering time: Summer and autumn

A tender perennial plant grown almost invariably as an annual. Flowers salverform, pink in color, in corymb-like panicles.

- Attracts butterflies
- Attracts slugs
- Prone to mildew

Verbena x ***hybrida*** 'Peaches and Cream' (Verbenaceae)

Common name: None
Height: 18in (45cm)
Spread: 20in (50cm)
Aspect: Sun
Soil: Well-drained, humus-rich
Hardiness: Zone 9
Propagation: Division in spring; stem-tip cuttings in late summer
Flowering time: Summer and autumn

A tender perennial plant grown usually as an annual. Flowers salverform, orange-pink, fading to apricot and then cream, borne in panicles.

- Attracts butterflies
- Attracts slugs
- Prone to mildew

Verbena x ***hybrida*** 'Quartz Burgundy' (Verbenaceae)

Common name: None
Height: 18in (45cm)
Spread: 20in (50cm)
Aspect: Sun
Soil: Humus-rich, well-drained
Hardiness: Zone 9
Propagation: Division in spring; stem-tip cuttings in late summer
Flowering time: Summer and autumn

A tender perennial grown almost invariably as an annual. Flowers salverform, burgundy, fading to pink, in panicles, in summer and autumn.

- Attracts butterflies
- Attracts slugs
- Prone to mildew

VERBENA x HYBRIDA 'RED CASCADE'

***Verbena* x *hybrida* 'Red Cascade'**
(Verbenaceae)

Common name: None
Height: 18in (45cm)
Spread: 20in (50cm)
Aspect: Sun
Soil: Well-drained, humus-rich
Hardiness: Zone 9
Propagation: Division in spring; stem-tip cuttings in late summer

Flowering time: Summer and again autumn

A tender perennial plant grown almost invariably as an annual. Flowers salverform, scarlet in color, borne in panicles, opening in summer and again in autumn.

- Attracts bees
- Attracts slugs
- Prone to mildew

Verbena x *hybrida* 'Sissinghurst' A.G.M. (Verbenaceae)

Common name: None
Height: 8in (20cm)
Spread: 2ft (60cm)
Aspect: Sun
Soil: Well-drained, humus-rich
Hardiness: Zone 9
Propagation: Division in spring; stem-tip cuttings in late summer
Flowering time: Late spring to autumn

A tender perennial grown almost invariably as an annual. Flowers salver-form, magenta-pink, in corymbs, from late spring.

- Attracts bees
- Attracts slugs
- Prone to mildew

Veronica spicata ssp. *incana* (Scrophulariaceae)

Common name: Wooly speedwell
Height: 1ft (30cm)
Spread: 1ft (30cm)
Aspect: Sun or part shade
Soil: Moist, well-drained, humus-rich, fertile
Hardiness: Zone 3
Propagation: Seed or division in autumn; division in spring
Flowering time: Early to late summer

Mat-forming plant. Leaves silver, hairy. Flowers star-shaped, blue, borne in dense terminal racemes.

- Attracts bees
- Handsome foliage
- Low allergen
- Prone to mildew

Veronica spicata **'Rotfuchs'**
(Scrophulariaceae)

Common name: None
Height: 1ft (30cm)
Spread: 1ft (30cm)
Aspect: Sun or part shade
Soil: Moist, well-drained, humus-rich, fertile
Hardiness: Zone 3
Propagation: Division in spring or autumn; seed in autumn
Flowering time: Early through to late summer

A mat-forming perennial plant. Flowers deep pink in color, star-shaped, borne in dense terminal racemes from early summer.

- Attracts bees
- Low allergen
- Prone to mildew

Viola **'Columbine' (Violaceae)**

Common name: None
Height: 8in (20cm)
Spread: 1ft (30cm)
Aspect: Sun or part shade
Soil: Moist, well-drained, humus-rich, fertile
Hardiness: Zone 7
Propagation: Division or stem-tip cuttings in spring
Flowering time: Spring and summer

An evergreen, short-lived perennial plant. Flowers lilac and white in color, streaked with purple.

- Evergreen
- Good cut flower
- Low allergen
- Scented flowers
- Attracts slugs
- Must deadhead
- Prone to mildew
- Short-lived

***Viola cornuta* 'Alba' A.G.M.**
(Violaceae)

Common name: None
Height: 6in (15cm)
Spread: 18in (45cm)
Aspect: Sun or part shade
Soil: Moist, humus-rich, fertile
Hardiness: Zone 7
Propagation: Seed when ripe, or in spring

Flowering time: From spring through to summer

A short-lived, evergreen, rhizomatous perennial plant. Flowers scented, white in color; flowers again later if sheared over.

- Evergreen
- Low allergen
- Scented flowers
- Attracts slugs
- Must deadhead
- Prone to mildew

Viola 'Etain' (Violaceae)

Common name: None
Height: 8in (20cm)
Spread: 1ft (30cm)
Aspect: Sun or part shade
Soil: Moist, well-drained, humus-rich, fertile
Hardiness: Zone 7
Propagation: Division or stem-tip cuttings in spring

Flowering time: Spring and again in summer

A low-growing, short-lived, evergreen perennial plant. Flowers cream, margined lilac, with orange-colored centers, in spring and summer.

- Evergreen
- Low allergen
- Attracts slugs
- Must deadhead
- Prone to mildew

***Viola* 'Jackanapes' A.G.M.**
(Violaceae)

Common name: None
Height: 8in (20cm)
Spread: 1ft (30cm)
Aspect: Sun or part shade
Soil: Moist, well-drained, humus-rich
Hardiness: Zone 7
Propagation: Division or stem-tip cuttings in spring

Flowering time: From spring through to summer

A short-lived, evergreen perennial plant. Flowers have chocolate-colored upper petals, and yellow, streaked purple, lower ones.

- Evergreen
- Low allergen
- Attracts slugs
- Must deadhead
- Prone to mildew

Zantedeschia aethiopica A.G.M.
(Araceae)

Common name: Arum lily
Height: 3ft (90cm)
Spread: 2ft (60cm)
Aspect: Sun
Soil: Wet or bog
Hardiness: Zone 8
Propagation: Seed in warmth when ripe; division in spring
Flowering time: Late spring to midsummer

A rhizomatous perennial plant. Leaves glossy-green. Flowers large, white spathes, with yellow spadices.

- Good cut flower
- Skin irritant
- Handsome foliage
- Poisonous

Zauschneria californica A.G.M.
(Onagraceae)

Common name: None
Height: 1ft (30cm)
Spread: 20in (50cm)
Aspect: Sun
Soil: Well-drained
Hardiness: Zone 8
Propagation: Seed or basal cuttings in spring
Flowering time: Late spring and early summer

A rhizomatous, evergreen perennial. Leaves gray-green in color. Flowers tubular, scarlet, borne in racemes.

- Evergreen
- Attracts slugs
- Handsome foliage

Zephyranthes candida
(Amaryllidaceae)

Common name: None
Height: 8in (20cm)
Spread: 3in (8cm)
Aspect: Sun; no winter wet
Soil: Moist, well-drained
Hardiness: Zone 9
Propagation: Seed in warmth when ripe; offsets in spring
Flowering time: Summer to early autumn

A bulbous perennial plant. Flowers crocus-like, solitary, white in color. A trouble-free plant.

section two
Shrubs

Shrubs are woody plants that usually have more than one stem arising at or near the ground, and they seldom reach more than 20ft (6m) in height; they differ from trees, which normally have only one stem and can grow to considerable heights.

Subshrubs either have stems that are woody only at the base, such as *Perovskias*, or have stems like *Fuchsias* that die back to some extent over winter. Subshrubs are often cultivated alongside perennials in mixed borders and given similar treatment. Both shrubs and subshrubs are generally long-lived, given correct conditions, and are easy to cultivate, requiring little attention.

Like perennials, shrubs can be evergreen or deciduous, and some of the latter have stunning autumn displays. Again, they vary widely in their degree of hardiness and the reader is advised to refer to the section on hardiness before buying. In cold climates, one can grown smaller, tender shrubs in containers and bring them indoors over winter; this is not possible with the larger varieties, which may be kept indoors all year round. Because the growth is above ground, it is obviously not effective to surface-mulch tender shrubs, but covering the plant with fleece or bubble polythene to insulate against the cold can help.

Certain shrubs are not suited to the small garden because of their height and spread; smaller shrubs and subshrubs, which will not overwhelm neighboring perennials, can be grown in mixed borders. As a general rule, shrubs do not tend to have a very long flowering season, but there are some notable exceptions, such as *Abelia* and *Abutilon*. Shrubs also have very different pruning requirements: some have to be pruned because they flower only on the growth of the previous season, and others for shape and size. The text highlights those plants unsuitable for small gardens and gives information on pruning.

As with perennials, some shrubs require acid soil conditions, and again these are indicated in the text. Good drainage is equally essential for shrubs as for perennials.

Abelia x *grandiflora* A.G.M. (Caprifoliaceae)

Common name: Glossy abelia
Height: 10ft (3m)
Spread: 12ft (4m)
Aspect: Sun
Soil: Fertile, well-drained
Hardiness: Zone 5
Propagation: Semi-ripe cuttings in late summer
Flowering time: Midsummer to autumn

A semi-evergreen or evergreen shrub. Leaves ovate, glossy green. Flowers in terminal panicles and axillary cymes, fragrant, funnel-shaped, white tinted pink. Prune in early spring only to remove wayward shoots.

- Evergreen
- Scented flowers
- Requires space

Abelia schumannii (Caprifoliaceae)

Common name: None
Height: 6ft (1.8m)
Spread: 10ft (3m)
Aspect: Sun
Soil: Well-drained, fertile
Hardiness: Zone 6
Propagation: Semi-ripe cuttings in late summer
Flowering time: Late summer through autumn

A deciduous, arching shrub. Leaves ovate, bronze, turning green. Flowers lilac-pink funnels with orange markings, borne in axillary cymes. Prune in early spring to remove wayward shoots.

- Scented flowers
- Requires space

ABUTILON (Malvaceae)
Flowering-maple

A genus consisting of some 150 species, from the subtropical and tropical regions of all five continents. They vary in their degree of hardiness, and most are Zone 8 or 9, although *A. theophrastii* is Zone 4. They may be evergreen or deciduous, and shrubs or trees – however, only the shrubs are featured here.

There are large numbers of hybrids. The flowers are bell-shaped, usually pendent, are available in all colors, and are borne for long periods from spring through to the autumn. They vary in their pruning requirements, and each plant covered is given a regime.

Though not generally completely hardy, they make excellent conservatory plants if grown in colder regions.

Abutilon 'Ashford Red' A.G.M.
(Malvaceae)

Common name: None
Height: 10ft (3m)
Spread: 10ft (3m)
Aspect: Sun
Soil: Well-drained, fertile
Hardiness: Zone 8
Propagation: Greenwood cuttings taken in summer
Flowering time: Spring to autumn

An erect or spreading evergreen shrub. Leaves ovate/rounded, mid-green in color. Flowers pendent or nodding, cup-shaped, red. Prune only lightly in summer.

- Evergreen
- Requires staking

Abutilon 'Boule de Neige'
(Malvaceae)

Common name: None
Height: 12ft (4m)
Spread: 10ft (3m)
Aspect: Sun
Soil: Well-drained, fertile
Hardiness Zone 8
Propagation: Greenwood cuttings in summer
Flowering time: All summer

An evergreen shrub. Leaves ovate. Flowers white, pendent. Prune only lightly in spring to maintain shape.

- Evergreen

Abutilon 'Canary Bird' A.G.M. (Malvaceae)

Common name: None
Height: 10ft (3m)
Spread: 10ft (3m)
Aspect: Sun
Soil: Well-drained, fertile
Hardiness: Zone 8
Propagation: Greenwood cuttings taken in summer
Flowering time: Spring to autumn

A vigorous, hybrid, evergreen shrub. Leaves ovate/rounded, mid-green in color. Flowers bell-shaped, pendent, yellow. Prune only lightly in spring to preserve shape.

• Evergreen   • Requires staking

Abutilon 'Cannington Peter' A.G.M. (Malvaceae)

Common name: None
Height: 6ft (1.8m)
Spread: 3ft (90cm)
Aspect: Sun
Soil: Well-drained, fertile
Hardiness: Zone 8
Propagation: Greenwood cuttings taken in summer
Flowering time: All summer

Leaves ovate/rounded, variegated yellow. Flowers deep maroon, bell-shaped, pendent. Very desirable. Prune only lightly in spring.

• Handsome foliage   • Short-lived

ABUTILON x SUNTENSE 'JERMYNS' A.G.M.

Abutilon 'Kentish Belle' A.G.M. (Malvaceae)

Common name: None
Height: 8ft (2.5m)
Spread: 6ft (1.8m)
Aspect: Sun
Soil: Fertile, well-drained
Hardiness: Zone 8
Propagation: Greenwood cuttings in summer
Flowering time: All summer and autumn

A tall, but extremely elegant, semi-evergreen shrub. Stems arching, with rows of pendent flowers, with yellow petals protruding from red calyces, throughout the summer and into autumn. Prune only lightly in spring to preserve shape.

• Requires staking

Abutilon x *suntense* 'Jermyns' A.G.M. (Malvaceae)

Common name: None
Height: 15ft (5m)
Spread: 6ft (2m)
Aspect: Sun
Soil: Fertile, well-drained
Hardiness: Zone 8
Propagation: Greenwood cuttings taken in summer
Flowering time: Late spring and early summer

A very tall, deciduous, fast-growing shrub. Leaves ovate, gray-green. Saucer-shaped flowers of deep purple from late spring and into summer. Prune only lightly in spring to preserve shape and remove wayward stems. Requires space: not suitable for the small garden.

• Requires staking

SHRUBS

Allamanda cathartica
(Apocynaceae)

Common name: None
Height: 52ft (16m)
Spread: 6ft (1.8m)
Aspect: Full sun
Soil: Moist, fertile
Hardiness: Zone 11
Propagation: Seed in heat in spring; greenwood cuttings, in spring-summer
Flowering time: Summer to autumn

A very large, evergreen, climbing shrub. Flowers in axillary and terminal cymes, trumpet-shaped, yellow. Prune to fit space, in spring or after flowering.

- Evergreen
- Poisonous
- Requires space
- Skin irritant

Angelonia gardneri
(Scrophulariaceae)

Common name: None
Height: 3ft (1m)
Spread: 2ft (60cm)
Aspect: Full sun
Soil: Well-drained, moist
Hardiness: Zone 9
Propagation: Seed in heat in spring
Flowering time: Summer

A subshrub from Brazil. Leaves hairy, broadly lance-shaped, toothed, mid-green in color. Flowers in terminal racemes, purple, with spreading lobes and white disc florets, all through summer. Best grown as an annual in cold areas.

- Must deadhead

Anisodontea capensis (Malvaceae)

Common name: None
Height: 3ft (90cm)
Spread: 32in (80cm)
Aspect: Full sun
Soil: Well-drained, fertile
Hardiness: Zone 9
Propagation: Seed in warmth in spring; semi-ripe cuttings in summer
Flowering time: Spring to autumn

A woody, evergreen, South African shrub. Leaves ovate/triangular, shallowly lobed, mid-green. Flowers solitary or in racemes of 2 or 3, cup-shaped, pale pink with a darker center. Prune lightly, only to preserve shape.

- Evergreen
- Drought-tolerant

Antirrhinum sempervirens (Scrophulariaceae)

Common name: None
Height: 8in (20cm)
Spread: 1ft (30cm)
Aspect: Full sun
Soil: Well-drained, fertile
Hardiness: Zone 7
Propagation: Seed in spring or autumn; softwood cuttings in summer
Flowering time: Early and again in midsummer

A dwarf, decumbent shrub. Leaves oblong/ovate, sticky-hairy, mid-green. Flowers white, with yellow palates and purple veins, from the leaf axils.
A. pulverulentum (Zone 9) is similar, with yellow flowers.

- Good cut flower
- Low allergen
- Must deadhead
- Prone to mildew
- Seeds everywhere
- Short-lived

ARGYRANTHEMUM (Asteraceae)

Argyranthemum

A genus of some 25 species of evergreen subshrubs from a wide range of habitats in Madeira and the Canary Islands. There are many hybrids in cultivation. The evergreen, pinnatisect foliage may be green or glaucous. The daisy-like flowers are solitary or in corymbs, and may be single, double, or anemone-centered. The flowering season is from late spring to early autumn, and they make excellent bedding plants. They are available in a range of colors from white, through yellow to pink. All are highly allergenic.
  Deadheading improves the length of flowering time.

Argyranthemum frutescens (Asteraceae)

Common name: Marguerite
Height: 28in (70cm)
Spread: 28in (70cm)
Aspect: Full sun
Soil: Well-drained
Hardiness: Zone 9
Propagation: Seed, in heat, in spring
Flowering time: All summer

A subshrub not grown often because of the many superior hybrids. Leaves pinnatisect, green. Flowers single, white, with a yellow disc. Prune after flowering to within 1in (2.5cm) of previous year's growth.

- Evergreen
- Good cut flower
- Highly allergenic
- Must deadhead

Argyranthemum 'Jamaica Primrose' A.G.M. (Asteraceae)

Common name: None
Height: 42in (1m)
Spread: 3ft (90cm)
Aspect: Full sun
Soil: Well-drained
Hardiness: Zone 9
Propagation: Greenwood cuttings in spring
Flowering time: All summer and autumn

A very handsome hybrid. Leaves pinnatisect, toothed, gray-green. Flowers solitary, single, yellow with a darker disc. A lovely standard plant. Prune after flowering to within 1in (2.5cm) of previous year's growth.

- Evergreen
- Good cut flower
- High allergen
- Must deadhead

Argyranthemum maderense A.G.M. (Asteraceae)

Common name: None
Height: 1ft (30cm)
Spread: 20in (50cm)
Aspect: Full sun
Soil: Well-drained
Hardiness: Zone 9
Propagation: Greenwood cuttings in spring; semi-ripe cuttings in summer
Flowering time: All summer

A compact species that comes from the Canaries. Leaves pinnatisect, toothed, gray-green. Ray florets lemon-colored, disc florets yellow. Prune after flowering to within 1in (2.5cm) of previous year's growth.

- Good cut flower
- Evergreen
- Handsome foliage
- High allergen
- Must deadhead

Argyranthemum 'Petite Pink' A.G.M. (Asteraceae)

Common name: None
Height: 1ft (30cm)
Spread: 1ft (30cm)
Aspect: Full sun
Soil: Well-drained
Hardiness: Zone 9
Propagation: Greenwood cuttings in spring; semi-ripe cuttings in summer
Flowering time: All summer

A compact, rounded, hybrid. Leaves pinnatisect, gray-green. Flowers solitary, single, pale pink, with yellow discs. Prune after flowering to within 1in (2.5cm) of previous year's growth.

- Evergreen
- Good cut flower
- Highly allergenic
- Must deadhead

Argyranthemum 'Sugar Button' (Asteraceae)

Common name: None
Height: 18in (45cm)
Spread: 18in (45cm)
Aspect: Full sun
Soil: Well-drained
Hardiness: Zone 9
Propagation: Greenwood cuttings taken in spring; semi-ripe cuttings taken in summer
Flowering time: Throughout the summer

A recent evergreen hybrid introduction to garden cultivation. Leaves pinnatisect, gray-green in color. Flowers solitary, double, white, with yellow-colored discs. Prune after flowering by cutting back stems to within 1in (2.5cm) of previous year's growth.

- Evergreen
- Good cut flower
- High allergen
- Must deadhead

Argyranthemum 'Summer Stars' (Asteraceae)

Common name: None
Height: 16in (40cm)
Spread: 16in (40cm)
Aspect: Full sun
Soil: Well-drained
Hardiness: Zone 9
Propagation: Greenwood cuttings in spring; semi-ripe cuttings in summer
Flowering time: All summer

Another recent clone. Leaves pinnatisect, toothed, gray-green. Flowers solitary, single, pale pink with deep pink basal regions, and yellow disc florets. Prune after flowering by cutting back to within 1in (2.5cm) of previous year's growth.

- Evergreen
- Good cut flower
- High allergen
- Must deadhead

List of other *Argyranthemum* cultivars given an Award of Garden Merit from the Royal Horticultural Scoiety (all Zone 9)

'Cornish Gold'
'Donington Hero'
gracile 'Chelsea Girl'
'Levada Cream'
'Mary Cheek'
'Quinta White'
'Snowstorm'
'Vancouver'
'Whiteknights'

Bomarea caldasii **A.G.M.**
(Alstroemeriaceae)

Common name: None
Height: 12ft (4m)
Spread: 3ft (90cm)
Aspect: Full sun
Soil: Moist, well-drained
Hardiness: Zone 9
Propagation: Seed in heat in spring; division in late winter or early spring
Flowering time: Late spring to autumn

A deciduous, twining, climbing shrub. Leaves oblong, mid-green in color. Inflorescence in spherical umbels of as many as 40, narrow, tubular, orange or brick-red flowers, spotted inside. Prune flowered shoots to the ground in autumn.

• Requires space

Bougainvillea glabra **A.G.M.**
(Nyctaginaceae)

Common name: None
Height: 25ft (7.6m)
Spread: 6ft (1.8m)
Aspect: Full sun
Soil: Well-drained, fertile
Hardiness: Zone 9
Propagation: Softwood cuttings in spring; semi-ripe cuttings in summer; layer in autumn
Flowering time: Summer to autumn

A large, evergreen climber. Flowers very small, white, insignificant. Bracts of white or magenta, in large clusters. Prune in early spring by cutting back side shoots to within 3–4 buds of permanent framework.

• Drought-tolerant • Requires space

BRUGMANSIA AUREA

Brachyglottis Dunedin group 'Sunshine' (Asteraceae)

Common name: None
Height: 5ft (1.5m)
Spread: 6ft (1.8m) or more
Aspect: Full sun
Soil: Well-drained
Hardiness: Zone 5
Propagation: Semi-ripe cuttings in summer
Flowering time: Summer through to autumn

An evergreen hybrid of garden origin. Leaves elliptic, gray-hairy. Flowers in loose terminal panicles, daisy-like, pale yellow, with darker yellow discs, from summer through to autumn. Good for coastal sites. Prune after flowering by deadheading, and removing any wayward shoots that spoil overall symmetry.

- Attracts bees
- Evergreen
- Handsome foliage
- Requires space

Brugmansia aurea (Solanaceae)

Common name: Angels' trumpets
Height: 30ft (10m)
Spread: 12ft (4m)
Aspect: Full sun
Soil: Moist, well-drained
Hardiness: Zone 9
Propagation: Seed in heat in spring
Flowering time: Summer through to autumn

A toxic, evergreen shrub. Leaves large, ovate, mid-green. Flowers night-scented, yellow (or white) pendent trumpets, up to 10in (24cm) long, borne freely from summer through to autumn. Prune by deadheading and removing any shoots that spoil symmetry after flowering. Needs space; not suitable for the smaller garden.

- Scented flowers
- Evergreen
- Poisonous
- Requires space

SHRUBS

***Brugmansia sanguinea* A.G.M.**
(Solanaceae)

Common name: None
Height: 30ft (9m)
Spread: 10ft (3m)
Aspect: Full sun
Soil: Sharply-drained, fertile
Hardiness: Zone 9
Propagation: Seed in heat in spring
Flowering time: Late spring to autumn

A highly toxic, very large shrub. Leaves large, ovate, wavy-edged, mid-green. Flowers tubular, pendent, orange/yellow trumpets, up to 10in (25cm) long. Prune by deadheading and removing any wayward shoots that spoil symmetry when flowering has finished.

- Poisonous
- Requires space

Bupleurum fruticosum (Apiaceae)

Common name: Shrubby hare's ear
Height: 6ft (1.8m)
Spread: 8ft (2.5m)
Aspect: Full sun
Soil: Well-drained
Hardiness: Zone 7
Propagation: Seed in spring
Flowering time: Midsummer to autumn

An evergreen, spreading shrub. Leaves narrow, obovate, blue-green. Flowers small, yellow stars, but borne in a large, domed, terminal umbel. Prune in spring to maintain symmetry; deadhead regularly.

- Attracts bees
- Drought-tolerant
- Evergreen
- Requires space
- Seeds everywhere

Caesalpinia pulcherrima (Caesalpiniaceae)

Common name: None
Height: 20ft (6m)
Spread: 16ft (5m)
Aspect: Sun
Soil: Moist, well-drained, fertile
Hardiness: Zone 9
Propagation: Soaked seed in heat in spring
Flowering time: Spring to autumn

A large, evergreen shrub. Leaves pinnate. Flowers bowl-shaped, in erect racemes of up to 40, yellow or orange-yellow, with red sepals and stamens. Prune by deadheading, and cutting out shoots to preserve symmetry.

- Evergreen
- Requires space

Calceolaria integrifolia A.G.M. (Scrophulariaceae)

Common name: Slipperflower, Slipperwort
Height: 3ft (90cm)
Spread: 1ft (30cm)
Aspect: Sun or half shade
Soil: Acid, gritty, fertile
Hardiness: Zone 9
Propagation: Seed or division in spring
Flowering time: All summer

A lax, evergreen subshrub. Leaves ovate/lance, toothed, gray-green. Flowers yellow, in cymes of up to 35. Best treated as an annual in cold areas.

- Evergreen
- Attracts slugs

Calluna vulgaris 'County Wicklow'
A.G.M. (Ericaceae)

Common name: Heather
Height: 10in (25cm)
Spread: 14in (35cm)
Aspect: Full sun
Soil: Acid, well-drained, humus-rich
Hardiness: Zone 4
Propagation: Layer in spring; semi-ripe cuttings in summer
Flowering time: Midsummer to autumn

A prostrate, compact cultivar. Flowers large, double, pale pink, in lengthy racemes. Prune after flowering to within 1in (2.5cm) of previous year's growth.

● Evergreen

Calluna vulgaris 'Kinlochruel'
A.G.M. (Ericaceae)

Common name: Heather
Height: 10in (25cm)
Spread: 16in (40cm)
Aspect: Full sun
Soil: Acid, well-drained, humus-rich
Hardiness: Zone 4
Propagation: Layer in spring; semi-ripe cuttings in summer
Flowering time: Summer to autumn

A handsome clone with leaves of bright green, which turn bronze in winter. Flowers white, double, in long racemes. Prune after flowering to within 1in (2.5cm) of previous year's growth.

● Evergreen

Calluna vulgaris 'Spring Torch'
(Ericaceae)

Common name: Heather
Height: 16in (40cm)
Spread: 30in (75cm)
Aspect: Full sun
Soil: Acid, humus-rich, well-drained
Hardiness: Zone 4
Propagation: Layer in spring; semi-ripe cuttings in summer
Flowering time: Midsummer to late autumn

A clone with mid-green, hairless leaves, orange in winter. Flowers bell-shaped, in racemes, mauve-pink. Prune after flowering to within 1in (2.5cm) of previous year's growth.

● Evergreen

CAMPSIS GRANDIFLORA

Calluna vulgaris 'Tib' A.G.M. (Ericaceae)

Common name: Heather, Ling
Height: 10in (25cm)
Spread: 16in (40cm)
Aspect: Full sun
Soil: Acid, well-drained, humus-rich
Hardiness: Zone 4
Propagation: Layer in spring; semi-ripe cuttings in summer
Flowering time: Summer

A clone of open habit. Leaves hairless, green. Flowers bell-shaped, double, pink, in long racemes for several weeks in summer. Prune back to within 1in (2.5cm) of the previous year's growth after flowering

- Evergreen

List of other *Calluna vulgaris* cultivars awarded the A.G.M. of the R.H.S (all Zone 4)

'Allegro'
'Annemarie'
'Anthony Davis'
'Battle of Arnhem'
'Beoley Gold'
'Dark Star'
'Darkness'
'Elsie Purnell'
'Finale'
'Firefly'
'Gold Haze'
'J.H. Hamilton'
'Jimmy Dyce'
'Joy Vanstone'
'Mair's Variety'
'Mullion'
'Orange Queen'
'Radnor'
'Red Star'
'Robert Chapman'
'Roland Haagen'
'Serlei Aurea'
'Silver Queen'
'Silver Rose'
'Sir John Charrington'
'Sister Anne'
'Spring Cream'
'Sunset'
'Underwoodii'
'White Lawn'
'Wickwar Flame'

Campsis grandiflora (Bignoniaceae)

Common name: Trumpetvine
Height: 30ft (9m)
Spread: 5ft (1.5m)
Aspect: Part shade
Soil: Moist, well-drained
Hardiness: Zone 7
Propagation: Seed in autumn; semi-ripe cuttings in summer
Flowering time: Summer to autumn

A robust, deciduous shrub. Flowers open funnels, red, in pendent panicles. Prune side shoots in late winter/early spring to within 3–4 buds of permanent framework.

- Prone to mildew
- Requires space
- Requires staking

SHRUBS

Caryopteris clandonensis (Verbenaceae)

Common name: None
Height: 3ft (1m)
Spread: 5ft (1.5m)
Aspect: Full sun
Soil: Well-drained, fertile
Hardiness: Zone 7
Propagation: Softwood cuttings in late spring
Flowering time: Late summer to early autumn

A dense erect, shrub. Leaves ovate, toothed, gray-green, and silver-hairy below. Flowers in cymes, axillary or terminal, dark blue, from late summer. Cut back to a low, permanent framework in early spring.

- Aromatic foliage
- Scented flowers

CEANOTHUS *(Rhamnaceae)*

California lilac

A genus consisting of some 55 species from southern N. America and Mexico. They occur on dry slopes from the coast to mountains, and vary considerably in their hardiness, therefore. Many hybrids are in cultivation. They have flowers in panicles or cymes, and the predominant color is blue, but pink and white forms exist. They are best grown in full sun, and in colder climates, must be sheltered from cold winds, and a sun-facing wall is ideal. Some are evergreen, but not all. Some are long-flowering, but not all. All, however, are highly allergenic.

Ceanothus 'Italian Skies' A.G.M. (Rhamnaceae)

Common name: None
Height: 5ft (1.5m)
Spread: 10ft (3m)
Aspect: Full sun
Soil: Well-drained, fertile
Hardiness: Zone 8
Propagation: Semi-ripe cuttings in summer
Flowering time: Late spring to early summer

A sprawling, evergreen, profuse-flowering shrub. Flowers in lateral and terminal conical cymes, bright blue, from late spring to early summer. Prune by deadheading, and to retain symmetry. Requires space; not for the small garden.

- Evergreen
- High allergen

Ceanothus 'Skylark' (Rhamnaceae)

Common name: None
Height: 6ft (1.8m)
Spread: 5ft (1.5m)
Aspect: Full sun
Soil: Well-drained, fertile
Hardiness: Zone 8
Propagation: Semi-ripe cuttings in summer
Flowering time: Late spring to early summer

An evergreen, compact, profuse-flowering shrub. Leaves oblong, toothed, glossy-green. Flowers in lateral and terminal panicles, dark blue in color from spring through to early summer. Prune to preserve symmetry and to deadhead.

- Evergreen
- Highly allergenic
- Requires space

Ceanothus thyrsiflorus repens A.G.M. (Rhamnaceae)

Common name: Blue blossom ceanothus
Height: 3ft (90cm)
Spread: 8ft (2.5m)
Aspect: Full sun
Soil: Well-drained, fertile
Hardiness: Zone 8
Propagation: Semi-ripe cuttings in summer
Flowering time: Late spring to early summer

An evergreen, sprawling, free-flowering shrub. Leaves ovate, toothed, glossy-green in color. Flowers borne in lateral and terminal panicles, pale blue, from late spring. Prune to preserve shape.

- Evergreen
- High allergen
- Requires space

Ceanothus x ***delileanus*** 'Topaze'
A.G.M. (Rhamnaceae)

Common name: None
Height: 5ft (1.5m)
Spread: 5ft (1.5m)
Aspect: Full sun
Soil: Well-drained, fertile
Hardiness: Zone 8
Propagation: Semi-ripe cuttings in summer
Flowering time: Midsummer to autumn

A deciduous, free-flowering shrub. Leaves oval, dark green. Flowers in terminal and axillary panicles, indigo blue. Prune to preserve symmetry, and to deadhead. Not for the small garden.

• High allergen

Ceratostigma willmottianum
A.G.M. (Plumbaginaceae)

Common name: Chinese plumbago
Height: 3ft (1m)
Spread: 5ft (1.5m)
Aspect: Full sun
Soil: Moist, well-drained
Hardiness: Zone 7
Propagation: Softwood cuttings, or suckers, in spring
Flowering time: Late summer

A deciduous shrub. Leaves bristly, lance-shaped, pointed, green, margined purple. Flowers pale blue, in terminal clusters. Prune early winter cutting back flowered shoots to within 1in (2.5cm) of previous year's growth.

• Prone to mildew

Cestrum elegans A.G.M.
(Solanaceae)

Common name: None
Height: 10ft (3m)
Spread: 10ft (3m)
Aspect: Sun or part shade
Soil: Well-drained, fertile
Hardiness: Zone 9
Propagation: Semi-ripe cuttings in summer
Flowering time: Summer to autumn

Arching shrub. Leaves linear, matt, mid-green. Flowers tubular, crimson (or purple), in compound, panicle-like cymes, followed by red berries. Not for the small garden.

• Evergreen   • Requires space

CESTRUM PARQUI A.G.M.

Cestrum 'Newellii' A.G.M.
(Solanaceae)

Common name: None
Height: 10ft (3m)
Spread: 10ft (3m)
Aspect: Sun or part shade
Soil: Well-drained, fertile
Hardiness: Zone 8
Propagation: Softwood cuttings in summer
Flowering time: Summer to autumn

An arching shrub. Leaves ovate, dark green. Flowers tubular, crimson, in dense, compound panicles, followed by purple berries. Prune to deadhead and preserve symmetry. Requires space.

• Evergreen

Cestrum parqui A.G.M.
(Solanaceae)

Common name: Chilean cestrum
Height: 6ft (1.8m)
Spread: 6ft (1.8m)
Aspect: Sun or half shade
Soil: Well-drained, fertile
Hardiness: Zone 8
Propagation: Softwood cuttings in summer
Flowering time: Summer to autumn

A deciduous, upright shrub from Chile. Leaves linear/lance, mid-green. Flowers, opening in summer and persisting through to autumn, are greenish-yellow in color, tubular, scented, borne in large axillary and terminal cymes, followed by brown berries. Prune annually, in spring, hard back to near the base to encourage new season's growth.

• Scented flowers

SHRUBS

Chamaecytisus purpureus (Leguminosae)

Common name: Purple broom
Height: 18in (45cm)
Spread: 2ft (60cm)
Aspect: Sun
Soil: Any, except shallow chalk
Hardiness: Zone 6
Propagation: Seed in spring or autumn
Flowering time: Early summer

A deciduous shrub. Leaves tripalmate, dark green, lobes obovate. Flowers in axillary clusters, pink or lilac, with darker throats. Prune after flowering by cutting back to buds or side shoots, low down.

- Drought-tolerant
- Must not be moved

Choisya 'Aztec Pearl' A.G.M. (Rutaceae)

Common name: None
Height: 8ft (2.5m)
Spread: 8ft (2.5m)
Aspect: Full sun
Soil: Well-drained, fertile
Hardiness: Zone 7
Propagation: Semi-ripe cuttings in summer
Flowering time: Late spring; late summer and autumn

An evergreen shrub. Flowers white, tinged pink, scented, in axillary cymes. Prune by deadheading and cutting out shoots which spoil symmetry.

- Aromatic foliage
- Scented flowers
- Attracts slugs
- Requires space

Choisya ternata A.G.M. (Rutaceae)

Common name: Mexican-orange
Height: 8ft (2.5m)
Spread: 8ft (2.5m)
Aspect: Full sun
Soil: Fertile, well-drained
Hardiness: Zone 7
Propagation: Semi-ripe cuttings in summer
Flowering time: Late spring; late summer and autumn

Leaves aromatic. Scented flowers, white, in axillary corymbs. Deadheading and removal of wayward shoots is all the pruning required.

- Aromatic foliage
- Evergreen
- Scented flowers
- Attracts slugs
- Requires space

CISTUS (Cistaceae)
Cistus

A genus of some 20 evergreen shrubs from stony or rocky areas in S. Europe, N. Africa, the Canaries, and Turkey. They have, like Day-lilies, flowers that last only one day, but that appear in succession over a long period from early to late summer. They can sometimes be short-lived. They should be grown in open, gritty soil in full sun. Prune to preserve symmetry, and deadhead, annually after flowering. They do not recover from being cut hard back, and old plants should be replaced.

Cistus x *dansereaui* (Cistaceae)

Common name: None
Height: 3ft (90cm)
Spread: 3ft (90cm)
Aspect: Full sun
Soil: Well-drained
Hardiness: Zone 8
Propagation: Seed as soon as ripe; softwood cuttings in summer
Flowering time: All summer

An upright shrub. Leaves lance-shaped, dark green. Flowers in terminal cymes, white, with crimson marks at the base of petals. Prune by deadheading and to preserve symmetry.

- Evergreen
- Short-lived
- Drought-tolerant

Cistus 'Elma' A.G.M. (Cistaceae)

Common name: None
Height: 6ft (1.8m)
Spread: 6ft (1.8m)
Aspect: Full sun
Soil: Well-drained
Hardiness: Zone 8
Propagation: Softwood or greenwood cuttings in summer
Flowering time: All summer

A bushy shrub. Leaves lance-shaped, glossy-green. Flowers in terminal cymes of up to 6, white, yellow stamens. Prune after flowering only by deadheading, and to keep symmetry.

- Drought-tolerant
- Requires space
- Evergreen
- Short-lived

Cistus ladanifer A.G.M. (Cistaceae)

Common name: Gum rock rose
Height: 6ft (1.8m)
Spread: 5ft (1.5m)
Aspect: Full sun
Soil: Well-drained
Hardiness: Zone 8
Propagation: Seed as soon as ripe; softwood or greenwood cuttings in summer
Flowering time: All summer

An upright shrub. Leaves aromatic, sticky, lance-shaped, dark green. Flowers white, with crimson marks at base of petals, borne on side shoots. Prune for symmetry in spring, and deadhead after flowering.

- Evergreen
- Drought-tolerant
- Requires space
- Short-lived

Cistus x *laxus* 'Snow White' (Cistaceae)

Common name: None
Height: 3ft (90cm)
Spread: 2ft (60cm)
Aspect: Full sun
Soil: Well-drained
Hardiness: Zone 8
Propagation: Softwood or greenwood cuttings in summer
Flowering time: Early spring and summer.

A hybrid, evergreen shrub. Leaves ovate/lanceolate, viscid, pubescent, green. Flowers white, with yellow centers. Prune for symmetry in spring; deadhead after flowering.

- Drought-tolerant
- Evergreen
- Short-lived

Cistus x *pulverulentus* 'Sunset' (Cistaceae)

Common name: None
Height: 3ft (90cm)
Spread: 2ft (60cm)
Aspect: Full sun
Soil: Well-drained
Hardiness: Zone 8
Propagation: Softwood or greenwood cuttings in summer
Flowering time: All summer

An evergreen shrub. Leaves oblong, gray-green. Flowers in terminal cymes, rose-pink, with yellow centers, borne profusely. Deadhead after flowering.

- Drought-tolerant
- Handsome foliage
- Short-lived

Cistus x purpureus A.G.M.
(Cistaceae)

Common name: None
Height: 4ft (1.2m)
Spread: 3ft (1m)
Aspect: Full sun
Soil: Well-drained
Hardiness: Zone 8
Propagation: Softwood or greenwood cuttings in summer
Flowering time: Summer

An evergreen shrub. Leaves oblong/obovate, dark green. Flowers large, in terminal cymes, deep pink, with a maroon spot at the base of each petal, over summer. Deadhead after flowering and prune for shape in spring.

- Evergreen
- Drought-tolerant
- Short-lived

CISTUS X SKANBERGII A.G.M.

***Cistus* x *skanbergii* A.G.M.**
(Cistaceae)

Common name: None
Height: 30in (75cm)
Spread: 3ft (90cm)
Aspect: Full sun
Soil: Well-drained
Hardiness: Zone 8
Propagation: Softwood or greenwood cuttings in summer
Flowering time: Throughout the summer

An evergreen, hybrid shrub. Leaves lance-shaped, gray-green. Flowers pale pink, in terminal cymes of up to 6, borne profusely. Deadhead after flowering.

- Drought-tolerant
- Short-lived
- Evergreen

***Clianthus puniceus* A.G.M.**
(Leguminosae)

Common name: Lobster claw
Height: 12ft (4m)
Spread: 10ft (3m)
Aspect: Full sun
Soil: Well-drained
Hardiness: Zone 8
Propagation: Seed in heat in spring; semi-ripe cuttings in summer
Flowering time: Spring to early summer

A large, evergreen, climbing shrub. Leaves narrow, oblong, green. Flowers bright red in color, shaped like lobster's claws, in pendent racemes from spring through to early summer. Prune after flowering to keep to required size and shape. Not suitable for the small garden.

- Evergreen
- Requires space

CORONILLA VALENTINA ssp. GLAUCA A.G.M.

Colutea arborescens (Leguminosae)

Common name: Bladder-senna
Height: 10ft (3m)
Spread: 10ft (3m)
Aspect: Full sun
Soil: Well-drained, fertile
Hardiness: Zone 5
Propagation: Seed in spring; greenwood cuttings in summer
Flowering time: Long period in summer

A robust shrub. Leaves pale green, pinnate. Flowers in racemes of up to 8, pea-like, yellow, followed by inflated, transparent seed pods. *Colutea* x *media* (Zone 6) is similar.

- Requires space
- Seeds everywhere

Convolvulus cneorum A.G.M. (Convolvulaceae)

Common name: Bindweed
Height: 2ft (60cm)
Spread: 3ft (90cm)
Aspect: Full sun
Soil: Well-drained
Hardiness: Zone 8
Propagation: Seed in heat, or softwood cuttings in spring
Flowering time: Late spring to summer

Shrub with linear/lance-shaped silky, silvery leaves. Flowers funnel-shaped, white with yellow centers, in axillary clusters. Deadhead and remove unwanted shoots after flowering.

- Low allergen
- Evergreen

Coronilla valentina ssp. *glauca* A.G.M. (Papilionaceae)

Common name: None
Height: 32in (80cm)
Spread: 32in (80cm)
Aspect: Full sun
Soil: Well-drained, fertile
Hardiness: Zone 9
Propagation: Seed in heat in spring
Flowering time: Late winter and early spring; late summer

A rounded, compact shrub. Leaves pinnate, blue-green. Flowers in axillary umbels, fragrant, pea-like, yellow. Prune by removing wayward shoots.

- Evergreen
- Handsome foliage
- Scented flowers

Cuphea cyanea (Lythraceae)

Common name: None
Height: 4ft (1.2m)
Spread: 3ft (90cm)
Aspect: Full sun, but not at midday
Soil: Well-drained, fertile
Hardiness: Zone 9
Propagation: Seed in warmth, or division, both in spring
Flowering time: Late spring through to autumn

A branching subshrub, with ovate midgreen leaves. Flowers are borne in terminal racemes, tubular, orange-red in color, with green tips. Prune in spring to within 1in (2.5cm) of previous year's growth to encourage new shoots.

● Attracts bees

Cuphea ignea A.G.M. (Lythraceae)

Common name: Cigarflower
Height: 30in (75cm)
Spread: 3ft (90cm)
Aspect: Full sun, but not midday
Soil: Well-drained, fertile
Hardiness: Zone 9
Propagation: Seed in heat, or division in spring
Flowering time: Late spring to autumn

A spreading shrub. Leaves glossy-green. Flowers solitary, long slim tubules, deep red with a dark red band and a white rim. Prune in spring by cutting back to within 1in (2.5cm) of previous year's growth to encourage new shoots.

● Attracts bees

CYTISUS (Leguminosae)
Broom

A genus of some 50 species of evergreen/deciduous shrubs; in nature they grow invariably on well-drained, acid sites. Brooms flower abundantly, the flowers being pea-like, sometimes fragrant, and borne in terminal, leafy, axillary racemes, or singly. Many hybrids are in cultivation.

They are low-allergen plants, suitable for gardeners with allergies. Brooms are drought-tolerant and thrive on poor soils. They should be pruned to remove wayward growths, and cut back annually after flowering to strong buds low down, or to young side shoots; they must not be pruned hard when mature. Brooms flower over the period from mid/late spring to early summer. All parts are poisonous, especially the seeds.

Cytisus 'Goldfinch' (Leguminosae)

Common name: None
Height: 5ft (1.5m)
Spread: 5ft (1.5m)
Aspect: Full sun
Soil: Acid, well-drained
Hardiness: Zone 6
Propagation: Ripewood cuttings in midsummer

Flowering time: Late spring to early summer

A compact, medium-sized, deciduous, hybrid shrub. Flowers are pale cream, with dark cerise wings, and the reverse of the petal is cerise.

- Drought-tolerant
- Poisonous
- Low allergen

Cytisus 'La Coquette' (Leguminosae)

Common name: None
Height: 5ft (1.5m)
Spread: 5ft (1.5m)
Aspect: Full sun
Soil: Acid, well-drained.
Hardiness: Zone 6
Propagation: Ripewood cuttings in midsummer
Flowering time: Late spring to early summer

A compact, medium-sized, deciduous, hybrid shrub. Flowers are striking in appearance: rose-red, with yellow-colored inside; the wings are deep orange, and the keel pale yellow, with rose-red markings.

- Drought-tolerant
- Poisonous
- Low allergen

Cytisus 'Lena' A.G.M. (Leguminosae)

Common name: None
Height: 4ft (1.2m)
Spread: 5ft (1.5m)
Aspect: Full sun
Soil: Acid, well-drained
Hardiness: Zone 6
Propagation: Ripewood cuttings in midsummer
Flowering time: Late spring to early summer

A spreading, but compact, deciduous, hybrid shrub. Flowers deep yellow, with the wings and the reverse of the standards bright red, borne in axillary clusters.

- Drought-tolerant
- Poisonous
- Low allergen

CYTISUS 'LENA' A.G.M.

Cytisus nigricans (Leguminosae)

Common name: None
Height: 5ft (1.5m)
Spread: 3ft (90cm)
Aspect: Full sun
Soil: Acid, well-drained
Hardiness: Zone 5
Propagation: Ripewood cuttings in midsummer
Flowering time: Late summer

An upright, compact, deciduous shrub. Leaves are tri-palmate; flowers yellow in color, and borne in terminal racemes.

- Drought-tolerant
- Low allergen
- Poisonous

Cytisus praecox albus (Leguminosae)

Common name: Warminster broom
Height: 5ft (1.5m)
Spread: 4ft (1.2m)
Aspect: Full sun
Soil: Acid, well-drained
Hardiness Zone 5
Propagation: Ripewood cuttings in summer
Flowering time: Mid through to late spring

Compact, deciduous shrub. Flowers in axillary clusters, white, pendent, borne on arching stems.

- Drought-tolerant
- Low allergen
- Poisonous

DABOECIA CANTABRICA ssp. SCOTICA 'WILLIAM BUCHANAN' A.G.M.

Daboecia cantabrica ssp. *scotica* 'Silverwells' A.G.M. (Ericaceae)

Common name: Irish heath
Height: 6in (15cm)
Spread: 20in (50cm)
Aspect: Sun or part shade
Soil: Acid, well-drained
Hardiness: Zone 6
Propagation: Ripewood cuttings in summer
Flowering time: Early summer to mid-autumn

A dwarf, compact, ericaceous shrub. Leaves shiny dark green above, densely hairy-silver below. Flowers in racemes, white, pendent. Prune in spring by cutting back flowered shoots to within 1in (2.5cm) of previous year's growth.

- Evergreen

Daboecia cantabrica ssp. *scotica* 'William Buchanan' A.G.M. (Ericaceae)

Common name: None
Height: 15in (38cm)
Spread: 2ft (60cm)
Aspect: Sun or part shade
Soil: Acid, well-drained
Hardiness: Zone 6
Propagation: Semi-ripe cuttings in midsummer
Flowering time: Early summer to late autumn

A compact, ericaceous shrub. Flowers in racemes, ovoid urns, crimson-purple in color. Prune in spring by cutting back to within about 1in (2.5cm) of previous year's growth to encourage new stems.

- Evergreen

Deutzia 'Mont Rose'

***Deutzia* 'Mont Rose'** (Hydrangeaceae)

Common name: None
Height: 4ft (1.2m)
Spread: 4ft (1.2m)
Aspect: Full sun, except at midday
Soil: Well-drained
Hardiness: Zone 5
Propagation: Softwood cuttings in summer; hardwood cuttings in autumn
Flowering time: Early summer

A deciduous, hybrid shrub. Flowers 5-petalled stars, pink-purple in color and yellow anthers, borne in panicles in early summer. Flowering is prolonged if plant is shaded from the effects of the midday sun. Flowers better as well if not crowded by other plants. Cut back flowered shoots to strong buds low down when flowering has finished.

- Low allergen

Deutzia pulchra (Hydrangeaceae)

Common name: None
Height: 8ft (2.5m)
Spread: 6ft (2m)
Aspect: Sun, except at midday
Soil: Well-drained
Hardiness: Zone 6
Propagation: Softwood cuttings in summer; hardwood cuttings in autumn
Flowering time: Late spring to early summer

A large shrub with very hairy, dark green leaves. Flowers star-shaped, white, tinged pink, in pendent panicles, from late spring to early summer. Cut back flowered shoots to strong buds, lower down, after flowering. Requires space; not suitable for the small garden.

- Low allergen
- Requires space
- Handsome foliage

ERICA (Ericaceae)
Heath

A genus of more than 700 species of evergreen shrubs from a wide variety of habitats in both hemispheres; most have in common a need for soil that is acid but some like it moist while others like it dry. They may be prostrate or tree-like. Of the 700 species, only a few *(EE arborea, carnea, cinerea, x darleyensis, erigena* and *vagans)* are widespread in cultivation, and many clones of these are to be found in the catalogs: some 73 cultivars have earned the Award of Garden Merit of the Royal Horticultural Society.

The flower of the heath can be distinguished from that of the heather by its prominent corolla and calyces (usually of green). All require full sun, with the notable exception of *E. vagans. Erica* cultivars require to be cut back after flowering to within 1in (2.5cm) of the previous year's growth. The lengthy listing of A.G.M. varieties is omitted, and the interested reader is referred to the specialist nurserymen's catalogs.

Erica carnea 'Winter Snow' (Ericaceae)

Common name: Spring heath
Height: 6in (15cm)
Spread: 18in (45cm)
Aspect: Sun or part shade
Soil: Acid, well-drained
Hardiness: Zone 5
Propagation: Semi-ripe cuttings in mid to late summer
Flowering time: Late winter and early spring

A low, spreading shrub with dark green leaves. Flowers white, urn-shaped, in one-sided racemes. Will tolerate alkaline soil only if mildly so.

- Evergreen
- Low allergen

Erica cinerea 'C.D. Eason' A.G.M. (Ericaceae)

Common name: None
Height: 10in (25cm)
Spread: 20in (50cm)
Aspect: Sun
Soil: Acid, well-drained
Hardiness: Zone 5
Propagation: Semi-ripe cuttings in mid-to late summer
Flowering time: Early summer to autumn

A clone that is makes a good groundcover plant. Leaves dark green in color. Flowers urn-shaped, bright magenta, borne in racemes.

- Evergreen
- Low allergen

Erica cinerea 'Domino' (Ericaceae)

Common name: None
Height: 2ft (60cm)
Spread: 32in (80cm)
Aspect: Sun
Soil: Acid, well-drained
Hardiness: Zone 5
Propagation: Semi-ripe cuttings between mid- and late summer
Flowering time: Early summer to autumn

An evergreen clone with dark, bottle-green leaves. Flowers urn-shaped, white in color, borne in racemes.

• Low allergen

Erica cinerea 'Pink Ice' A.G.M. (Ericaceae)

Common name: None
Height: 8in (20cm)
Spread: 14in (35cm)
Aspect: Sun
Soil: Acid, well-drained
Hardiness: Zone 5
Propagation: Semi-ripe cuttings in mid- to late summer
Flowering time: Early summer to autumn

A twiggy, dwarf, compact clone. Leaves bronze in winter, deep green in color during summer season. Flowers clear pink in color, urn-shaped, borne in racemes.

• Evergreen
• Low allergen

ERICA x DARLEYENSIS 'DARLEY DALE'

***Erica* x *darleyensis* 'Darley Dale'
(Ericaceae)**

Common name: Darley heath
Height: 1ft (30cm)
Spread: 20in (50cm)
Aspect: Sun
Soil: Acid, well-drained
Hardiness: Zone 6
Propagation: Semi-ripe cuttings in mid- to late summer
Flowering time: Late winter and early spring

A small-growing bushy, ericaceous shrub. Leaves mid-green, tipped with cream in spring. Flowers urn-shaped, shell pink in color, though darkening with time, borne in racemes. Develops into a good groundcover plant.

- Evergreen
- Handsome foliage
- Low allergen

***Erica cinerea* 'Stephen Davis'
A.G.M. (Ericaceae)**

Common name: None
Height: 8in (20cm)
Spread: 15in (38cm)
Aspect: Sun
Soil: Acid, well-drained
Hardiness: Zone 5
Propagation: Semi-ripe cuttings in mid- to late summer
Flowering time: Early summer to autumn

A striking clone. Foliage dark green. Flower vivid dark pink, in racemes.

- Evergreen
- Low allergen

SHRUBS

Erica x *darleyensis* 'George Rendall' (Ericaceae)

Common name: Darley heath
Height: 1ft (30cm)
Spread: 2ft (60cm)
Aspect: Sun
Soil: Acid, well-drained
Hardiness: Zone 6
Propagation: Semi-ripe cuttings in mid- to late summer
Flowering time: Late winter to early spring

A very handsome clone for garden cultivation. Leaves are mid-green in color and lance-shaped. Flowers are urn-shaped, a rich pink color, and borne in racemes.

- Evergreen
- Low allergen

Erica erigena 'Irish Dusk' A.G.M. (Ericaceae)

Common name: None
Height: 2ft (60cm)
Spread: 18in (45cm)
Aspect: Sun
Soil: Acid, well-drained
Hardiness: Zone 8
Propagation: Semi-ripe cuttings in mid- to late summer
Flowering time: Late autumn to late spring

A half-hardy, ericaceous shrub. Leaves dark gray-green. Flowers urn-shaped, honey-scented, rose-pink in color.

- Evergreen
- Handsome foliage
- Low allergen
- Scented flowers

Erica gracilis (Ericaceae)

Common name: None
Height: 20in (50cm)
Spread: 20in (50cm)
Aspect: Sun
Soil: Acid, well-drained
Hardiness: Zone 10
Propagation: Semi-ripe cuttings in mid- to late summer
Flowering time: Autumn to spring

A tender, compact shrub. Flowers urn-shaped, cerise, pink or white, in whorls of 4. Requires a warm greenhouse or conservatory in cold areas.

- Evergreen
- Low allergen

ERYSIMUM 'BOWLES' MAUVE'

***Eriogonum umbellatum* var. *torreyanum* (Polygonaceae)**

Common name: Sulphur flower
Height: 1ft (30cm)
Spread: 3ft (1m)
Aspect: Sun
Soil: Sharply drained
Hardiness: Zone 7
Propagation: Seed in autumn; cuttings in spring
Flowering time: All summer

A spreading subshrub with shiny dark green leaves. Flowers yellow, in umbels, yellow, bracted. Pruning requirements minimal, only for shape.

- Drought-tolerant
- Must not be moved

***Erysimum* 'Bowles' Mauve' (Brassicaceae)**

Common name: Wallflower
Height: 42in (1m)
Spread: 2ft (60cm)
Aspect: Sun
Soil: Well-drained, fertile
Hardiness: Zone 7
Propagation: Softwood cuttings, with a heel, in spring or summer
Flowering time: Early spring to autumn

An evergreen, woody subshrub, producing gray-green leaves. Flowers mauve in color, borne in racemes. Short-lived, and becoming less floriferous with age.

- Drought-tolerant
- Evergreen
- Handsome foliage
- Attracts slugs
- Must deadhead
- Prone to mildew
- Short-lived

SHRUBS

Escallonia 'Donard Radiance'
A.G.M. (Escalloniaceae)

Common name: None
Height: 8ft (2.5m)
Spread: 8ft (2.5m)
Aspect: Full sun
Soil: Well-drained, fertile
Hardiness: Zone 8
Propagation: Softwood cuttings in early summer; semi-ripe cuttings in late summer
Flowering time: Early through to midsummer

A half-hardy evergreen shrub. Leaves glossy, toothed, dark green. Flowers chalice-shaped, rich pink in color, borne in short racemes from the early summer onwards. Prune lightly by deadheading, and to preserve symmetry, annually in spring. Requires space; not suitable for the small garden.

- Evergreen
- Requires space
- Drought-tolerant
- Low allergen

Escallonia rubra 'Crimson Spire'
A.G.M. (Escalloniaceae)

Common name: None
Height: 15ft (5m)
Spread: 15ft (5m)
Aspect: Sun
Soil: Well-drained, fertile
Hardiness: Zone 8
Propagation: Softwood cuttings in early summer; semi-ripe cuttings in late summer
Flowering time: Summer to early autumn

A very large, half-hardy, evergreen shrub. Leaves glossy, dark green. Flowers in panicles, tubular, dark crimson, abundantly, from summer onwards. Prune by deadheading, and remove wayward shoots to preserve symmetry, annually in spring. Requires space; not for the small garden.

- Evergreen
- Requires space
- Drought-tolerant
- Low allergen

Other Escallonias with an A.G.M. of the Royal Horticultural Society

'Apple Blossom'
'Edinensis'
'Iveyi'
'Langleyensis'
'Peach Blossom'
'Pride of Donard'

FREMONTODENDRON CALIFORNICUM

***Euryops pectinatus* A.G.M.**
(Asteraceae)

Common name: None
Height: 3ft (90cm)
Spread: 3ft (90cm)
Aspect: Full sun
Soil: Well-drained, fertile
Hardiness: Zone 8
Propagation: Seed in heat in spring; semi-ripe cuttings in summer

Flowering time: Early summer through to autumn; extends into winter in mild regions

A half-hardy shrub. Leaves pinnatisect, hairy, gray. Flowers single or in clusters, borne on long stems, yellow in color. Prune lightly when flowering has finished.

- 🟢 Good cut flower
- 🔴 High allergen

Fremontodendron californicum
(Sterculiaceae)

Common name: Flannel-bush
Height: 20ft (6m)
Spread: 12ft (4m)
Aspect: Full sun
Soil: Well-drained, fertile
Hardiness: Zone 8
Propagation: Seed in heat in spring
Flowering time: Late spring to mid-autumn

A half-hardy, semi-evergreen or evergreen shrub. Leaves dark green. Flowers large, single, yellow saucers.

- 🟢 Drought-tolerant
- 🔴 High allergen
- 🔴 Requires space
- 🔴 Skin irritant

SHRUBS

FUCHSIA (Onagraceae)
Fuchsia

A genus of only some 100 or so species, but more than 8,000 hybrids are in cultivation. The genus is renowned for its free-flowering and long-flowering qualities: it flowers from summer to late autumn. Degree of hardiness varies within the genus, from Zone 6 to Zone 9, so it is important to check the hardiness before buying a plant. The pendent flower is quite unique: the upper part is composed of sepals that form a perianth tube, at the lower end of which the sepals are spread out. Below is a cup- or bell-shaped corolla formed by the petals; in some species the petals are absent, or much reduced. The number of petals varies from 4, in single flowers, through 5–7 in double flowers, to 8 or more in fully double flowers. The perianth and corolla can be the same color or different colors. The flowers are followed by berries, usually containing many seeds. Fuchsias may be evergreen or deciduous, and the leaves are lance-shaped to ovate, usually toothed and mid-green, although a number of handsome variegated cultivars are in cultivation. They should be cut back to their permanent framework in early spring. An Award of Garden Merit of the Royal Horticultural Society has been given to 56 Fuchsias.

Fuchsia 'Bicentennial' (Onagaaceae)

Common name: None
Height: 18in (45cm)
Spread: 2ft (60cm)
Aspect: Sun or part shade
Soil: Moist, well-drained
Hardiness: Zone 9
Propagation: Softwood cuttings in spring
Flowering time: Summer through to late autumn

A tender Fuchsia, with arching stems bearing fully double flowers, with pale orange-pink sepals and magenta petals.

- Attracts bees
- Low allergen

Fuchsia 'Coralle' A.G.M. (Onagraceae)

Common name: None
Height: 3ft (90cm)
Spread: 2ft (60cm)
Aspect: Sun or part shade
Soil: Moist, well-drained
Hardiness: Zone 9
Propagation: Softwood cuttings in spring
Flowering time: Summer to late autumn

Leaves olive-green, velvety. Flowers in terminal clusters, upturned sepals, tubes orange-red, corollas salmon-pink.

- Attracts bees
- Low allergen

FUCHSIA 'LYE'S UNIQUE'

Fuchsia 'Happy Wedding' (Onagraceae)

Common name: None
Height: 1ft (30cm)
Spread: 18in (45cm)
Aspect: Sun or half shade
Soil: Moist, well-drained, fertile
Hardiness: Zone 8
Propagation: Softwood cuttings, in spring
Flowering time: Summer through to late autumn

A half-hardy cultivar. Flowers semi-double, tube and sepals in shell pink.

- Attracts bees
- Low allergen

Fuchsia 'Love's Reward' (Onagraceae)

Common name: None
Height: 18in (45cm)
Spread: 18in (45cm)
Aspect: Sun or part shade
Soil: Moist, well-drained, fertile
Hardiness: Zone 8
Propagation: Softwood cuttings in spring
Flowering time: Summer to autumn

An upright shrub with single, medium-sized flowers. Sepals and tubes pale pink, corollas of violet-blue.

- Attracts bees
- Low allergen

Fuchsia 'Lye's Unique' (Onagraceae)

Common name: None
Height: 2ft (60cm)
Spread: 18in (45cm)
Aspect: Sun or half shade
Soil: Moist, well-drained, fertile
Hardiness: Zone 8
Propagation: Softwood cuttings in spring
Flowering time: Summer through to autumn

A free-flowering shrub. Flowers single, sepals and tubes of white, corollas of a deep salmon color.

- Attracts bees
- Low allergen

FUCHSIA 'MADAME CORNELISSEN'

***Fuchsia* 'Madame Cornelissen'
(Onagraceae)**

Common name: None
Height: 3ft (90cm)
Spread: 1ft (30cm)
Aspect: Sun or half shade
Soil: Moist, well-drained, fertile
Hardiness: Zone 6
Propagation: Softwood cuttings in spring

Flowering time: Summer through to late autumn

A hardy Fuchsia shrub. Flowers double or semi-double, with red-colored tubes and sepals, and a corolla of a pure white color.

- Attracts bees
- Low allergen

Fuchsia 'Phenomenal' (Onagraceae)

Common name: None
Height: 1ft (30cm)
Spread: 1ft (30cm)
Aspect: Sun or part shade
Soil: Moist, well-drained, fertile
Hardiness: Zone 7
Propagation: Softwood cuttings in spring
Flowering time: Summer through to late autumn

A hardy Fuchsia with very large, double flowers. Sepals and tube red, corolla mauve-purple.

- Attracts bees
- Low allergen

Fuchsia 'Reading Show' (Onagraceae)

Common name: None
Height: 1ft (30cm)
Spread: 1ft (30cm)
Aspect: Sun or part shade
Soil: Moist, well-drained, fertile
Hardiness: Zone 8
Propagation: Softwood cuttings in spring
Flowering time: Summer to autumn

A handsome, large-flowered cultivar. Flowers have tube and sepals of bright red, and a deep blue-colored corolla.

- Attracts bees
- Low allergen

Fuchsia 'Thalia' A.G.M. (Onagraceae)

Common name: None
Height: 3ft (90cm)
Spread: 3ft (90cm)
Aspect: Sun or part shade
Soil: Moist, well-drained, fertile
Hardiness: Zone 9
Propagation: Softwood cuttings in spring
Flowering time: Midsummer to late autumn

A very desirable cultivar. Flowers are very long-tubed, borne in profusion in terminal clusters. Flowers have red tubes and sepals, and orange-colored petals. Tender.

- Attracts bees
- Low allergen

Garrya elliptica (Garryaceae)

Common name: Silk tassel bush
Height: 12ft (4m)
Spread: 12ft (4m)
Aspect: Sun or part shade
Soil: Well-drained
Hardiness: Zone 8
Propagation: Seed in spring; semi-ripe cuttings in summer
Flowering time: Midwinter through to early spring

A half-hardy shrub. Leaves leathery, glossy, or matt gray-green. Male plants have the more attractive flowers, females have brown berries. Flowers are catkins, pendent, gray-green. Prune only to deadhead, and to preserve symmetry. Requires space.

- Evergreen

Genista hispanica (Papilionaceae)

Common name: Spanish gorse
Height: 30in (75cm)
Spread: 5ft (1.5m)
Aspect: Full sun
Soil: Well-drained
Hardiness: Zone 6
Propagation: Seed in autumn or spring
Flowering time: Late spring to early summer

A dense, mound-forming, deciduous shrub. Leaves green above, hairy below. Flowers in terminal racemes, pea-like, golden yellow. Prune lightly; do not cut into old wood.

- Drought-tolerant
- Low allergen

Genista lydia A.G.M.
(Papilionaceae)

Common name: Broom
Height: 2ft (60cm)
Spread: 3ft (1m)
Aspect: Full sun
Soil: Well-drained
Hardiness: Zone 7
Propagation: Seed in spring or autumn
Flowering time: Late spring and early summer

A spreading deciduous shrub. Stems gray-green. Leaves blue-green. Flowers yellow, in short racemes, in late spring and early summer. Prune very lightly to preserve symmetry.

- Drought-tolerant
- Handsome foliage
- Low allergen

Grevillea 'Canberra Gem' A.G.M.
(Proteaceae)

Common name: None
Height: 12ft (4m)
Spread: 15ft (4.5m)
Aspect: Full sun
Soil: Acid or neutral, fertile
Hardiness: Zone 9
Propagation: Semi-ripe cuttings in summer
Flowering time: Late winter to late summer, but also at other times

A large, tender shrub. Leaves linear, green above, hairy-silky below. Flowers petalless, calyx red, waxy, in dense racemes. Prune in early spring by removing wayward shoots.

- Evergreen
- Handsome foliage
- Requires space
- Skin irritant

Grevillea rosmarinifolia A.G.M.
(Proteaceae)

Common name: None
Height: 10ft (3m)
Spread: 15ft (4.5m)
Aspect: Full sun
Soil: Acid to neutral, fertile
Hardiness: Zone 9
Propagation: Semi-ripe cuttings in summer
Flowering time: Spring to late summer

A tender shrub. Leaves narrow, gray-green above, downy below. Flowers without petals, calyx pink or yellow, borne in racemes.

- Evergreen
- Handsome foliage
- Requires space
- Skin irritant

Grindelia chiloensis (Asteraceae)

Common name: None
Height: 3ft (90cm)
Spread: 3ft (90cm)
Aspect: Sun
Soil: Well-drained
Hardiness: Zone 6
Propagation: Seed in spring; semi-ripe cuttings in summer
Flowering time: Throughout the summer

An evergreen subshrub. Basal rosette of gray-green leaves. Flowers solitary, semi-double, yellow in color, borne on long stems. Minimal pruning is required.

- Drought-tolerant
- Evergreen
- Good cut flower
- Requires staking

x *Halimiocistus sahucii* A.G.M. (Cistaceae)

Common name: None
Height: 18in (45cm)
Spread: 3ft (90cm)
Aspect: Full sun
Soil: Sharply drained
Hardiness: Zone 8
Propagation: Semi-ripe cuttings in late summer
Flowering time: Late spring and again in early summer

An evergreen, spreading shrub. Leaves dark green. Flowers white, like rock-roses, with yellow centers, in umbel-like cymes, in late spring and early summer. Minimal pruning is required.

- Evergreen
- Drought-tolerant

Halimium ocymoides A.G.M. (Cistaceae)

Common name: None
Height: 2ft (60cm)
Spread: 3ft (1m)
Aspect: Full sun
Soil: Sharply drained
Hardiness: Zone 8
Propagation: Seed, in heat, in spring; semi-ripe cuttings in late summer
Flowering time: Early summer

Leaves gray-green, downy, white. Flowers golden yellow, maroon centers, in terminal panicles. Deadhead in spring.

- Evergreen
- Drought-tolerant

HEBE (Scrophulariaceae)
Hebe

This is a genus consisting of about 100 evergreen shrubs, which are usually grown for their attractive evergreen foliage value, but some also have a reasonably long flowering season, with flowers being borne in spikes, racemes, or panicles. Species vary in their degrees of hardiness, from tender to fully hardy, so check the hardiness of specimens before making a purchase. They will grow in sun or in part shade but they dislike cold, drying winds. Smaller specimens are idea for rock gardens.

In general, Hebes make excellent plants for a seaside location. The soil should be moist, but well-drained, and not too rich. Most hebes require very little in the way of pruning, apart from the removal of wayward or damaged stems to preserve symmetry.

Hebe albicans A.G.M. (Scrophulariaceae)

Common name: None
Height: 2ft (60cm)
Spread: 3ft (90cm)
Aspect: Sun or part shade
Soil: Moist, well-drained
Hardiness: Zone 8
Propagation: Seed when ripe; semi-ripe cuttings in late summer
Flowering time: Early and midsummer

A mound-forming, evergreen shrub. Leaves gray-green. Flowers white, medium-sized, in short terminal racemes. Prune by deadheading, and to preserve symmetry.

- Evergreen
- Handsome foliage
- Low allergen
- Prone to mildew

Hebe x *franciscana* 'Blue Gem' A.G.M. (Scrophulariaceae)

Common name: None
Height: 5ft (1.5m)
Spread: 5ft (1.5m)
Aspect: Sun or part shade
Soil: Moist, well-drained
Hardiness: Zone 7
Propagation: Semi-ripe cuttings with bottom heat in late summer
Flowering time: Summer through to autumn

A spreading shrub. Leaves mid-green. Flowers mauve in color, borne in dense axillary racemes. Prune by deadheading, and remove stems as necessary to preserve symmetry.

- Evergreen
- Low allergen

Hebe 'Great Orme' A.G.M.
(Scrophulariaceae)

Common name: None
Height: 4ft (1.2m)
Spread: 4ft (1.2m)
Aspect: Sun or part shade
Soil: Moist, well-drained
Hardiness: Zone 8
Propagation: Semi-ripe cuttings with bottom heat in late summer
Flowering time: Summer to autumn

An evergreen, open shrub. Leaves glossy-green. Flowers bright pink, ageing to white, borne on dense axillary spikes.

- Evergreen
- Handsome foliage
- Low allergen

Hebe hulkeana (Scrophulariaceae)

Common name: None
Height: 2ft (60cm)
Spread: 2ft (60cm)
Aspect: Sun or part shade
Soil: Moist, well-drained
Hardiness: Zone 9
Propagation: Semi-ripe cuttings with bottom heat in late summer
Flowering time: Spring to early summer

An open, upright evergreen shrub. Leaves glossy, mid-green, edged red. Flowers lavender, lilac, or white, in terminal panicles, from late spring to early summer. Prune by deadheading.

- Evergreen
- Handsome foliage
- Low allergen

Hebe ochracea 'James Stirling' A.G.M. (Scrophulariaceae)

Common name: None
Height: 3ft (1m)
Spread: 4ft (1.2m)
Aspect: Sun or part shade
Soil: Moist, well-drained
Hardiness: Zone 6
Propagation: Semi-ripe cuttings with bottom heat, in late summer
Flowering time: Spring and early summer

Shrub, with whipcord leaves, ochre-yellow. Flowers small, white, in axillary racemes. Prune by deadheading. Do not cut hard back.

- Evergreen
- Low allergen

Hebe 'Youngii' (Scrophulariaceae)

Common name: None
Height: 8in (20cm)
Spread: 2ft (60cm)
Aspect: Sun or part shade
Soil: Moist, well-drained
Hardiness: Zone 8
Propagation: Semi-ripe cuttings, with bottom heat, in late summer
Flowering time: Several weeks in summer

An evergreen, mat-forming shrub. Leaves dark green, perhaps margined red. Flowers large, violet with white throats, in axillary racemes. Prune by deadheading, and remove stems as necessary to preserve symmetry.

- Evergreen
- Low allergen

Helianthemum 'Ben Hope'
(Cistaceae)

Common name: Sunrose
Height: 1ft (30cm)
Spread: 1ft (30cm)
Aspect: Sun
Soil: Well-drained, fertile
Hardiness: Zone 6
Propagation: Softwood cuttings in late spring/early summer
Flowering time: Spring to early summer

A spreading shrub. Leaves pale gray-green, downy. Flowers single, saucer-shaped, red, with orange centers. Cut back flowered shoots to within 1in (2.5cm) of previous year's growth.

- Drought tolerant
- Evergreen
- Low allergen

Helianthemum 'Coppernob'
(Cistaceae)

Common name: Sunrose
Height: 1ft (30cm)
Spread: 1ft (30cm)
Aspect: Sun
Soil: Well-drained, fertile
Hardiness: Zone 6
Propagation: Softwood cuttings in late spring/early summer
Flowering time: Mid-spring to summer

Leaves gray-green. Flowers of deep copper, with a bronze-crimson center, in cymes. After flowering, cut back flowered shoots to within 1in (2.5cm) of previous year's growth.

- Drought-tolerant
- Evergreen
- Low allergen

HELIANTHEMUM 'RASPBERRY RIPPLE'

Helianthemum 'Fireball' (Cistaceae)

Common name: Sunrose
Height: 8in (20cm)
Spread: 1ft (30cm)
Aspect: Full sun
Soil: Well-drained, fertile
Hardiness: Zone 6
Propagation: Softwood cuttings from spring to early summer
Flowering time: Late spring through to midsummer

An evergreen subshrub. Leaves gray-green. Flowers fully double, bright red in color, borne in cymes. After flowering, cut back flowered shoots to within 1in (2.5cm) of previous year's growth.

- Drought-tolerant
- Evergreen
- Low allergen

Helianthemum 'Raspberry Ripple' (Cistaceae)

Common name: Sunrose
Height: 8in (20cm)
Spread: 1ft (30cm)
Aspect: Full sun
Soil: Well-drained, fertile
Hardiness: Zone 6
Propagation: Softwood cuttings from spring to early summer
Flowering time: Late spring through to midsummer

A very attractive, evergreen subshrub. Leaves dark gray-green in color. Flowers white, with purple-pink centers, the color radiating to the margins of the petals. After flowering, cut back flowered shoots to within 1in (2.5cm) of previous year's growth.

- Drought-tolerant
- Evergreen
- Low allergen

SHRUBS

Heliotropium arborescens 'Marine' A.G.M. (Boraginaceae)

Common name: Heliotrope
Height: 18in (45cm)
Spread: 18in (45cm)
Aspect: Full sun
Soil: Moist, well-drained, fertile
Hardiness: Zone 10
Propagation: Semi-ripe cuttings in summer
Flowering time: Throughout the summer

A tender, short-lived, bushy shrub, often grown as an annual in cold climates. Leaves wrinkled, dark green in color. Flowers perfumed, deep violet-blue, borne in flattened cymes, for long periods in summer.

- Scented flowers
- Attracts butterflies
- Skin irritant
- Short-lived

Hibiscus rosa-sinensis hybridus (Malvaceae)

Common name: None
Height: 15ft (4.5m)
Spread: 10ft (3m)
Aspect: Full sun
Soil: Moist, well-drained, humus-rich
Hardiness: Zone 9
Propagation: Seed in heat, or softwood cuttings, in spring
Flowering time: Summer through to autumn

A large, tender evergreen shrub, with glossy-green leaves. Flowers solitary, single, 5-petaled, in a range of colors or bicolored (*as above*). Minimal pruning required, except to retain symmetry.

- Evergreen
- Handsome foliage
- Low allergen
- Prone to mildew
- Requires space

HIBISCUS SYRIACUS 'BLUE BIRD' A.G.M.

Hibiscus rosa-sinensis **hybridus** (Malvaceae)

Common name: None
Height: 15ft (4.5m)
Spread: 10ft (3m)
Aspect: Full sun
Soil: Moist, well-drained, humus-rich
Hardiness: Zone 9
Propagation: Seed in heat, or softwood cuttings, in spring
Flowering time: Summer to autumn

Shrub with glossy-green leaves. Flowers solitary, single, in a range of colors or single (yellow and reflexed). Minimal pruning required.

- 🟢 Evergreen
- 🟢 Handsome foliage
- 🔴 Prone to mildew
- 🔴 Requires space

Hibiscus syriacus 'Blue Bird' A.G.M. (Malvaceae)

Common name: Shrub althea
Height: 8ft (2.5m)
Spread: 4ft (1.2m)
Aspect: Full sun
Soil: Moist, well-drained, humus-rich
Hardiness: Zone 5
Propagation: Softwood cuttings in late spring
Flowering time: Late summer to mid-autumn

A medium-sized, hardy, deciduous shrub. Leaves toothed, dark green. Flowers large, single or in pairs, blue with red centers.

- 🟢 Low allergen
- 🔴 Prone to mildew
- 🔴 Requires space

SHRUBS

Hibiscus syriacus 'Hamabo' A.G.M. (Malvaceae)

Common name: None
Height: 8ft (2.5m)
Spread: 4ft (1.2m)
Aspect: Sun
Soil: Moist, humus-rich, well-drained
Hardiness: Zone 5
Propagation: Softwood cuttings yaken in late spring

Flowering time: Late summer through to mid-autumn

A medium-sized, hardy, deciduous shrub. Flowers single, large, pale pink in color with a crimson eye. Minimal pruning required except to preserve symmetry.

- Low allergen
- Prone to mildew
- Requires space

HYDRANGEA (Hydrangeaceae)
Hydrangea

A genus of about 80 species from Asia, and both N. and S. America. The flowers may be in corymbs or panicles, composed of large sterile flowers and small fertile flowers. The cultivars of the common Hydrangea, *Hydrangea macrophylla*, can be divided into two groups:

Hortensias: These 'mophead' cultivars have rounded flowerheads, composed of sterile flowers.

Lacecaps: These have flattened flowerheads, with fertile, small central flowers, surrounded by large sterile flowers.

Additionally, some cultivars of *Hydrangea serrata* are also called 'Lacecaps', and this is the best species for small gardens (see *H. serrata* 'Bluebird').

The color of the flowers depends on the availability of ions of aluminum in the ground. Blue flowers ensue when the soil is acid at a pH of below 5.5. Pink flowers ensue when the pH is greater than 5.5. White flowers are not influenced by pH. Flower color can be manipulated artificially by the use of a 'blueing' compound.

Hydrangeas may be evergreen or deciduous; some are climbers and others are trees. All parts are poisonous, and contact with foliage may irritate the skin. The flower heads can be dried for winter decoration.

Hydrangea macrophylla 'Blaumeise'
(Hydrangeaceae)

Common name: None
Height: 6ft (1.8m)
Spread: 8ft (2.5m)
Aspect: Sun or part shade
Soil: Moist, well-drained, fertile
Hardiness: Zone 5
Propagation: Softwood cuttings in early summer

Flowering time: Mid- and late summer

Lacecap, Leaves glossy, dark green. Flowers in flattened corymbs, with many central, cream-colored fertile flowers, and a few peripheral lilac-colored sterile flowers.

- Can be dried
- Low allergen
- Poisonous
- Prone to mildew
- Skin irritant

Hydrangea macrophylla 'Lady Nobuko'® (Hydrangeaceae)

Common name: Common hydrangea
Height: 4ft (1.2m)
Spread: 3ft (1m)
Aspect: Sun or half shade
Soil: Moist, well-drained, fertile
Hardiness: Zone 5
Propagation: Softwood cuttings in early summer
Flowering time: Mid- through to late summer

A Hortensia hydrangea. Leaves veined, matt green. Flowers in mopheads, large, sterile, deep pink in color, margined white, opening in mid- and late summer. Prune by cutting back to the first bud below the flowerhead in early spring after the danger of frosts is over. Requires space; not suitable for the small garden.

- Can be dried
- Low allergen
- Prone to mildew
- Poisonous
- Skin irritant
- Requires space

Hydrangea macrophylla 'Leuchtfeuer' (Hydrangeaceae)

Common name: None
Height: 6ft (1.8m)
Spread: 6ft (1.8m)
Aspect: Sun or half shade
Soil: Moist, well-drained, fertile, humus-rich
Hardiness: Zone 5
Propagation: Softwood cuttings in early summer
Flowering time: Mid- through to late summer

A Hortensia hydrangea. Leaves glossy green. Flowers in mopheads, large, sterile, cerise-pink. Prune in early spring by cutting back to the first bud below the flowerhead after the danger of frosts is over. Requires space; not suitable for the small garden.

- Can be dried
- Low allergen
- Poisonous
- Prone to mildew
- Requires space
- Skin irritant

HYDRANGEA 'SANDRA'®

Hydrangea 'Sabrina'®
(Hydrangeaceae)

Common name: None
Height: 4ft (1.2m)
Spread: 3ft (90cm)
Aspect: Sun or part shade
Soil: Moist, well-drained, humus-rich
Hardiness: Zone 5
Propagation: Softwood cuttings in early summer
Flowering time: Mid- through to late summer

A Hortensia hydrangea recently introduced from the Netherlands. Flowers in mopheads, large, sterile, pale pink in color with a darker edge. Prune in early spring after the danger of frost is over by cutting back to the first bud below the flowerhead.

- Can be dried
- Low allergen
- Attracts slugs
- Poisonous
- Prone to mildew
- Skin irritant

Hydrangea 'Sandra'®
(Hydrangeaceae)

Common name: None
Height: 4ft (1.2m)
Spread: 3ft (90cm)
Aspect: Sun or part shade
Soil: Moist, well-drained, humus-rich
Hardiness: Zone 5
Propagation: Softwood cuttings in early summer
Flowering time: Mid- through to late summer

A Lacecap hydrangea recently introduced from the Netherlands. Flat corymbs of small central flowers, green, fading to white, and peripheral, large white flowers. Prune in early spring after the danger of frost is over to the first bud below the flowerhead.

- Can be dried
- Low allergen
- Attracts slugs
- Poisonous
- Prone to mildew
- Skin irritant

SHRUBS

Hydrangea paniculata
(Hydrangeaceae)

Common name: Panicle hydrangea
Height: 22ft (7m)
Spread: 8ft (2.5m)
Aspect: Sun or part shade
Soil: Moist, well-drained, humus-rich
Hardiness: Zone 3
Propagation: Softwood cuttings in early summer
Flowering time: Late summer to autumn

A large, deciduous shrub. Conical panicles of small cream-colored, fertile flowers, and large white, sterile flowers. In spring, prune previous year's shoots to within a few buds of the wood. Requires space; not suitable for the small garden

- Can be dried
- Low allergen
- Poisonous
- Prone to mildew
- Requires space

***Hydrangea* 'Preziosa' A.G.M.**
(Hydrangeaceae)

Common name: None
Height: 5ft (1.5m)
Spread: 5ft (1.5m)
Aspect: Sun or part shade
Soil: Acid, moist, well-drained, humus-rich
Hardiness: Zone 5
Propagation: Softwood cuttings in early summer
Flowering time: Late summer and early autumn

A Hortensia hydrangea. Sterile flowers in spherical corymbs, white, on alkaline soil, deep purple-pink on acid soil, in late summer and early autumn. Prune by cutting back to the first bud below the flowerhead in early spring after the danger of frost is over.

- Can be dried
- Low allergen
- Attracts slugs
- Prone to mildew
- Poisonous
- Skin irritant

Hydrangea quercifolia A.G.M. (Hydrangeaceae)

Common name: Oak–leaved hydrangea
Height: 6ft (2m)
Spread: 8ft (2.5m)
Aspect: Sun or part shade
Soil: Moist, well-drained, humus-rich
Hardiness: Zone 5
Propagation: Softwood cuttings in early summer
Flowering time: Summer and early autumn

A large, deciduous shrub. Leaves turn bronze in winter. Flowers open in conical panicles, both large sterile and small fertile being white from summer onwards. Prune by cutting back to the first bud below the flowerhead in early spring, after the danger of frost is over.

- Can be dried
- Low allergen
- Attracts slugs
- Prone to mildew
- Poisonous
- Skin irritant

Hydrangea serrata 'Bluebird' A.G.M. (Hydrangeaceae)

Common name: Tea-of-heaven
Height: 4ft (1.2m)
Spread: 4ft (1.2m)
Aspect: Sun or part shade
Soil: Moist, well-drained, humus-rich
Hardiness: Zone 6
Propagation: Softwood cuttings in early summer
Flowering time: Long period from summer to autumn

A compact cultivar. Leaves turn red in autumn. Lacecap corymbs of small, blue, fertile flowers surrounded by large, pale blue, sterile ones. Prune in early spring by cutting back to the first bud below the flowerhead after the danger of frost is over.

- Can be dried
- Low allergen
- Attracts slugs
- Poisonous
- Prone to mildew
- Skin irritant

HYPERICUM (Clusiaceae)
Hypericum

A genus of more than 400 species from all parts of the world; they may be annual, perennial or shrubs, evergreen or deciduous. The flowers are invariably yellow, with prominent yellow stamens, and are borne over long periods in some instances; some species have fruits after flowering. There is such a wide divergence in cultural requirement that it is difficult to generalize. Similarly, the shrubby species have quite different pruning requirements, depending on whether they are evergreen or deciduous. The dwarf species require full sun and sharp drainage, whereas the larger species will grow in sun or part shade, and also like well-drained soil.

Hypericum calycinum (Clusiaceae)

Common name: Rose of Sharon
Height: 2ft (60cm)
Spread: Indefinite
Aspect: Sun or part shade
Soil: Moist, well-drained
Hardiness: Zone 6
Propagation: Division in spring or autumn
Flowering time: Midsummer through to mid-autumn

A rampant, evergreen shrub that spreads by sending out runners. Flowers open in cymes or can be single, yellow, saucer-shaped. Good ground cover, even if planted in dry shade. Cut back hard to the ground in spring to encourage new growth.

- Drought-tolerant
- Invasive
- Evergreen
- Low allergen

Hypericum 'Hidcote' A.G.M. (Clusiaceae)

Common name: None
Height: 4ft (1.2m)
Spread: 5ft (1.5m)
Aspect: Sun or part shade
Soil: Moist, well-drained
Hardiness: Zone 7
Propagation: Greenwood or semi-ripe cuttings in summer
Flowering time: Midsummer through to early autumn

A semi-evergreen/evergreen shrub. Flowers large, bright yellow, borne in corymb-like cymes, from midsummer to early autumn. Prune hard back, close to the base, in early spring to encourage new growth.

- Low allergen

Hypericum x *inodorum* 'Elstead'
(Clusiaceae)

Common name: None
Height: 4ft (1.2m)
Spread: 4ft (1.2m)
Aspect: Sun or part shade
Soil: Moist, well-drained
Hardiness: Zone 8
Propagation: Greenwood or semi-ripe cuttings in summer
Flowering time: Summer to autumn

A bushy, semi-evergreen shrub with aromatic leaves. Flowers in cymes, small, star-shaped, yellow, followed by large red fruits. Prune in early spring by cutting back fairly hard to low wood.

- Handsome foliage
- Low allergen

Hypericum olympicum forma *uniflorum* 'Citrinum' A.G.M.
(Clusiaceae)

Common name: None
Height: 10 in (25cm)
Spread: 1ft (30cm)
Aspect: Sun
Soil: Sharply drained
Hardiness: Zone 6
Propagation: Semi-ripe or greenwood cuttings in summer
Flowering time: Summer

A dwarf deciduous shrub. Flowers in cymes of up to 5, star-shaped, pale lemon-yellow flowers in summer. Good in a rock garden. Cut back fairly hard in early spring.

- Low allergen

Hypericum 'Rowallane' A.G.M.
(Clusiaceae)

Common name: None
Height: 6ft (1.8m)
Spread: 3ft (1m)
Aspect: Sun or part shade
Soil: Moist, well-drained
Hardiness: Zone 8
Propagation: Semi-ripe or softwood cuttings in summer.
Flowering time: Summer to autumn

A large, half-hardy, semi-evergreen shrub. Flowers in cymes, saucer-shaped, golden yellow, from late summer to autumn. Prune in late spring by cutting back hard to low permanent wood. Requires space.

- Low allergen

Iberis sempervirens (**Brassicaceae**)

Common name: Evergreen candytuft
Height: 1ft (30cm)
Spread: 20in (50cm)
Aspect: Sun
Soil: Moist, well-drained, fertile
Hardiness: Zone 4
Propagation: Softwood cuttings in late spring
Flowering time: Late spring through to early summer

An evergreen subshrub. Flowers small, carried in flat, corymb-like racemes, white colored, perhaps flushed with pink. Cut back hard annually after flowering has finished to within 1in (2.5cm) of previous year's growth to encourage new shoots.

- Attracts butterflies
- Evergreen
- Low allergen

Ixora coccinea (Rubiaceae)

Common name: None
Height: 6ft (1.8m)
Spread: 6ft (1.8m)
Aspect: Sun, but not at midday
Soil: Moist, fertile, well-drained; dry in winter
Hardiness: Zone 10
Propagation: Semi-ripe cuttings, with bottom heat, in summer
Flowering time: Late spring to early summer

A large, evergreen, tender shrub. Flowers scented, 4-petaled, carried in corymb-like cymes, yellow, red, orange, or pink in color. Prune annually in spring by lightly cutting back to preserve symmetry. Not suitable for the small garden.

- Evergreen
- Scented flowers
- Requires space

Justicia carnea (Acanthaceae)

Common name: None
Height: 6ft (1.8m)
Spread: 3ft (90cm)
Aspect: Part shade
Soil: Moist, well-drained, fertile
Hardiness: Zone 10
Propagation: Seed in heat, or softwood cuttings, in spring
Flowering time: Summer and autumn

A large, tender, evergreen shrub. Leaves glossy-green. Flowers borne in dense, axillary or terminal spikes, 2-lipped, tubular, pink in color. Prune annually by deadheading, and light cutting back in spring to preserve symmetry. Not suitable for the small garden.

- Evergreen
- Handsome foliage
- Requires space

KERRIA JAPONICA 'PLENIFLORA' A.G.M.

Kerria japonica **'Pleniflora' A.G.M. (Rosaceae)**

Common name: Kerria
Height: 10ft (3m)
Spread: 10ft (3m)
Aspect: Sun or part shade
Soil: Well-drained, fertile
Hardiness: Zone 4
Propagation: Greenwood cuttings taken in summer
Flowering time: Mid and late spring

A large, deciduous, spreading shrub. Flowers large, double, solitary, yellow. Prune annually when flowering has finished by cutting back to strong buds, low down.

- Good cut flower   • Requires space

Kolkwitzia amabilis **'Pink Cloud' A.G.M. (Caprifoliaceae)**

Common name: Beauty bush
Height: 10ft (3m)
Spread: 12ft (4m)
Aspect: Sun or part shade
Soil: Well-drained, fertile
Hardiness: Zone 4
Propagation: Greenwood cuttings, or suckers, in spring
Flowering time: Spring to early summer

A large, suckering, deciduous shrub. Flowers bell-shaped, pink, with yellow throats, in terminal corymbs, from late spring to early summer. Prune a quarter of flowered shoots back to the base annually, after flowering. Not suitable for the small garden.

- Low allergen   • Requires space

LAVANDULA STOECHAS A.G.M.

Lantana camara 'Radiation' (Verbenaceae)

Common name: Common lantana
Height: 6ft (1.8m)
Spread: 6ft (1.8m)
Aspect: Full sun
Soil: Moist, well-drained, fertile
Hardiness: Zone 10
Propagation: Semi-ripe cuttings with bottom heat, in summer
Flowering time: Late spring through to late autumn

A tender, evergreen, medium-sized shrub. Flowers in flat heads, bicolored red and orange. Deadhead regularly and remove wayward shoots in spring.

- Attracts butterflies
- Poisonous
- Prone to mildew
- Skin irritant

Lavandula stoechas A.G.M. (Lamiaceae)

Common name: French lavender
Height: 2ft (60cm)
Spread: 2ft (60cm)
Aspect: Sun
Soil: Well-drained, fertile
Hardiness: Zone 8
Propagation: Seed in spring; semi-ripe cuttings in summer
Flowering time: Late spring through to early summer

A half-hardy, evergreen subshrub. Leaves gray-green, aromatic. Scented flowers, purple in color, borne in dense spikes topped by purple bracts. Cut flowered shoots back in spring to within 1in (2.5cm) of previous year's growth.

- Attracts bees
- Can be dried
- Evergreen
- Handsome foliage
- Scented flowers

Lavatera 'Barnsley' A.G.M.
(**Malvaceae**)

Common name: Herb tree-mallow
Height: 6ft (1.8m)
Spread: 4ft (1.2m)
Aspect: Sun
Soil: Well-drained, fertile
Hardiness: Zone 7
Propagation: Softwood cuttings in early summer
Flowering time: All summer

A short-lived, evergreen subshrub. Leaves gray-green. Flowers large, saucer-shaped, white with a red-colored eye, borne in racemes. Prune in early spring by cutting back close to the base. Not suitable for the small garden.

- Drought-tolerant
- Evergreen
- Good cut flower
- Handsome foliage
- Requires space
- Short-lived

Lavatera 'Bredon Springs'
(**Malvaceae**)

Common name: Herb tree-mallow
Height: 6ft (1.8m)
Spread: 4ft (1.2m)
Aspect: Sun
Soil: Well-drained, fertile
Hardiness: Zone 8
Propagation: Softwood cuttings in early summer
Flowering time: All summer

A short-lived, evergreen subshrub. Leaves gray-green. Flowers large saucers, dusky pink, in racemes. Prune in early spring by cutting back hard, close to the base.

- Drought-tolerant
- Evergreen
- Good cut flower
- Handsome foliage
- Requires space
- Short-lived

LAVATERA 'CANDY FLOSS'

Lavatera 'Burgundy Wine' (Malvaceae)

Common name: Herb tree-mallow
Height: 4ft (1.2m)
Spread: 3ft (90cm)
Aspect: Sun
Soil: Well-drained, fertile
Hardiness: Zone 7
Propagation: Softwood cuttings in early summer
Flowering time: All summer

A evergreen subshrub. Leaves gray-green. Flowers large, dark pink, with darker veins, in racemes. Suitable for a small garden. Prune in early spring by cutting back close to the base.

- Drought-tolerant
- Evergreen
- Good cut flower
- Handsome foliage
- Short-lived

Lavatera 'Candy Floss' (Malvaceae)

Common name: Herb tree-mallow
Height: 6ft (1.8m)
Spread: 4ft (1.2m)
Aspect: Sun
Soil: Well-drained, fertile
Hardiness: Zone 8
Propagation: Softwood cuttings in early summer
Flowering time: All summer

A short-lived, evergreen subshrub. Foliage gray-green. Flowers large, pale pink in color, saucer-shaped, in racemes throughout the summer. Prune in early spring by cutting back hard, close to the base, to encourage new growth. Not suitable for the small garden.

- Drought-tolerant
- Evergreen
- Good cut flower
- Handsome foliage
- Requires space
- Short-lived

Leptospermum scoparium 'Nicholsii Nanum' A.G.M. (Myrtaceae)

Common name: None
Height: 6in (15cm)
Spread: 18in (45cm)
Aspect: Sun or part shade
Soil: Well-drained, fertile
Hardiness: Zone 8
Propagation: Semi-ripe cuttings with bottom heat taken in summer
Flowering time: Late spring to early summer

A charming, dwarf, evergreen, half-hardy, prostrate shrub. Leaves aromatic, green. Flowers single, red, borne in profusion. Prune after flowering only to deadhead and maintain shape.

- Evergreen

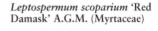

Leptospermum scoparium 'Red Damask' A.G.M. (Myrtaceae)

Common name: None
Height: 10ft (3m)
Spread: 10ft (3m)
Aspect: Sun or part shade
Soil: Well-drained, fertile
Hardiness: Zone 8
Propagation: Semi-ripe cuttings with bottom heat taken in summer
Flowering time: Late spring to early summer

A large, half-hardy, evergreen shrub. Leaves aromatic, dark green in color. Flowers solitary, double, dark red, borne profusely from late spring to summer. Prune lightly after flowering by deadheading, and remove any warward shoots to preserve symmetry.

- Evergreen
- Aromatic leaves
- Requires space

LONICERA x BROWNII 'DROPMORE SCARLET'

Leycesteria formosa (Caprifoliaceae)

Common name: Formosa-honeysuckle
Height: 6ft (1.8m)
Spread: 6ft (1.8m)
Aspect: Sun or part shade
Soil: Any well-drained, fertile
Hardiness: Zone 7
Propagation: Softwood cuttings in summer; seed in autumn
Flowering time: Summer to autumn

An upright shrub with hollow stems. Flowers in pendent spikes, white, surrounded by reddish-purple bracts, followed by red berries. Prune in spring to a medium or low framework.

- Requires space

Linum arboreum A.G.M. (Linaceae)

Common name: Flax
Height: 1ft (30cm)
Spread: 1ft (30cm)
Aspect: Full sun
Soil: Sharply drained, humus-rich
Hardiness: Zone 8
Propagation: Semi-ripe cuttings in summer
Flowering time: Late spring to summer

Leaves in rosettes, bluish-green. Flowers funnel-shaped, yellow, in terminal cymes, opening in succession.

- Evergreen
- Attracts slugs
- Drought-tolerant

Lonicera x *brownii* 'Dropmore Scarlet' (Caprifoliaceae)

Common name: None
Height: 12ft (4m)
Spread 30in (75cm)
Aspect: Sun or part shade
Soil: Moist, well-drained, humus-rich, fertile
Hardiness: Zone 5
Propagation: Greenwood cuttings in summer, hardwood cuttings in autumn
Flowering time: All summer

A semi-evergreen, twining, climbing shrub. Leaves blue-green. Flowers bright scarlet, tubular, in terminal whorls. Regular pruning not necessary; prune only to fit into available space.

- Scented flowers
- Poisonous

SHRUBS

Lonicera pericyclamenum 'Serotina' A.G.M. (Caprifoliaceae)

Common name: Late Dutch honeysuckle
Height: 22ft (7m)
Spread: 3ft (1m)
Aspect: Sun or part shade
Soil: Well-drained, humus-rich, fertile
Hardiness: Zone 4
Propagation: Greenwood cuttings in summer; hardwood cuttings in autumn
Flowering time: Mid-to late summer

A deciduous, twining climber. Flowers tubular, scented, creamy-white, streaked red, followed by red berries. Prune after flowering.

- Scented flowers
- Poisonous
- Drought-tolerant
- Requires space

Mimulus aurantiacus A.G.M. (Scrophulariaceae)

Common name: Monkey-flower
Height: 3ft (90cm)
Spread: 3ft (90cm)
Aspect: Full sun
Soil: Well-drained, humus-rich
Hardiness: Zone 8
Propagation: Seed in autumn or spring; division in autumn
Flowering time: Summer to autumn

Leaves sticky, glossy-green. Flowers trumpet-shaped, with wavy margins, red, yellow or orange, in leafy racemes. Prune in spring by deadheading and by removing wayward shoots.

- Evergreen
- Prone to mildew
- Handsome foliage
- Short-lived
- Low allergen

Mimulus puniceus (Scrophulariaceae)

Common name: None
Height: 5ft (1.5m)
Spread: 5ft (1.5m)
Aspect: Full sun
Soil: Well-drained, humus-rich, fertile
Hardiness: Zone 9
Propagation: Softwood cuttings in summer; semi-ripe cuttings in midsummer
Flowering time: Spring to late summer

Flowers orange-red, in leafy racemes. Prune in spring by deadheading and removing any wayward shoots.

- Low allergen
- Attracts slugs
- Prone to mildew

NERIUM OLEANDER

Nerium oleander (**Apocynaceae**)

Common name: Oleander
Height: 20ft (6m)
Spread: 9ft (2.7m)
Aspect: Sun
Soil: Moist, well-drained, fertile, dry in winter
Hardiness: Zone 9
Propagation: Semi-ripe cuttings, with bottom heat, in summer

Flowering time: Throughout summer

An evergreen shrub. Leaves grayish-green. Flowers pink, red, or white, in cymes of up to 80. Prune annually in spring by deadheading, and to maintain symmetry.

- Evergreen
- Poisonous
- Requires space
- Skin irritant

Nicotiana glauca (Solanaceae)

Common name: Tree tobacco
Height: 10ft (3m)
Spread: 10ft (3m)
Aspect: Sun or part shade
Soil: Moist, well-drained, fertile
Hardiness: Zone 8
Propagation: Seed in heat in spring
Flowering time: Long periods in summer

A fast-growing, large, half-hardy, evergreen shrub. Leaves blue-gray. Flowers narrow tubular, bright yellow in color. Cut back in early spring to a low, permanent framework. Grows into a large plant; not suitable for the small garden.

- Evergreen
- Handsome foliage
- Requires space
- Skin irritant

Olearia 'Henry Travers' A.G.M. (Asteraceae)

Common name: Daisy bush
Height: 8ft (2.5m)
Spread: 6ft (2m)
Aspect: Full sun
Soil: Well-drained, fertile
Hardiness: Zone 8
Propagation: Semi-ripe cuttings, with bottom heat, in summer
Flowering time: Early and midsummer

A large, rounded, evergreen shrub. Leaves gray-green, leathery. Flowers solitary single daisy-like, lilac, with purple centers, from early summer. Deadhead and remove shoots that spoil symmetry after flowering. Requires space; not suitable for the small garden.

- Evergreen
- High allergen

OSTEOSPERMUM (*Asteraceae*)

Osteospermum

A genus consisting of about 70 evergreen species from Arabia and South Africa; they are mostly tender or half-hardy, but a few species are hardy. The flowers are daisy-like, single, and solitary or borne in panicles. Flowering is from late spring to autumn, especially if regularly deadheaded. The color range is wide, and some have differing ray and disc florets. They must be given a sunny position as the flowers do not open in the shade. Large numbers of hybrids are now coming into cultivation.

Osteospermums make excellent groundcover plants where they can be left in the open ground all year round. They make good cut flowers, but are highly allergenic and prone to downy mildew.

OSTEOSPERMUM CAULESCENS A.G.M.

Osteospermum 'Buttermilk' A.G.M. (Asteraceae)

Common name: None
Height: 2ft (60cm)
Spread: 2ft (60cm)
Aspect: Sun
Soil: Well-drained, humus-rich
Hardiness: Zone 9
Propagation: Softwood cuttings in spring; semi-ripe cuttings in summer
Flowering time: Late spring to autumn

An evergreen subshrub. Flowers daisy-like, with primrose ray florets, and dark mauve disc florets. Usually treated as an annual.

- Evergreen
- Good cut flower
- High allergen
- Must deadhead
- Prone to mildew

Osteospermum caulescens (= 'White Pim') A.G.M. (Asteraceae)

Common name: None
Height: 4in (10cm)
Spread: 2ft (60cm)
Aspect: Full sun
Soil: Well-drained, humus-rich
Hardiness: Zone 8
Propagation: Seed in heat in spring
Flowering time: Late spring through to autumn

A prostrate, evergreen subshrub. Flowers daisy-like, solitary, white, with gray centers. Deadheading is all the pruning that is required.

- Evergreen
- High allergen
- Must deadhead

SHRUBS 287

Osteospermum 'Nairobi Purple'
(Asteraceae)

Common name: None
Height: 6in (15cm)
Spread: 3ft (90cm)
Aspect: Full sun
Soil: Well-drained, humus-rich
Hardiness: Zone 8
Propagation: Softwood cuttings in spring; semi-ripe cuttings in summer
Flowering time: Late spring through to autumn

A sprawling, evergreen subshrub. Flowers daisy-like, solitary, single, purple, with black centers. Deadheading prolongs flowering. Usually treated as an annual.

- Evergreen
- High allergen
- Must deadhead

Osteospermum 'Whirligig' A.G.M.
(Asteraceae)

Common name: None
Height: 2ft (60cm)
Spread: 2ft (60cm)
Aspect: Full sun
Soil: Well-drained, humus-rich
Hardiness: Zone 8
Propagation: Softwood cuttings in spring; semi-ripe cuttings in summer
Flowering time: Late spring to autumn

A sprawling, evergreen subshrub. Flowers single, solitary daisies, with crimped ray florets of purple or white, and dark blue centers. Deadheading prolongs flowering.

- Good cut flower
- Evergreen
- High allergen
- Must deadhead

Pachystachys lutea A.G.M.
(Acanthaceae)

Common name: None
Height: 3ft (90cm)
Spread: 30in (75cm)
Aspect: Full sun
Soil: Moist, well-drained, fertile
Hardiness: Zone 10
Propagation: Softwood cuttings with bottom heat, in summer
Flowering time: Spring and summer

An erect, evergreen shrub. Flowers tubular, 2-lipped, white, with yellow bracts, in long, terminal spikes. Deadhead, and prune for shape when flowering has finished.

- Evergreen

Penstemon isophyllus A.G.M. (Scrophulariaceae)

Common name: None
Height: 28in (70cm)
Spread: 18in (45cm)
Aspect: Sun or part shade
Soil: Well-drained, fertile
Hardiness: Zone 9
Propagation: Seed or division in spring
Flowering time: Early to late summer

An evergreen subshrub. Leaves purple-tinged. Flowers tubular, red in color, open in one-sided racemes.

- Evergreen
- Handsome foliage
- Low allergen
- Attracts slugs
- Must deadhead
- Prone to mildew

Pentas lanceolata (Rubiaceae)

Common name: None
Height: 6ft (1.8m)
Spread: 3ft (90cm)
Aspect: Full sun
Soil: Well-drained, fertile
Hardiness: Zone 10
Propagation: Seed in heat in spring; softwood cuttings at any time
Flowering time: Spring to autumn

An evergreen subshrub. Leaves hairy, glossy-green. Flowers open in domed corymbs, long-tubed, pink, white, blue, or lilac. Prune in spring by deadheading and remove wayward shoots to keep to the required size and preserve symmetry.

- Evergreen
- Handsome foliage

***Pericallis lanata* 'Kew' form
(Asteraceae)**

Common name: None
Height: 3ft (90cm)
Spread: 1ft (30cm)
Aspect: Sun (but not midday), or part shade
Soil: Well-drained, fertile
Hardiness: Zone 9
Propagation: Seed in heat in spring or summer; semi-ripe cuttings in summer
Flowering time: Winter through to late summer

A subshrub originating from Tenerife. Leaves 5–7-lobed, mid-green in color. Scented flowers, solitary or in corymbs, daisy-like, ray florets mauve, disc florets purple.

• Scented flowers

PHILADELPHUS 'BELLE ETOILE' A.G.M.

Perovskia 'Blue Spire' A.G.M.
(Lamiaceae)

Common name: None
Height: 4ft (1.2m)
Spread: 3ft (1m)
Aspect: Sun
Soil: Well-drained, fertile
Hardiness: Zone 6
Propagation: Softwood cuttings in spring; semi-ripe cuttings in summer.
Flowering time: Late summer and early autumn

A deciduous subshrub. Leaves aromatic, silver-gray. Flowers tubular, violet-blue in color, borne in panicles, from late summer through to early autumn. Prune by cutting back to a low, permanent framework, annually, in spring.

- Handsome foliage
- Drought-tolerant
- Aromatic foliage

Philadelphus 'Belle Etoile' A.G.M.
(Hydrangeaceae)

Common name: Mock orange
Height: 4ft (1.2m)
Spread: 8ft (2.5m)
Aspect: Sun or part shade
Soil: Well-drained
Hardiness: Zone 5
Propagation: Softwood cuttings in summer; hardwood cuttings in autumn
Flowering time: Late spring to early summer

A large, deciduous shrub. Flowers pineapple-scented, cup-shaped, white, with pale purple centers, in racemes from late spring. Prune back annually after flowering to basal or lower strong buds. Requires space; not suitable for the small garden.

- Scented flowers
- Prone to mildew
- High allergen

Philadelphus 'Voie Lactee'
(**Hydrangeaceae**)

Common name: Mock orange
Height: 8ft (2.5m)
Spread: 6ft (2m)
Aspect: Sun or part shade
Soil: Well-drained
Hardiness: Zone 5
Propagation: Softwood cuttings in summer; hardwood cuttings in autumn.
Flowering time: Late spring to early summer

A large, deciduous, arching shrub. Flowers highly scented, white, borne in racemes, from late spring onwards. Cut back annually after flowering to lower, or basal, strong buds. Requires space; not suitable for the small garden.

- Scented flowers
- Prone to mildew
- High allergen

Phlomis fruticosa A.G.M.
(**Lamiaceae**)

Common name: None
Height: 4ft (1.2m)
Spread: 5ft (1.5m)
Aspect: Sun
Soil: Well-drained, fertile
Hardiness: Zone 7
Propagation: Seed in heat, in spring; softwood cuttings in summer
Flowering time: Early through to midsummer

An evergreen subshrub. Leaves gray-green in color. Flowers deadnettle-like, yellow, in whorls. Prune annually after flowering by deadheading and to preserve shape and symmetry.

- Can be dried
- Drought-tolerant
- Evergreen
- Good cut flower
- Handsome foliage

PHYGELIUS AEQUALIS 'SENSATION' (PBR)

Phygelius aequalis
(Scrophulariaceae)

Common name: None
Height: 3ft (90cm)
Spread: 3ft (90cm)
Aspect: Sun
Soil: Moist, well-drained, fertile
Hardiness: Zone 8
Propagation: Suckers, soft woodcuttings, or seed, all taken in spring
Flowering time: Throughout the summer

A half-hardy, evergreen shrub. Flowers long tubular, pendent, pink with yellow throats, in panicles. Prune in spring by cutting back hard or by deadheading and for shape.

- Evergreen
- Invasive

Phygelius aequalis 'Sensation' (PBR)
(Scrophulariaceae)

Common name: None
Height: 4ft (1.2m)
Spread: 3ft (90cm)
Aspect: Sun
Soil: Moist, well-drained, fertile
Hardiness: Zone 8
Propagation: Separate suckers, or softwood cuttings, in spring
Flowering time: Summer through to autumn

A half-hardy, evergreen subshrub. Flowers long, tubular, cerise in color, borne in panicles throughout summer period. Prune in spring by cutting back hard, or by deadheading, as required.

- Evergreen
- Invasive

Phygelius aequalis 'Yellow Trumpet' A.G.M. (Scrophulariaceae)

Common name: None
Height: 4ft (1.2m)
Spread: 3ft (90cm)
Aspect: Sun
Soil: Moist, well-drained, fertile
Hardiness: Zone 8
Propagation: Separate suckers, or softwood cuttings, in spring
Flowering time: All summer

A half-hardy, evergreen, suckering subshrub. Flowers long, tubular, yellow, in panicles. Prune in spring, by cutting back hard, or by deadheading and pruning for shape or symmetry.

- 🟢 Evergreen
- 🔴 Invasive

Phygelius x *rectus* (Scrophulariaceae)

Common name: None
Height: 4ft (1.2m)
Spread: 4ft (1.2m)
Aspect: Sun
Soil: Moist, well-drained, fertile
Hardiness: Zone 8
Propagation: Separate suckers, or take softwood cuttings in spring
Flowering time: Most of the summer

An evergreen, suckering, subshrub. Flowers long, tubular, pale red in color, borne in panicles. Prune in spring either by cutting back hard, or by deadheading, as required.

- 🟢 Evergreen
- 🔴 Invasive

Phygelius x *rectus* 'Moonraker' (Scrophulariaceae)

Common name: None
Height: 5ft (1.5m)
Spread: 5ft (1.5m)
Aspect: Sun
Soil: Moist, well-drained, fertile
Hardiness: Zone 8
Propagation: Separate suckers, or take softwood cuttings, in spring
Flowering time: Throughout the summer

An evergreen, suckering subshrub. Flowers long, tubular, creamy-yellow in color, borne in panicles. Prune in spring by cutting back hard, or deadheading and pruning for shape or symmetry.

- 🟢 Evergreen
- 🔴 Invasive
- 🔴 Requires space

Pieris formosa (Ericaceae)

Common name: None
Height: 15ft (5m)
Spread: 12ft (4m)
Aspect: Sun or part shade
Soil: Acid, moist, well-drained, humus-rich
Hardiness: Zone 6
Propagation: Seed in spring; softwood, or semi-ripe cuttings, with bottom heat, in summer
Flowering time: Mid- to late spring

A large evergreen shrub. Leaves glossy-green. Flowers white-colored, small, urn-shaped, borne in pendent or semi-erect panicles, opening from mid- to late spring. Prune only to deadhead or to maintain symmetry, in autumn. Requires space; notsuitable for the small garden.

- Evergreen
- Low allergen
- Handsome foliage
- Poisonous

Plumbago auriculata A.G.M. (Plumbaginaceae)

Common name: None
Height: 20ft (6m)
Spread: 10ft (3m)
Aspect: Full sun
Soil: Well-drained, fertile
Hardiness: Zone 9
Propagation: Seed in heat in spring; take semi-ripe cuttings with bottom heat in summer
Flowering time: Summer through to late autumn

A large, evergreen, climbing shrub. Flowers long-tubed, sky blue, in dense racemes. Prune in early spring by cutting back to within 3 or 4 buds of permanent framework.

- Evergreen
- Requires space

Plumeria alba (Apocynaceae)

Common name: None
Height: 20ft (6m)
Spread: 12ft (4m)
Aspect: Full sun
Soil: Well-drained, fertile
Hardiness: Zone 10
Propagation: Seed in heat or take ripe cuttings of leafless stem tips in spring
Flowering time: Summer through to autumn

A large, deciduous shrub. Flowers salverform, white, with yellow eyes. Pruning is minimal, except to maintain shape and size.

- Scented flowers
- Poisonous
- Requires space

Plumeria rubra (Apocynaceae)

Common name: None
Height: 22ft (7m)
Spread: 15ft (4.5m)
Aspect: Full sun
Soil: Well-drained, fertile
Hardiness: Zone 10
Propagation: Seed in heat, or ripe cuttings of leafless stem tips, in spring
Flowering time: Summer through to late autumn

A large, deciduous shrub. Flowers salverform, rose-pink, with yellow eyes. Minimal pruning required, except for shape and size. Superb specimen plant for the garden.

- Scented flowers
- Poisonous
- Requires space

POTENTILLA FRUTICOSA 'GOLDFINGER' A.G.M.

Polygala myrtifolia (Polygalaceae)

Common name: None
Height: 8ft (2.5m)
Spread: 6ft (1.8m)
Aspect: Sun or part shade
Soil: Sharply-drained, humus-rich, fertile
Hardiness: Zone 9
Propagation: Seed in heat in spring
Flowering time: Spring through to autumn, or even longer in some regions

A large, evergreen shrub. Flowers pink-purple, in short, terminal racemes. Pruning is minimal: deadhead, and cut out shoots which spoil symmetry. Not suitable for the small garden.

- Evergreen
- Requires space

Potentilla fruticosa 'Abbotswood' A.G.M. (Rosaceae)

Common name: Bush cinquefoil
Height: 3ft (90cm)
Spread: 5ft (1.5m)
Aspect: Sun
Soil: Well-drained
Hardiness: Zone 2
Propagation: Greenwood cuttings in early summer
Flowering time: Late spring to autumn

A hardy, deciduous shrub. Leaves dark green. Flowers flat, white, in cymes. Prune in spring by cutting back flowered shoots to within 1in (2.5cm) of previous year's growth.

- Attracts bees
- Requires space
- Low allergen

Potentilla fruticosa 'Goldfinger' A.G.M. (Rosaceae)

Common name: Bush cinquefoil
Height: 4ft (1.2m)
Spread: 4ft (1.2m)
Aspect: Sun
Soil: Well-drained
Hardiness: Zone 2
Propagation: Greenwood cuttings in early summer
Flowering time: Late spring to autumn

A hardy, deciduous shrub. Flowers flat, rich yellow in color, in cymes. Prune in spring by cutting back flowered shoots to within 1in (2.5cm) of previous year's growth.

- Attracts bees
- Low allergen

Potentilla fruticosa 'Pretty Polly' (Rosaceae)

Common name: Bush cinquefoil
Height: 20in (50cm)
Spread: 30in (75cm)
Aspect: Sun
Soil: Well-drained
Hardiness: Zone 2
Propagation: Greenwood cuttings in early summer
Flowering time: Late spring to mid-autumn

A dwarf, hardy, deciduous shrub. Flowers flat, pale pink, in cymes. Prune in spring by cutting back flowered shoots to within 1in (2.5cm) of previous year's growth.

- Attracts bees
- Low allergen

Punica granatum flore plena A.G.M. (Punicaceae)

Common name: None
Height: 20ft (6m)
Spread: 15ft (4.5m)
Aspect: Full sun
Soil: Well-drained, fertile
Hardiness: Zone 9
Propagation: Seed in heat in spring; semi-ripe cuttings, with bottom heat, in summer
Flowering time: All summer

A deciduous shrub. Leaves glossy-green. Flowers double, orange-red, followed by fruits. Prune (if wall-trained) by cutting back to within 2–4 buds of permanent framework; if not, prune wayward shoots after flowering.

- Handsome foliage
- Requires space

Rhodanthemum hosmariense A.G.M. (Asteraceae)

Common name: None
Height: 1ft (30cm)
Spread: 1ft (30cm)
Aspect: Sun
Soil: Sharply-drained, fertile
Hardiness: Zone 8
Propagation: Seed in spring; softwood cuttings in early summer
Flowering time: Early spring to autumn; all year in warmth

A sprawling subshrub. Leaves intensely silver. Flowers daisy-like, single, solitary, white, with yellow centers and silver bracts.

- Drought-tolerant
- High allergen
- Handsome foliage

Romneya coulteri **A.G.M.**
(Papaveraceae)

Common name: Matilija-poppy
Height: 8ft (2.5m)
Spread: Indefinite
Aspect: Full sun
Soil: Well-drained, fertile
Hardiness: Zone 7
Propagation: Seed when ripe; division in spring

Flowering time: Long period throughout summer

A tall, invasive, deciduous subshrub. Leaves glaucous gray-green. Flowers solitary, scented, large single cups, white with yellow centers.

- Handsome foliage
- Scented flowers
- Invasive
- Requires space
- Requires staking

ROSA (Rosaceae)
Rose

A genus of about 150 species of deciduous shrubs and climbers. They can be subdivided into old-fashioned and modern categories, and the members of the latter group can be either long-flowering or repeat-flowering (remontant). Roses prefer a position in sun, but will tolerate some shade. They prefer soil to be moist but well-drained, and rich in humus. It is not advisable to dig up old plants and replace them with new stock without first digging out the old soil and replacing it with fresh.

Roses are best planted during winter or early spring. Most roses have been grafted onto wild rose rootstock, and it is important not to bury the grafted area, as suckers are then more likely to appear: these are shoots from the rootstock and must be cut out. Many modern roses are registered by trademark, and/or protected by Plant Breeders Rights, and such varieties are indicated by ®, ™ or (PBR) in the following text.

Roses are prone to a battery of diseases, pests, insects, and ruminants, and the reader is referred to specialist texts for details of these, and their prevention and cure.

Rosa 'Ballerina' A.G.M.

Common name: None
Height: 5ft (1.5m)
Spread: 4ft (1.2m)
Aspect: Sun
Soil: Moist, well-drained, humus-rich, fertile
Hardiness: Zone 6
Propagation: Bud in summer; hardwood cuttings in autumn
Flowering time: Summer to autumn

A modern polyantha shrub rose. Flowers single, pale pink, with white centers, in large rounded clusters. Prune in late summer by cutting back to up to a third, as required.

- Good cut flower
- Prone to mildew

Rosa banksiae 'Lutea' A.G.M.

Common name: Banks rose
Height: 40ft (12m)
Spread: 20ft (6m)
Aspect: Sun
Soil: Moist, well-drained, humus-rich, fertile
Hardiness: Zone 6
Propagation: Bud in summer; hardwood cuttings in autumn
Flowering time: Late spring and through to early summer

A climbing, banksian species rose. Scented flowers, double, yellow, in clusters. In first 2 years, cut out dead wood and side shoots. After that, cut out a third of flowered stems at base after flowering.

- Good cut flower
- Low allergen
- Scented flowers
- Prone to mildew
- Requires space

Rosa 'Blue Moon'®

Common name: None
Height: 3ft (90cm)
Spread: 28in (70cm)
Aspect: Sun
Soil: Moist, well-drained, humus-rich, fertile
Hardiness: Zone 7
Propagation: Bud in summer; hardwood cuttings in autumn
Flowering time: Summer to autumn

A large-flowered, modern bush (hybrid tea) rose. Flowers scented, double, lilac-mauve. Prune in late winter or early spring by cutting back main stems to within about 10in (25cm) of the ground.

- Good cut flower
- Low allergen
- Scented flowers
- Prone to mildew

Rosa 'Charles de Mills' A.G.M.

Common name: None
Height: 5ft (1.5m)
Spread: 5ft (1.5m)
Aspect: Sun
Soil: Moist, well-drained, humus-rich, fertile
Hardiness: Zone 5
Propagation: Bud in summer; hardwood cuttings in autumn
Flowering time: All summer

An old-fashioned, thornless, Gallica rose. Flowers scented, fully double, magenta. Prune in late summer by cutting back main stems by a third, and side shoots by two-thirds.

- Good cut flower
- Low allergen
- Scented flowers
- Needs space
- Prone to mildew

Rosa 'Compassion'® A.G.M.

Common name: None
Height: 10ft (3m)
Spread: 8ft (2.5m)
Aspect: Sun
Soil: Moist, well-drained, humus-rich, fertile
Hardiness: Zone 7
Propagation: Bud in summer
Flowering time: Summer to autumn

A modern climbing rose with double, scented, salmon-pink flowers. Prune in first 2 years only to cut out dead wood; thereafter, cut main stems back in winter or early spring to desired height, and side shoots by two-thirds.

- Good cut flower
- Low allergen
- Scented flowers
- Needs space
- Prone to mildew

Rosa 'De Rescht' A.G.M.

Common name: None
Height: 4ft (1.2m)
Spread: 3ft (90cm)
Aspect: Sun
Soil: Moist, well-drained, humus-rich, fertile
Hardiness: Zone 5
Propagation: Bud in summer
Flowering time: Throughout the summer

An old, Damask Portland rose. Flowers double, deep purple-pink in color. Prune main stems back lightly, or by up to one third, just after flowering has finished.

- Good cut flower
- Low allergen
- Scented flowers
- Prone to mildew

Rosa 'Double Delight'®

Common name: None
Height: 3ft (90cm)
Spread: 2ft (60cm)
Aspect: Sun
Soil: Moist, well-drained, humus-rich, fertile
Hardiness: Zone 7
Propagation: Bud in summer
Flowering time: Summer to autumn

A modern, large-flowered bush (hybrid tea) rose. Flowers double, scented, pale pink, margined red. Prune in late winter/early spring by cutting back main stems to within 10in (25cm) of the ground.

- Good cut flower
- Low allergen
- Scented flowers
- Prone to mildew

Rosa 'Elina' A.G.M.® (PBR)

Common name: None
Height: 4ft (1.2m)
Spread: 30in (75cm)
Aspect: Sun
Soil: Moist, well-drained, humus-rich, fertile
Hardiness: Zone 7
Propagation: Bud in summer
Flowering time: Summer to autumn

A modern, large-flowered bush (hybrid tea) rose. Flowers scented, double, ivory-colored, with lemon centers. Prune in late winter/early spring by cutting back main stems to within 10in (25cm) of the ground.

- Good cut flower
- Low allergen
- Scented flowers
- Prone to mildew

Rosa 'Ena Harkness'

Common name: None
Height: 15ft (4.5m)
Spread: 3ft (90cm)
Aspect: Sun
Soil: Moist, well-drained, humus-rich, fertile
Hardiness: Zone 7
Propagation: Bud in summer
Flowering time: Summer to autumn

A vigorous climbing rose with scented, double, pendent, crimson-colored flowers. In the first 2 years, cut out any dead wood; thereafter, prune the main shoots back to the desired height, and the side shoots by about two-thirds.

- Good cut flower
- Low allergen
- Scented flowers
- Prone to mildew

Rosa 'Flower Carpet' A.G.M. (PBR)

Rosa 'Flower Carpet' A.G.M. (PBR)

Common name: None
Height: 30in (75cm)
Spread: 4ft (1.2m)
Aspect: Sun
Soil: Moist, well-drained, humus-rich, fertile
Hardiness: Zone 4
Propagation: Bud in summer
Flowering time: Summer through to autumn

A robust, ground-cover rose. Flowers double, dark rose-pink, in clusters, borne freely. Prune in late winter/spring by cutting back to outward-facing buds at levels to suit size requirements of garden and situation.

• Low allergen   • Prone to mildew

Rosa 'Fragrant Cloud'

Common name: None
Height: 30in (75cm)
Spread: 2ft (60cm)
Aspect: Sun
Soil: Moist, well-drained, humus-rich fertile
Hardiness: Zone 7
Propagation: Bud in summer
Flowering time: Summer to autumn

A compact, large-flowered (hybrid tea) bush rose. Flowers double, highly-scented, dusky scarlet. Prune in late winter/early spring by cutting back to within 10in (25cm) of the ground.

- Good cut flower
- Prone to mildew
- Low allergen
- Scented flowers

Rosa 'Fred Loads' A.G.M.

Common name: None
Height: 6ft (1.8m)
Spread: 3ft (90cm)
Aspect: Sun
Soil: Moist, well-drained, humus-rich, fertile
Hardiness: Zone 7
Propagation: Bud in summer
Flowering time: Summer to autumn

A robust, cluster-flowered, polyantha bush rose. Flowers vermilion-orange in color, in many-flowered clusters. Prune in late winter/early spring by cutting back to within 10in (25cm) of the ground.

- Good cut flower
- Prone to mildew
- Low allergen

Rosa 'Fulton Mackay' (PBR)

Common name: None
Height: 30in (75cm)
Spread: 2ft (60cm)
Aspect: Sun
Soil: Moist, well-drained, humus-rich, fertile
Hardiness: Zone 7
Propagation: Bud in summer
Flowering time: Summer through to autumn

A compact, large-flowered (hybrid tea) bush rose. Flowers double, scented, apricot, flushed pink. Prune in late winter/early spring by cutting back to within 10in (25cm) of the ground.

- Good cut flower
- Prone to mildew
- Low allergen
- Scented flowers

Rosa 'Golden Wedding' (PBR)

Common name: None
Height: 3ft (90cm)
Spread: 2ft (60cm)
Aspect: Sun
Soil: Moist, well-drained, humus-rich, fertile
Hardiness: Zone 5
Propagation: Bud in summer
Flowering time: Summer to autumn

A large-flowered, bush (hybrid tea) rose. Flowers double, yellow. Prune in spring by cutting back to within 10in (25cm) of the ground.

- Good cut flower
- Prone to mildew
- Low allergen

Rosa 'Gertrude Jekyll' A.G.M. ® (PBR)

Common name: None
Height: 4ft (1.2m)
Spread: 3ft (90cm)
Aspect: Sun
Soil: Moist, well-drained, humus-rich, fertile
Hardiness: Zone 7
Propagation: Bud in summer
Flowering time: Summer through to autumn

A large-flowered shrub rose. Flowers scented, double, pink. Prune back main stems by up to a third, and side shoots by two-thirds or as required, after flowering.

- Good cut flower
- Prone to mildew
- Low allergen
- Scented flowers

ROSA 'GORDON'S COLLEGE' (PBR)

Rosa 'Gordon's College' (PBR)

Common name: None
Height: 3ft (90cm)
Spread: 2ft (60cm)
Aspect: Sun
Soil: Moist, well-drained, humus-rich, fertile
Hardiness: Zone 5
Propagation: Bud in summer
Flowering time: Summer to autumn

A large-flowered floribunda rose. Flowers rich pink in color. Very disease-resistant. Prune in spring by cutting back to within about 10in (25cm) of the ground.

- Good cut flower
- Low allergen

Rosa 'Happy Times' (Rosaceae)

Common name: None
Height: 1ft (30cm)
Spread: 1ft (30cm)
Aspect: Sun
Soil: Moist, well-drained, humus-rich, fertile
Hardiness: Zone 5
Propagation: Bud in summer
Flowering time: Summer to autumn

A dwarf, miniature, bush rose. Flowers rich pink, in clusters. Prune by cutting back main stems by up to a third, and side stems by two-thirds, after flowering.

- Good cut flower
- Prone to mildew
- Low allergen

Rosa 'Joseph's Coat' (Rosaceae)

Common name: None
Height: 4ft (1.2m)
Spread: 3ft (90cm)
Aspect: Sun
Soil: Moist, well-drained, fertile
Hardiness: Zone 4
Propagation: Bud in summer
Flowering time: Summer through to autumn

A robust shrub or climbing rose. Flowers double, yellow in color suffused with pink, in clusters. Prune main stems by up to a third, and side stems by up to two-thirds, when flowering has finished.

- Good cut flower
- Prone to mildew
- Low allergen

Rosa 'Lady MacRobert'

Common name: None
Height: 4ft (1.2m)
Spread: 3ft (90cm)
Aspect: Sun
Soil: Moist, well-drained, humus-rich, fertile
Hardiness: Zone 4
Propagation: Bud in summer
Flowering time: Summer to autumn

A cluster-flowered (floribunda) bush rose Flowers double, pink, with cream centers. Prune in late winter or early spring by cutting back to within 10in (25cm) of the ground.

- Good cut flower
- Prone to mildew
- Low allergen

Rosa 'Lavender Lassie' A.G.M.

Common name: None
Height: 4ft (1.2m)
Spread: 3ft (90cm)
Aspect: Sun
Soil: Moist, well-drained, humus-rich, fertile
Hardiness: Zone 5
Propagation: Bud in summer
Flowering time: Summer to autumn

A hybrid musk rose. Flowers double, medium-sized, pink, in clusters. Prune in spring by cutting back to within 10in (25cm) of the ground.

- Good cut flower
- Prone to mildew
- Low allergen
- Scented flowers

ROSA 'ORANGES AND LEMONS' (PBR)

Rosa 'Mme. Isaac Pereire' A.G.M.

Common name: None
Height: 7ft (2m)
Spread: 6ft (1.8m)
Aspect: Sun
Soil: Moist, well-drained, humus-rich, fertile
Hardiness: Zone 7
Propagation: Bud in summer
Flowering time: Summer to autumn

A robust, bourbon shrub or climbing rose. Flowers double, scented, deep pink. Prune in late winter/early spring by cutting back main stems by a third, and side shoots by two-thirds.

- Good cut flower
- Low allergen
- Scented flowers
- Prone to mildew
- Requires space

Rosa 'National Trust'

Common name: None
Height: 2ft (60cm)
Spread: 2ft (60cm)
Aspect: Sun
Soil: Moist, well-drained, humus-rich, fertile
Hardiness: Zone 7
Propagation: Bud in summer
Flowering time: Summer to autumn

A dwarf, large-flowered bush (hybrid tea) rose. Flowers double, scarlet, borne freely. Prune back up to within 10in (25cm) of the ground in late winter or early spring.

- Good cut flower
- Low allergen
- Prone to mildew

Rosa 'Oranges and Lemons' (PBR)

Common name: None
Height: 32in (80cm)
Spread: 2ft (60cm)
Aspect: Sun
Soil: Moist, well-drained, fertile, humus-rich
Hardiness: Zone 6
Propagation: Bud in summer
Flowering time: Summer to autumn

A robust, cluster-flowered (floribunda) bush rose. Flowers double, orange, striped scarlet, fading to pinkish-red. Prune in late winter to early spring by cutting back to within 18in (45cm) of the ground.

- Good cut flower
- Prone to mildew

SHRUBS

Rosa 'Paul Ricault'

Common name: None
Height: 5ft (1.5m)
Spread: 4ft (1.2m)
Aspect: Sun
Soil: Moist, well-drained, humus-rich, fertile
Hardiness: Zone 7
Propagation: Bud in summer
Flowering time: Summer to autumn

A hybrid perpetual rose; habit arching and lax. Flowers double, scented, deep pink in color. Prune back in late winter/early spring to within 10in (25cm) of the ground.

- Good cut flower
- Low allergen
- Scented flowers
- Prone to mildew

Rosa 'Pink Grootendorst' A.G.M.

Common name: None
Height: 5ft (1.5m)
Spread: 3ft (90cm)
Aspect: Sun
Soil: Moist, well-drained, humus-rich, fertile
Hardiness: Zone 3
Propagation: Bud in summer
Flowering time: Summer to autumn

An upright, dense, Rugosa rose. Flowers double, rose-pink in color, borne in crowded clusters of blooms. Prune main shoots by cutting back, when flowering has finished, by up to one-third, and side shoots by up to two-thirds.

- Good cut flower
- Prone to mildew
- Low allergen

Rosa 'Queen Mother' A.G.M. (PBR)

Common name: None
Height: 16in (40cm)
Spread: 2ft (60cm)
Aspect: Sun
Soil: Moist, well-drained, fertile, humus-rich
Hardiness: Zone 6
Propagation: Bud in summer
Flowering time: Summer to autumn

A dwarf, cluster-flowered (floribunda) bush patio rose. Flowers flat, clear pink. Prune in late winter to early spring by cutting back main stems and side shoots by up to a half.

- Good cut flower
- Prone to mildew
- Low allergen

Rosa 'Samaritan' (PBR)

Common name: None
Height: 28in (70cm)
Spread: 2ft (60cm)
Aspect: Sun
Soil: Moist, well-drained, humus-rich, fertile
Hardiness: Zone 7
Propagation: Bud in summer
Flowering time: Summer to autumn

A large-flowered bush (hybrid tea) rose. Flowers double, scented, pink, ageing to red, in wide sprays. Prune in early spring by cutting back to within 10in (25cm) of the ground.

- Good cut flower
- Prone to mildew
- Low allergen
- Scented flowers

Rosa 'Warm Wishes' (PBR)

Common name: None
Height: 3ft (90cm)
Spread: 2ft (60cm)
Aspect: Sun
Soil: Moist, well-drained, humus-rich, fertile
Hardiness: Zone 5
Propagation: Bud in summer
Flowering time: Summer to autumn

A large-flowered bush (hybrid rea) rose. Flowers double, scented, peach-pink in color. Prune in spring by cutting back to within 10in (25cm) of the ground.

- Good cut flower
- Prone to mildew
- Low allergen
- Scented flowers

Rosa 'William Quarrier' (PBR)

Rosa 'William Quarrier' (PBR)

Common name: None
Height: 3ft (90cm)
Spread: 2ft (60cm)
Aspect: Sun
Soil: Moist, well-drained, humus-rich, fertile
Hardiness: Zone 6
Propagation: Bud in summer
Flowering time: Summer to autumn

A cluster-flowered (polyantha) bush rose. Flowers large, peach-colored, borne in clusters. Prune in late winter to early spring by cutting back to within 10in (25cm) of the ground.

- Good cut flower
- Low allergen
- Prone to mildew

Santolina rosmarinifolia (Asteraceae)

Common name: Cotton lavender
Height: 20in (50cm)
Spread: 3ft (1m)
Aspect: Sun
Soil: Well-drained, fertile
Hardiness: Zone 7
Propagation: Seed in autumn or spring
Flowering time: Summer

A shrub with aromatic, green leaves. Flowers solitary, bright yellow, on long stems. Prune in spring by cutting back flowered shoots to within 1in (2.5cm) of previous year's growth.

- Evergreen
- Drought tolerant
- High allergen

Senecio cineraria (Asteraceae)

Common name: Silver groundsel
Height: 2ft (60cm)
Spread: 2ft (60cm)
Aspect: Sun
Soil: Sharply-drained
Hardiness: Zone 8
Propagation: Seed in spring
Flowering time: Midsummer

An evergreen subshrub, grown usually as a foliage plant by pinching out the flower buds. Flowers yellow, daisy-like, in flat corymbs. Prune only to deadhead and maintain symmetry.

- Evergreen
- Drought tolerant
- Good cut flower
- Seeds everywhere
- Poisonous
- High allergen

Senecio vira-vira A.G.M. (Asteraceae)

Common name: None
Height: 2ft (60cm)
Spread: 3ft (90cm)
Aspect: Sun
Soil: Sharply-drained, fertile
Hardiness: Zone 6
Propagation: Seed in spring; semi-ripe cuttings in summer
Flowering time: Summer to autumn

An evergreen subshrub. Leaves ferny, gray-green. Flowers composed only of disc florets, off-white, in loose corymbs. Prune by deadheading, and to maintain shape.

- Attracts bees
- Evergreen
- Handsome foliage
- High allergen
- Poisonous

Senna didymobotrya
(Caesalpiniaceae)

Common name: None
Height: 8ft (2.5m)
Spread: 10ft (3m)
Aspect: Sun
Soil: Moist, well-drained
Hardiness: Zone 10
Propagation: Seed in heat in spring
Flowering time: Late summer through to mid-autumn

An upright or spreading evergreen shrub. Flowers golden yellow in color, borne in tall upright racemes topped by buds covered by black bracts, opening from late summer onwards. Prune minimally; cut out wayward shoots to maintain shape and symmetry. Not suitable for the small garden.

- Evergreen
- Requires space

Solanum laciniatum (Solanaceae)

Common name: None
Height: 6ft (1.8m)
Spread: 5ft (1.5m)
Aspect: Sun
Soil: Alkaline, moist, well-drained, fertile
Hardiness: Zone 9
Propagation: Semi-ripe cuttings with bottom heat in summer
Flowering time: Summer through to autumn

A robust, evergreen shrub. Leaves pinnatisect, mid-green. Flowers dark blue, in axillary cymes. Prune by deadheading, and cutting back shoots that spoil symmetry, in spring.

- Evergreen
- Poisonous
- Handsome foliage
- Requires space

Solanum rantonnetti (Solanaceae)

Common name: Paraguay nightshade
Height: 6ft (1.8m)
Spread: 6ft (1.8m)
Aspect: Sun
Soil: Alkaline, moist, well-drained, fertile
Hardiness: Zone 9
Propagation: Semi-ripe cuttings with bottom heat in summer
Flowering time: Summer to mid-autumn

An evergreen shrub. Leaves shiny green. Flowers violet-blue saucers, in axillary clusters. Prune in spring by deadheading and cutting out shoots that spoil symmetry.

- Evergreen
- Poisonous
- Handsome foliage
- Requires space

Spiraea japonica 'Goldflame' A.G.M. (Rosaceae)

Common name: Japanese spirea
Height: 30in (75cm)
Spread: 30in (75cm)
Aspect: Sun
Soil: Moist, well-drained, fertile
Hardiness: Zone 5
Propagation: Greenwood cuttings in summer
Flowering time: Mid- and late summer

A deciduous shrub. Leaves yellow, turning green. Flowers bowl-shaped, pink, in terminal corymbs. Prune annually, after flowering, by cutting back 25 percent of shoots to the base.

- Low allergen

TWEEDIA CAERULEA A.G.M.

Spiraea japonica 'Shirobana' A.G.M. (Rosaceae)

Common name: Japanese spirea
Height: 2ft (60cm)
Spread: 2ft (60cm)
Aspect: Sun
Soil: Moist, well-drained, fertile
Hardiness: Zone 5
Propagation: Greenwood cuttings in summer
Flowering time: Mid- through to late summer

A compact deciduous shrub. Flowers bowl-shaped, colored pink and white at the same time, borne in terminal corymbs. Prune annually when flowering has finished by cutting back 25percent of stems to the base.

● Low allergen

Streptosolen jamesonii A.G.M. (Solanaceae)

Common name: Orange streptosolen
Height: 10ft (3m)
Spread: 8ft (2.5m)
Aspect: Sun
Soil: Moist, well-drained, fertile
Hardiness: Zone 9
Propagation: Softwood cuttings, with bottom heat in early summer
Flowering time: Late spring through to late summer

A large evergreen, semi-scandent shrub. Flowers tubular, orange-yellow, in large terminal corymbs. Deadhead after flowering, and prune in spring for size and shape. Not suitable for small gardens

● Evergreen   ● Requires space

Tweedia caerulea A.G.M. (Asclepiadaceae)

Common name: None
Height: 3ft (90cm)
Spread: 8in (20cm)
Aspect: Sun
Soil: Moist, well-drained, fertile
Hardiness: Zone 10
Propagation: Seed in spring; softwood cuttings in summer
Flowering time: Summer to autumn

An erect, twining, evergreen subshrub. Flowers sky-blue, ageing to purple, in few-flowered cymes. Prune in spring by cutting back flowered shoots to within 2–4 buds of permanent framework.

● Good cut flower

SHRUBS

***Verbascum* 'Letitia' A.G.M.**
(Scrophulariaceae)

Common name: None
Height: 10in (25cm)
Spread: 1ft (30cm)
Aspect: Sun
Soil: Sharply-drained poor
Hardiness: Zone 7
Propagation: Division in spring; root cuttings in winter
Flowering time: Summer to autumn

A dwarf, evergreen subshrub. Leaves gray-green. Flowers flat, yellow, with reddish centers, in short racemes.

- Attracts bees
- Drought-tolerant
- Evergreen
- Handsome foliage
- Prone to mildew

Viburnum tinus (Caprifoliaceae)

Common name: Laurestinus viburnum
Height: 10ft (3m)
Spread: 10ft (3m)
Aspect: Sun or part shade
Soil: Moist, well-drained, fertile
Hardiness: Zone 7
Propagation: Semi-ripe cuttings in summer
Flowering time: Late winter and early spring

An evergreen shrub. Flowers small, salveriform, white, in flattened, terminal cymes. Minimal pruning required, but will tolerate being cut hard back if required.

- Evergreen
- Poisonous
- Requires space

***Vinca major* 'Variegata' A.G.M.**
(Apocynaceae)

Common name: Big periwinkle
Height: 18in (45cm)
Spread: Indefinite
Aspect: Sun or part shade
Soil: Humus-rich, moisture-retentive
Hardiness: Zone 7
Propagation: Division between autumn and spring
Flowering time: Spring to summer

A prostrate evergreen shrub, but which can be tied into an upright position. Foliage green, margined cream. Flowers star-shaped, lilac-blue. Can be cut back in early spring.

- Evergreen
- Handsome foliage
- Invasive
- Poisonous

**_Vinca minor_ 'Alba Variegata'
(Apocynaceae)**

Common name: Periwinkle, Myrtle
Height: 8in (20cm)
Spread: Indefinite
Aspect: Sun or part shade
Soil: Humus-rich, moisture-retentive
Hardiness: Zone 4
Propagation: Division from autumn to spring

Flowering time: Spring through to summer

A prostrate, evergreen shrub. Leaves margined cream. Flowers white. Can be cut back in early spring as hard as necessary to prevent spreading into unwanted areas.

- Evergreen
- Handsome foliage
- Invasive
- Poisonous

section three
Annuals

A plant that flowers, sets seed, and dies in a single season is termed an annual, whereas a plant that makes leaf in its first season, then flowers, sets seed, and dies in the second season is a biennial. Both are conventionally classified as hardy or half-hardy, and their culture is handled differently.

Hardy annuals can withstand frost and can be sown *in situ* in autumn. If treated like a biennial and sown in autumn for flowering the next season, annuals will flower much earlier and bloom much longer than if they are sown in early spring. Half-hardly annuals can only be sown when all danger of frost is past and, as a result, flowering will be comparatively late and short-lived. In order to ensure half-hardy annuals have a long flowering season, they must be sown in heat in late winter or early spring and planted out after the last frost.

The terms 'annual' and 'biennial' are sometimes erroneously assumed to be synonymous with 'bedding plant' but many tender perennials bloom in their first year from seed and are handled as if they were annuals. These three categories of plant are all grouped together as bedding plants, and can be grown in beds or borders exclusive to them; this method of display was common in Victorian times and is again popular today.

Many bedding plants require frequent deadheading if long flowering is to be attained, otherwise they will set seed and cease flowering. The Common snapdragon, *Antirrhinum majus*, is one popular bedding plant that must be deadheaded on a regular basis if it is to be kept flowering; on the other hand the Sultan snapweed, *Impatiens walleriana*, is an example of a plant that will remain flowering without.

Bedding plants are used extensively to cover gaps left by early-flowering plants in beds and borders, and are also the mainstay of containers and hanging baskets. They will continue to flower well into the winter, or if planted up with perennials they may flower all winter provided the containers are taken into a warm environment before the plants have been exposed to a first frost.

Ageratum houstonianum (**Asteraceae**)

Common name: None
Height: 18in (45cm)
Spread: 1ft (30cm)
Aspect: Full sun
Soil: Moist, well-drained
Hardiness: Zone 8
Propagation: Seed in heat in spring
Flowering time: Midsummer through to first frost

A compact, mound-forming annual. Leaves oval, downy, dull green. Flowers borne in panicles, of up to 40, blue, pink or white. Deadheading prolongs flowering.

- High allergen
- Must deadhead

Anchusa capensis (**Boraginaceae**)

Common name: None
Height: 7in (18cm)
Spread: 5in (12cm)
Aspect: Full sun
Soil: Well-drained, humus-rich
Hardiness: Zone 9
Propagation: Seed in heat in spring
Flowering time: Throughout the summer

An erect annual or biennial. Leaves narrow lance-shaped, rough, mid-green in color. Flowers open saucers, borne in panicles, bright blue with a white-colored throat.

- Attracts bees
- Low allergen

BRACHYCOME IBERIDIFOLIA

Argemone mexicana (**Papaveraceae**)

Common name: Mexican prickle-poppy
Height: 3ft (90cm)
Spread: 16in (40cm)
Aspect: Full sun
Soil: Sharply-drained, poor
Hardiness: Zone 8
Propagation: Seed in heat in early spring
Flowering time: Summer to autumn

A clump-forming annual from southern U.S.A. and Central America. Leaves elliptic, deeply-lobed, silver-veined, blue-green, very spiny. Flowers solitary, scented, poppy-like, yellow.

- Drought-tolerant
- Handsome foliage
- Must deadhead
- Seeds everywhere

Borago officinalis (**Boraginaceae**)

Common name: Common borage
Height: 2ft (60cm)
Spread: 18in (45cm)
Aspect: Sun or part shade
Soil: Well-drained
Hardiness: Zone 7
Propagation: Seed *in situ* in spring
Flowering time: Long period during summer

A strongly growing, branching annual with basal and stem leaves; the former are ovate, bristly, dull green, the latter are lance-shaped. The flowers are in branched cymes, star-shaped, 5-petaled, blue. Deadhead to prevent seeding.

- Prone to mildew
- Seeds everywhere

Brachycome iberidifolia (**Asteraceae**)

Common name: Swan River daisy
Height: 18in (45cm)
Spread: 15in (38cm)
Aspect: Full sun
Soil: Well-drained, fertile
Hardiness: Zone 8
Propagation: Seed in heat in spring
Flowering time: All summer

A spreading annual from Australia. Leaves pinnatisect, downy gray-green in color. Flowers are secented and may be white, purple, or blue.

- Drought-tolerant
- Scented flowers
- Attracts slugs
- Must deadhead

ANNUALS

Bracteantha bracteata Monstrosum group (Asteraceae)

Common name: None
Height: 5ft (1.5m)
Spread: 1ft (30cm)
Aspect: Full sun
Soil: Moist, well-drained
Hardiness: Zone 8
Propagation: Seed in heat in spring
Flowering time: Late spring to autumn

A perennial from Australia, grown universally as an annual. Leaves lance-shaped, gray-green. Flowers solitary, terminal, papery, in a color range of white, yellow, pink, or red.

- Can be dried
- High allergen
- Short-lived

Calceolaria Herbeohybrida group (Scrophulariaceae)

Common name: None
Height: 18in (45cm)
Spread: 1ft (30cm)
Aspect: Sun or part shade
Soil: Acid, gritty, fertile
Hardiness: Zone 9
Propagation: Seed, surface-sown, in spring or late summer
Flowering time: Throughout the summer

Compact biennials. Leaves ovate, hairy, mid-green. Flowers in cymes of up to 15, yellow orange, or bicolored. Excellent in hanging baskets.

- Attracts slugs

Calendula officinalis (Asteraceae)

Common name: Pot marigold
Height: 28in (70cm)
Spread: 18in (45cm)
Aspect: Sun or part shade
Soil: Any, but well-drained
Hardiness: Zone 6
Propagation: Seed in spring
Flowering time: Summer to autumn

An annual with inverse lance-shaped, aromatic, hairy, leaves of mid-green. Flowers daisy-like, double or single, in yellow, orange, apricot, or cream, borne profusely.

- Aromatic foliage
- Drought-tolerant
- High allergen
- Must deadhead
- Prone to mildew

Callistephus chinensis (Asteraceae)

Common name: China aster
Height: 2ft (60cm)
Spread: 18in (45cm)
Aspect: Full sun
Soil: Moist, well-drained, fertile
Hardiness: Zone 8
Propagation: Seed in heat in early spring
Flowering time: Late summer to autumn

A monotypic genus of annual. Leaves ovate, toothed, mid-green. Flowers single or double, like chrysanthemums, in all colors and shades.

- Good cut flower

Campanula medium (Campanulaceae)

Common name: Canterbury bells
Height: 3ft (90cm)
Spread: 1ft (30cm)
Aspect: Sun or part shade
Soil: Well-drained, fertile
Hardiness: Zone 8
Propagation: Seed in autumn or spring
Flowering time: Spring through to summer

A very popular biennial. Leaves basal, lance-shaped, mid-green. Flowers in racemes, bell-shaped, single or double, in white, pink, or blue. Will repeat-flower if sheared over after the first blooms are spent.

- Good cut flower   • Attracts slugs

Centaurea cyanus 'Diadem' (Asteraceae)

Common name: Cornflower
Height: 30in (75cm)
Spread: 6in (15cm)
Aspect: Full sun
Soil: Well-drained
Hardiness: Zone 7
Propagation: Seed *in situ* in spring or autumn

Flowering time: Late spring through to midsummer

An upright annual. Leaves lance-shaped, entire, mid-green. Flowers deep blue in color.

- Good cut flower
- High allergen
- Must deadhead
- Must not be moved

CHRYSANTHEMUM CARINATUM

Cerinthe major **'Purpurascens'**
(Boraginaceae)

Common name: Honeywort
Height: 18in (45cm)
Spread: 1ft (30cm)
Aspect: Sun
Soil: Well-drained
Hardiness: Zone 7
Propagation: Seed in spring
Flowering time: Spring onwards

An annual from the Mediterranean area. Leaves heart-shaped, blue-green in color, blotched white when young. Flowers tubular, green, yellow, or purple, blue underneath, and surrounded by blue bracts.

• Handsome foliage   • Seeds everywhere

Chrysanthemum carinatum
(Asteraceae)

Common name: Tricolor chrysanthemum
Height: 2ft (60cm)
Spread: 1ft (30cm)
Aspect: Sun
Soil: Well-drained, fertile
Hardiness: Zone 8
Propagation: Seed in spring
Flowering time: Summer through to autumn

An annual from Morocco. Leaves succulent, pinnatisect, bright green. Flowers single, solitary, daisy-like in red, yellow, and white, surrounding a central dark disc.

• Good cut flower   • Attracts slugs
                    • Must deadhead

ANNUALS

Chrysanthemum coronarium
(Asteraceae)

Common name: None
Height: 32in (80cm)
Spread: 32in (80cm)
Aspect: Full sun
Soil: Well-drained, fertile
Hardiness: Zone 7
Propagation: Seed in spring
Flowering time: Spring through to summer

An annual from the Mediterranean region. Leaves ferny, pale green. Flowers single, daisy-like, pale cream to white in color.

- Good cut flower
- Attracts slugs
- Must deadhead

Clarkia amoena (Portulacaceae)

Common name: None
Height: 30in (75cm)
Spread: 1ft (30cm)
Aspect: Sun or part shade
Soil: On the acid side, fertile, well-drained
Hardiness: Zone 10
Propagation: Seed *in situ* in spring
Flowering time: Throughout the summer

An attractive and robust annual from California. Leaves lance-shaped, toothed, mid-green in color. Flowers single or double, funnel-shaped, paper-thin, in pastel shades, borne in clusters on long, leafy shoots.

- Good cut flower
- Must not be moved

CONSOLIDA AJACIS

Cleome hassleriana (Capparidaceae)

Common name: Spiderflower
Height: 5ft (1.5m)
Spread: 18in (45cm)
Aspect: Full sun
Soil: Sharply-draining, fertile
Hardiness: Zone 10
Propagation: Seed in heat in spring
Flowering time: All summer, if deadheaded

An erect annual. Stems hairy. Leaves palmate, hairy, toothed, mid-green. Flowers scented, spider-like, white, pink, or purple in color, borne in dense terminal racemes.

- Drought-tolerant
- Good cut flower
- Scented flowers
- High allergen
- Must deadhead

Consolida ajacis (Ranunculaceae)

Common name: Larkspur
Height: 4ft (1.2m)
Spread: 1ft (30cm)
Aspect: Full sun
Soil: Well-drained, fertile
Hardiness: Zone 10
Propagation: Seed *in situ* in spring
Flowering time: All summer

A little- to well-branched annual with finely dissected fern-like foliage. Flowers single or double, spurred, in upright spikes, open to densely packed, in pastel or rich shades of violet, blue, pink, or white.

- Can be dried
- Good cut flower
- Handsome foliage
- Attracts slugs
- Poisonous
- Prone to mildew

ANNUALS 331

Cosmos bipinnatus Sonata series A.G.M. (Asteraceae) (1)

Common name: Common cosmos
Height: 4ft (1.2m)
Spread: 18in (45cm)
Aspect: Full sun
Soil: Moist, well-drained, fertile
Hardiness: Zone 10
Propagation: Seed in heat in spring
Flowering time: All summer, if deadheaded

A tall, erect annual, with pinnatisect mid-green leaves. Flowers solitary, saucer-shaped, deep red with yellow-colored centers.

- Handsome foliage
- High allergen
- Must deadhead

Cosmos bipinnatus Sonata series A.G.M. (Asteraceae) (2)

Common name: Common cosmos
Height: 4ft (1.2m)
Spread: 18in (45cm)
Aspect: Full sun
Soil: Moist, well-drained, fertile
Hardiness: Zone 10
Propagation: Seed in heat in spring
Flowering time: All summer, if deadheaded

An annual with ferny foliage. Flowers solitary, saucer-shaped, pink, with yellow-colored centers.

- Handsome foliage
- High allergen
- Must deadhead

Cynoglossum amabile A.G.M.
(Boraginaceae)

Common name: Chinese forget-me-not
Height: 2ft (60cm)
Spread: 1ft (30cm)
Aspect: Sun or part shade
Soil: Moist, well-drained
Hardiness: Zone 7
Propagation: Seed *in situ* in mid-spring

Flowering time: Late summer

A bushy, upright, slow-growing annual or biennial. Leaves gray-green in color, hairy, obovate. Flowers sky blue, borne in one-sided terminal cymes.

- Handsome foliage
- Must not be moved

Dimorphotheca sinuata (Asteraceae)

Common name: Winter Cape-marigold
Height: 1ft (30cm)
Spread: 1ft (30cm)
Aspect: Full sun
Soil: Well-drained, fertile, open
Hardiness: Zone 9
Propagation: Seed in heat in spring
Flowering time: Summer through to autumn

An erect annual from South Africa. Leaves coarsely-toothed, aromatic. Flowers borne on stiff stems, single, solitary, in colors of yellow, orange, white, or pink, with a brown-violet center.

- Aromatic foliage
- Must deadhead
- Good cut flower

Dorotheanthus bellidiformis (Aizoaceae)

Common name: None
Height: 6in (15cm)
Spread: 1ft (30cm)
Aspect: Full sun
Soil: Sharply-drained, poor
Hardiness: Zone 9
Propagation: Seed in heat in early spring
Flowering time: All summer

A colorful, low-growing annual. Leaves fleshy, cylindrical, glistening, green. Flowers single, solitary, daisies in a myriad of colors, but opening only in sunshine.

- Drought-tolerant
- Attracts slugs
- Handsome foliage

Echium vulgare 'Dwarf Bedder' (Boraginaceae)

Common name: Common viper's bugloss
Height: 3ft (90cm)
Spread: 1ft (30cm)
Aspect: Full sun
Soil: Well-drained, fertile
Hardiness: Zone 7
Propagation: Seed in spring, or in autumn for the next year
Flowering time: All summer, if deadheaded

An upright, compact biennial. Leaves white-hairy. Flowers bell-shaped, with a prominent green calyx, in shades of pink, blue, or white.

- Attracts slugs
- Must deadhead

Eschscholzia californica A.G.M.
(**Papaveraceae**)

Common name: Californian poppy
Height: 1ft (30cm)
Spread: 6in (15cm)
Aspect: Full sun
Soil: Well-drained
Hardiness: Zone 6
Propagation: Seed *in situ* in spring
Flowering time: Many weeks during summer

A hardy annual with finely-divided leaves of gray-green. Flowers single, usually orange in color, but may be white, yellow, or red.

- Drought-tolerant
- Good cut flower
- Handsome foliage

Eustoma grandiflorum
(**Gentianaceae**)

Common name: Russell prairie-gentian
Height: 3ft (90cm)
Spread: 1ft (30cm)
Aspect: Full sun
Soil: Well-drained, fertile
Hardiness: Zone 9
Propagation: Seed in heat in autumn or early spring
Flowering time: Throughout the summer

An annual from south U.S.A. Leaves glaucous gray-green. Flowers wide bells, lilac or white, with dark centers. Suitable for the hot dry garden.

- Good cut flower
- Prone to mildew
- Handsome foliage

Felicia bergeriana (**Asteraceae**)

Common name: Kingfisher-daisy
Height: 10in (25cm)
Spread: 10in (25cm)
Aspect: Full sun
Soil: Well-drained
Hardiness: Zone 9
Propagation: Seed in heat in spring
Flowering time: All summer and early autumn

A tender annual from South Africa. Leaves hairy, gray-green in color. Flowers solitary, single, blue daisies, with yellow-colored centers, opening only in sunshine. A good specimen for hot; dry gardens.

- Handsome foliage
- High allergen

GAILLARDIA PULCHELLA

Gaillardia pulchella (Asteraceae)

Common name: Painted gaillardia
Height: 18in (45cm)
Spread: 1ft (30cm)
Aspect: Full sun
Soil: Well-drained
Hardiness: Zone 8
Propagation: Seed in heat in spring, or *in situ* in early summer
Flowering time: Summer through to autumn

An upright annual from south U.S.A. and Mexico. Flowers have red, yellow, or red/yellow, ray florets, and purple-colored disc florets.

- Drought-tolerant
- Good cut flower
- Attracts slugs
- High allergen
- Must deadhead

Helianthus annuus (Asteraceae)

Common name: Common sunflower
Height: 15ft (5m)
Spread: 2ft (60cm)
Aspect: Full sun
Soil: Moist, humus-rich, fertile
Hardiness: Zone 10
Propagation: Seed in heat in late winter, or *in situ* in spring
Flowering time: All summer

A very tall, fast-growing annual. Leaves rough, hairy, dark green. Flowers large, solitary or branched, single or double, single- or multicolored in yellow or red. Never allow seedlings to dry out. Seeds are edible.

- Attract bees
- Good cut flower
- Attracts slugs
- Prone to mildew
- Skin irritant

IBERIS UMBELLULATA 'FANTASIA'

***Iberis umbellulata* 'Fantasia'**
(Brassicaceae)

Common name: Globe candytuft
Height: 1ft (30cm)
Spread: 10in (25cm)
Aspect: Sun
Soil: Well-drained, fertile
Hardiness: Zone 7
Propagation: Seed *in situ* in spring
Flowering time: Spring to summer

An annual with a bushy habit. Flowers scented, small, borne in flattened corymbs, in a range of colors.

- Low allergen
- Scented flowers
- Attracts slugs
- Must deadhead
- Must not be moved

Impatiens balfourii (Balsaminaceae)

Common name: None
Height: 3ft (90cm)
Spread 1ft (30cm)
Aspect: Sun or part shade
Soil: Moist, well-drained, humus-rich
Hardiness: Zone 10
Propagation: Seed in heat in early spring
Flowering time: Summer through to early autumn

A tender annual. Flowers bicolored, white and rich mauve.

● Seeds everywhere

Impatiens glandulifera (Balsaminaceae)

Common name: None
Height: 6ft (1.8m)
Spread 2ft (60cm)
Aspect: Shade
Soil: Moist,
Hardiness: Zone 10
Propagation: Seed in spring
Flowering time: Summer to autumn

A weed of woods and waste places. Flowers scented, red, rose, lavender, or white, interior spotted yellow. Seed capsules explosive.

● Scented flowers   ● Seeds everywhere

Ipomoea purpurea (Convolvulaceae)

Common name: None
Height: 10ft (3m)
Spread: 3ft (90cm)
Aspect: Full sun
Soil: Well-drained, fertile
Hardiness: Zone 7
Propagation: Seed in heat in spring
Flowering time: Long periods in summer

An annual, twining climber. Flowers trumpet-shaped, purple, blue, pink, or white in color, or white striped with these colors, borne in cymes.

● Prone to mildew

Lathyrus odoratus 'Winston Churchill' A.G.M.

Lathyrus odoratus 'Winston Churchill' A.G.M. (Papilionaceae)

Common name: Sweet pea
Height: 6ft (1.8m)
Spread: 2ft (60cm)
Aspect: Sun or light shade
Soil: Well-drained, humus-rich, fertile
Hardiness: Zone 5
Propagation: Seed, after soaking, in autumn or spring
Flowering time: Summer through to early autumn

A popular annual that needs little introduction. Leaves dark green, stems winged. Flowers borne on long stems, scented, in all colors (except yellow) or bicolored. Seeds poisonous.

- Good cut flower
- Scented flowers
- Attracts slugs
- Must deadhead
- Poisonous
- Prone to mildew

Lavatera trimestris (Malvaceae)

Common name: Herb tree-mallow
Height: 5ft (1.5m)
Spread: 5ft (1.5m)
Aspect: Sun
Soil: Well-drained, fertile
Hardiness: Zone 8
Propagation: Seed *in situ* in late spring
Flowering time: Throughout the summer

An annual with a bushy habit. Flowers solitary, open, funnel-shaped in colors of pink, rose-red, or white.

- Drought-tolerant
- Good cut flower
- Must not be moved

Limnanthes douglasii A.G.M. (Limnanthaceae)

Common name: Meadow-foam
Height: 6in (15cm)
Spread: 2ft (60cm)
Aspect: Sun
Soil: Moist, well-drained, fertile
Hardiness: Zone 8
Propagation: Seed *in situ* in spring or autumn
Flowering time: Summer through to autumn

A half-hardy annual. Leaves toothed, glossy. Flowers yellow-colored cups with white centers.

- Attracts bees
- Scented flowers
- Must not be moved

Lupinus texensis (Papilionaceae)

Common name: None
Height: 1ft (30cm)
Spread: 10in (25cm)
Aspect: Sun
Soil: Sharply-drained
Hardiness: Zone 9
Propagation: Seed in spring or autumn
Flowering time: All summer, if deadheaded

A bushy, upright annual. Flowers borne in dense racemes, deep blue or purple in color. Seeds poisonous.

- Drought-tolerant
- Attracts slugs
- Must deadhead
- Poisonous

Mentzelia lindleyi (Loasaceae)

Common name: Lindley mentzelia
Height: 28in (70cm)
Spread: 10in (25cm)
Aspect: Full sun
Soil: Well-drained, fertile
Hardiness: Zone 9
Propagation: Seed *in situ* in spring
Flowering time: Early through to late summer

A tender annual suitable for the hot, dry garden. Leaves pinnatifid, gray-green in color. Flowers night-scented, solitary, or in few-flowered cymes, yellow with orange centers. Cut back hard to obtain a second flush of flowers in late summer.

- Handsome foliage
- Scented flowers

***Nemesia strumosa* 'Carnival' series
(Scrophulariaceae)**

Common name: Pouch nemesia
Height: 1ft (30cm)
Spread: 6in (15cm)
Aspect: Full sun
Soil: Acidic, moist, well-drained
Hardiness: Zone 9
Propagation: Seed in heat in spring
Flowering time: Mid- through to late summer

A strain of compact, dwarf habit. Flowers in a range of colors, with darker veins and pale throats, borne in terminal racemes.

- Good cut flower

***Nemesia strumosa* 'K.L.M.' strain
(Scrophulariaceae)**

Common name: Pouch nemesia
Height: 1ft (30cm)
Spread: 6in (15cm)
Aspect: Sun
Soil: Acidic, moist, well-drained, fertile
Hardiness: Zone 9
Propagation: Seed in heat in spring
Flowering time: Early through to late summer

A strain of compact, dwarf habit. Flowers 2-lipped, bicolored, in terminal racemes.

- Good cut flower

Nemesia strumosa 'National Ensign' strain (Scrophulariaceae)

Common name: Pouch nemesia
Height: 1ft (30cm)
Spread: 6in (15cm)
Aspect: Sun
Soil: Acidic, moist, well-drained
Hardiness: Zone 9
Propagation: Seed in heat in spring
Flowering time: Early through to late summer

A strain of compact, dwarf habit. Flowers 2-lipped, bicolored, in terminal racemes.

• Good cut flower

Nicandra physaloides 'Violacea' (Solanaceae)

Common name: Apple-of-Peru
Height: 3ft (90cm)
Spread: 1ft (30cm)
Aspect: Full sun
Soil: Moist, well-drained, fertile
Hardiness: Zone 8
Propagation: Seed in heat in spring
Flowering time: Summer to autumn

An upright, half-hardy annual. Flowers short-lived, bell-shaped, pale violet-blue, with white centers in the upper leaf axils, followed by brown berries.

• Seeds everywhere

Nicotiana langsdorfii A.G.M. (Solanaceae)

Common name: None
Height: 5ft (1.5m)
Spread: 15in (38cm)
Aspect: Sun or part shade
Soil: Moist, well-drained, fertile
Hardiness: Zone 9
Propagation: Seed in heat in spring
Flowering time: Long periods in summer

A tall, tender, sticky annual. Leaves in a basal rosette. Flowers tubular, nodding, apple-green, borne in tall, slender panicles.

• Scented flowers   • Skin irritant

Nicotiana **'Domino Lime Green'**
A.G.M. (Solanaceae)

Common name: None
Height: 2ft (60cm)
Spread: 10in (25cm)
Aspect: Sun or half shade
Soil: Moist, well-drained, fertile
Hardiness: Zone 7
Propagation: Seed in heat in spring
Flowering time: All summer

An upright, hardy annual. Flowers lime green in color, salveriform, borne abundantly throughout the summer season.

- Scented flowers   • Skin irritant

Nigella damascena **'Miss Jekyll'**
A.G.M (Ranunculaceae)

Common name: Love-in-a-mist
Height: 20in (50cm)
Spread: 10in (25cm)
Aspect: Full sun
Soil: Well-drained
Hardiness: Zone 10
Propagation: Seed *in situ* in spring
Flowering time: Throughout the summer

An upright annual with very finely divided green leaves. Flowers terminal borne on tall stems, sky blue in color, and surrounded by an attractive ruff of foliage.

- Handsome foliage • Must not be moved

NIGELLA HISPANICA 'CURIOSITY'

Nigella hispanica 'Curiosity'
(Ranunculaceae)

Common name: None
Height: 30in (75cm)
Spread: 18in (45cm)
Aspect: Sun
Soil: Well-drained
Hardiness: Zone 10
Propagation: Seed *in situ* in spring
Flowering time: Long periods in summer

An upright annual with finely divided, ferny foliage. Flowers terminal borne on tall stems, solitary or paired, scented, bright blue in color, with black eyes and deep red stamens.

- Handsome foliage
- Scented flowers
- Must not be moved

ANNUALS

OENOTHERA BIENNIS

Oenothera biennis (**Onagraceae**)

Common name: Common evening primrose
Height: 5ft (1.5m)
Spread: 2ft (60cm)
Aspect: Full sun
Soil: Sharply-drained
Hardiness: Zone 4
Propagation: Seed in early summer for next season
Flowering time: Summer to autumn

A tall annual, grown usually as a biennial. Leaves in a basal rosette. Flowers bowl-shaped, scented, pale yellow darkening to deep yellow, borne in leafy racemes.

- Drought-tolerant
- Scented flowers
- Attracts slugs

Onopordum acanthium (Asteraceae)

Common name: None
Height: 10ft (3m)
Spread: 3ft (90cm)
Aspect: Sun
Soil: Well-drained, fertile
Hardiness: Zone 6
Propagation: Seed in autumn or spring
Flowering time: Several weeks in summer

A very tall, tap-rooted, rosette-forming biennial. Leaves spiny, gray-green. Flowers thistle-like, purple in color, surrounded by spiny bracts.

- Handsome foliage
- Attracts slugs
- Seeds everywhere

Papaver commutatum A.G.M. (Papaveraceae)

Common name: None
Height: 18in (45cm)
Spread: 6in (15cm)
Aspect: Full sun
Soil: Well-drained, fertile
Hardiness: Zone 8
Propagation: Seed in spring
Flowering time: Several weeks in summer

An annual upright, branched poppy. Flowers solitary, bright scarlet, with black basal spots.

- Drought-tolerant
- Low allergen
- Must not be moved
- Prone to mildew
- Seeds everywhere

Papaver dubium (Papaveraceae)

Common name: None
Height: 2ft (60cm)
Spread: 8in (20cm)
Aspect: Sun
Soil: Well-drained, fertile
Hardiness: Zone 7
Propagation: Seed in spring
Flowering time: All summer

An upright, angular, hairy annual, with pinnatisect leaves of blue-green. Flowers solitary, single, pale red or pink in color.

- Drought-tolerant
- Handsome foliage
- Low allergen
- Seeds everywhere

Phacelia campanularia (Hydrophyllaceae)

Common name: Harebell phacelia
Height: 1ft (30cm)
Spread: 6in (15cm)
Aspect: Full sun
Soil: Well-drained, fertile
Hardiness: Zone 9
Propagation: Seed *in situ* in spring
Flowering time: Spring through to summer

An upright annual. Leaves aromatic. Flowers upward-facing, dark blue-colored bells.

- Attracts bees
- Skin irritant

Phlox drummondii 'Beauty' series (Polemoniaceae)

Common name: Drummond phlox
Height: 9in (23cm)
Spread: 10in (25cm)
Aspect: Full sun
Soil: Well-drained, fertile
Hardiness: Zone 6
Propagation: Seed in heat in early spring
Flowering time: Late spring through to autumn

An erect or spreading, bushy annual. Flowers salverform, in colors of white, red, pink, blue, or purple, with contrasting basal markings, borne in cymes.

- Low allergen
- Prone to mildew

PORTULACA GRANDIFLORA

Phlox drummondii 'Dolly' series
(Polemoniaceae)

Common name: Annual/Drummond phlox
Height: 6in (15cm)
Spread: 6in (15cm)
Aspect: Full sun
Soil: Well-drained, fertile
Hardiness: Zone 6
Propagation: Seed in heat in spring
Flowering time: Spring to late summer

A dwarf clone of bushy, hardy annuals. Flowers salveriform, single-colored or bicolored, in a range of colors, in cymes.

● Low allergen   ● Prone to mildew

Portulaca grandiflora
(Portulacaceae)

Common name: Sunplant, Common portulaca
Height: 8in (20cm)
Spread: 6in (15cm)
Aspect: Full sun
Soil: Sharply-drained, poor
Hardiness: Zone 10
Propagation: Seed in heat in spring
Flowering time: All summer

A prostrate annual. Leaves narrow, cylindrical, fleshy. Flowers single or double, pink, red, orange, yellow, or white. Suitable for hot, dry gardens.

● Drought-tolerant
● Handsome foliage

Salpiglossis sinuata 'Casino' series A.G.M. (Solanaceae)

Common name: Painted-tongue
Height: 2ft (60cm)
Spread: 1ft (30cm)
Aspect: Full sun
Soil: Moist, well-drained, humus-rich
Hardiness: Zone 8
Propagation: Seed in spring or autumn
Flowering time: Summer through to autumn

A short-lived perennial, grown almost always as an annual. Flowers funnel-shaped, solitary, in a wide range of colors, and sometimes heavily-veined. Suitable for the hot, dry garden.

- Good cut flower
- Must deadhead

Sanvitalia procumbens (Asteraceae)

Common name: Trailing sanvitalia
Height: 8in (20cm)
Spread: 18in (45cm)
Aspect: Sun
Soil: Humus-rich, well-drained, fertile
Hardiness: Zone 7
Propagation: Seed *in situ* in autumn or spring
Flowering time: Summer through to early autumn

A sprawling, hardy annual. Flowers single, daisy-like, yellow in color, with black centers. Good specimen for hanging baskets.

- High allergen
- Must not be moved

Schizanthus pinnatus (**Solanaceae**)

Common name: Butterfly-flower
Height: 20in (50cm)
Spread: 1ft (30cm)
Aspect: Sun
Soil: Moist, well-drained, fertile
Hardiness: Zone 10
Propagation: Seed in heat in spring
Flowering time: Spring to autumn

An erect annual. Flowers 2-lipped, in a range of colors, and spotted, open cymes. Pinch out seedlings to make bushy and dwarf.

- Good cut flower
- Requires staking

Senecio elegans (**Asteraceae**)

Common name: None
Height: 2ft (60cm)
Spread: 18in (45cm)
Aspect: Sun
Soil: Well-drained
Hardiness: Zone 9
Propagation: Seed in heat in spring
Flowering time: All summer

A tender annual. Flowers have red-purple ray florets and yellow disc florets, in corymbs.

- Attracts bees
- High allergen
- Poisonous

Silybum marianum (**Asteraceae**)

Common name: None
Height: 5ft (1.5m)
Spread: 3ft (90cm)
Aspect: Sun
Soil: Well-drained
Hardiness: Zone 7
Propagation: Seed *in situ* in late spring
Flowering time: Summer to autumn, in the year after sowing

A biennial, with a basal rosette of glossy, marbled, leaves, often grown for its foliage. Flowers thistle-like, scented, purple-pink in color.

- Good cut flower
- Attracts slugs
- Handsome foliage
- Scented flowers

TAGETES (Asteraceae)
Marigold

A genus of only 50 species, but one that provides us with some of our most popular and widely-used annuals, derived from *Tt. patula, erecta,* and *tenuifolia*. Four principal hybrid annual types are recognized:

African marigolds, derived from *T. erecta*. These have pinnate leaves, and large, fully-double, pompon-like flowers of yellow or orange. Flowers are borne from spring to autumn. These are especially useful in formal bedding schemes.

French marigolds, derived from *T. patula*. These have pinnate leaves. The solitary, double, and occasionally single, flowers have ray florets of yellow, brown, or orange (or combinations of these). The disc florets are the same or different colors; flowering is from late spring to autumn. They are useful in the front of mixed borders.

Afro-French marigolds, derived from *Tt. erecta* and *patula*. These have pinnate leaves. The small flowers, which may be single or double, in yellow and orange, are marked red or brown. They grow in cymes or solitary, from late spring to autumn.

Signet marigolds, derived from *T. tenuifolia*. These have pinnate leaves. The single flowers are rich in disc florets of yellow or orange, but lack ray florets. Flowering is from late spring to autumn.

Marigolds like full sun and soil that is well-drained. The foliage may cause skin irritation. They are highly allergenic, and prone to attack by slugs. Marigolds require to be deadheaded to keep them flowering.

Tagetes erecta 'Antigua' series (Asteraceae)

Common name: African marigold
Height: 1ft (30cm)
Spread: 18in (45cm)
Aspect: Sun
Soil: Well-drained, fertile
Hardiness: Zone 9
Propagation: Seed *in situ* in late spring, or in heat in early spring
Flowering time: Late spring through to early autumn

A strain of African marigold. Leaves ferny. Produces double flowers in colors of yellow, orange, lemon, or primrose.

- Handsome foliage
- Attracts slugs
- High allergen
- Must deadhead
- Skin irritant

***Tagetes patula* 'Beaux' series**
(Asteraceae)

Common name: Afro-French marigold
Height: 14in (35cm)
Spread: 18in (45cm)
Aspect: Sun
Soil: Well-drained, fertile
Hardiness: Zone 9
Propagation: Seed in heat in early, or *in situ* in late spring
Flowering time: Spring to late summer

A compact, free-flowering Afro-French marigold. Leaves ferny. Flowers densely double, golden yellow.

- Handsome foliage
- Attracts slugs
- High allergen
- Must deadhead
- Skin irritant

***Tagetes patula* 'Boy' series**
(Asteraceae)

Common name: French marigold
Height: 6in (15cm)
Spread: 1ft (30cm)
Aspect: Sun
Soil: Well-drained, fertile
Hardiness: Zone 9
Propagation: Seed *in situ* in late spring, or in heat in early spring
Flowering time: Late spring to autumn

A strain of compact French marigolds. Leaves ferny. Flowers large, double, in colors of yellow, orange, or red, with yellow or orange crests.

- Handsome foliage
- Attracts slugs
- High allergen
- Must deadhead

***Tagetes patula* 'Orange Boy'**
(Asteraceae)

Common name: French marigold
Height: 6in (15cm)
Spread: 1ft (30cm)
Aspect: Sun
Soil: Well-drained, fertile
Hardiness: Zone 9
Propagation: Seed in heat in early spring, or *in situ* in late spring
Flowering time: Spring to late summer

A very compact, free-flowering strain. Leaves ferny. Flowers double, crested, bright orange.

- Handsome foliage
- Attracts slugs
- High allergen
- Must deadhead
- Skin irritant

***Tagetes tenuifolia* 'Lemon Gem'**
(Asteraceae)

Common name: None
Height: 16in (40cm)
Spread: 18in (45cm)
Aspect: Sun
Soil: Well-drained, fertile
Hardiness: Zone 9
Propagation: Seed in heat in early spring, or *in situ* in late spring
Flowering time: Late spring to late summer

A compact, dwarf strain of Signet marigolds. Leaves ferny. Flowers single, lemon-yellow.

- Handsome foliage
- Attracts slugs
- High allergen
- Must deadhead
- Skin irritant

***Tagetes tenuifolia* 'Tangerine Gem'**
(Asteraceae)

Common name: None
Height: 16in (40cm)
Spread: 18in (45cm)
Aspect: Sun
Soil: Well-drained, fertile
Hardiness: Zone 9
Propagation: Seed in heat in early spring, or *in situ* in late spring
Flowering time: Late spring through to late summer

A compact, dwarf strain of Signet marigolds. Leaves ferny. Flowers single, orange-colored with deep orange centers.

- Handsome foliage
- Attracts slugs
- High allergen
- Must deadhead
- Skin irritant

Torenia fournieri 'Clown' series
(Scrophulariaceae)

Common name: None
Height: 10in (25cm)
Spread: 9in (23cm)
Aspect: Part shade
Soil: Moist, well-drained, fertile
Hardiness: Zone 9
Propagation: Seed in heat in spring
Flowering time: All summer

An upright annual. Flowers tubular, flared, 2-lipped, purple, lavender, white, or pink in terminal or axillary racemes.

Torenia fournieri 'Panda' series
(Scrophulariaceae)

Common name: None
Height: 8in (20cm)
Spread: 9in (23cm)
Aspect: Part shade
Soil: Moist, well-drained, fertile
Hardiness: Zone 9
Propagation: Seed in heat, in spring
Flowering time: Several weeks in summer

An erect annual. Flowers tubular, flared, 2-lipped, in colors of purple, pink, white, or lavender, borne in terminal or axillary racemes.

Tropaeolum 'Alaska' series A.G.M.
(Tropaeolaceae)

Common name: None
Height: 1ft (30cm)
Spread: 18in (45cm)
Aspect: Sun
Soil: Poor, well-drained
Hardiness: Zone 8
Propagation: Seed in heat in early spring, or *in situ* in late spring
Flowering time: Summer through to autumn

A compact, dwarf strain with leaves speckled and marked white. Flowers single, in a range of colors. Leaves and flowers edible.

- Handsome foliage
- Attracts slugs
- Seeds everywhere

Tropaeolum 'Empress of India'
(Tropaeolaceae)

Common name: None
Height: 1ft (30cm)
Spresd: 18in (45cm)
Aspect: Sun
Soil: Poor, well-drained
Hardiness: Zone 8
Propagation: Seed in heat in early spring, or *in situ* in late spring
Flowering time: Summer through to autumn

A compact, dwarf annual. Flowers semi-double, scarlet. Leaves and flowers edible.

- Attracts slugs
- Seeds everywhere

ZINNIA ELEGANS 'THUMBELINA' SERIES

Tropaeolum majus (**Tropaeolaceae**)

Common name: Common nasturtium
Height: 10ft (3m)
Spread: 15ft (4.5m)
Aspect: Sun
Soil: Poor, well-drained
Hardiness: Zone 8
Propagation: Seed in heat in early spring, or *in situ* in late spring
Flowering time: Summer through to autumn

A robust, annual climber or scrambler. Flowers long-spurred, orange, red, or yellow in color. Leaves and flowers both edible.

- Attracts slugs
- Seeds everywhere

Zinnia elegans 'Thumbelina' series (**Asteraceae**)

Common name: Common zinnia
Height: 6in (15cm)
Spread: 18in (45cm)
Aspect: Sun
Soil: Well-drained, humus-rich, fertile
Hardiness: Zone 8
Propagation: Seed in heat in early spring, or *in situ* in late spring
Flowering time: Long periods in summer

A dwarf, spreading annual. Flowers single or double, in a range of colors; weather-resistant. Deadheading prolongs flowering.

- High allergen
- Prone to mildew

ANNUALS

Appendices

Evergreen long-flowering perennials

Acanthus spinosus
Aeonium cuneatum
Anthemis punctata
Anthemis tinctoria
Bellis perennis
Calceolaria biflora
Calceolaria 'Sunset Red'
Campanula persicifolia
Catharanthus roseus
Chrysogonum virginianum
Cobaea scandens
Corydalis lutea
Eccremocarpus scaber
Erysimum linifolium
Gazania
Happlopappus glutinosus
Hemerocallis 'Corky'
Hemerocallis 'Green Flutter'
Hemerocallis 'Stafford'
Heuchera 'Red Spangles'
x *Heucherella alba*
Hypericum cerastioides
Lapageria rosea
Omphalodes cappadocica
Origanum laevigatum
Osteospermum jucundum
Passiflora coerulea
Passiflora quadrangularis
Pelargonium peltatum
Pelargonium tricolor
Pelargonium zonale
Penstemon heterophyllus
Pulmonaria rubra
Pulmonaria saccharata
Thunbergia alata
Verbascum 'Helen Johnson'
Viola 'Columbine'
Viola 'Etain'
Zauschneria californica

Evergreen long-flowering shrubs

Abelia in variety
Abutilon in variety
Allamanda cathartica
Anisodontea capensis
Argyranthemum in variety
Bougainvillea glabra
Brachglottis 'Sunshine'
Bupleurum fruticosum
Caesalpinia pulcherrima
Calceolaria integrifolia
Calluna in variety
Ceanothus 'Skylark'
Ceanothus thyrsiflorus
Choisya 'Aztec Pearl'
Cistus in variety
Coronilla valentina ssp. *glauca*
Daboecia in variety
Dendromecon rigida
Erica carnea in variety
Erica cinerea in variety
Erica darleyensis in variety
Erica gracilis in variety
Erysimum 'Bowles' Mauve'
Grevillea in variety
Grindelia chiloensis
Hebe in variety
Helianthemum in variety
Hibiscus rosa-sinensis
Hypericum calycinum
Iberis sempervirens
Justicia carnea
Lavandula stoechas
Lavatera in variety
Leptospermum scoparium
Lithodora diffusa
Lupinus arboreus
Mimulus aurantiacus
Nerium oleander
Nicotiana glauca
Osteospermum in variety
Pachystachys lutea
Penstemon isophyllus
Pentas lanceolata
Phlomis fruticosa
Phygelius in variety
Plumbago auriculata
Polygala myrtifolia
Senecio vira-vira
Solanum laciniatum
Solanum rantonetti
Streptosolen jamesonii
Verbascum 'Letitia'
Viburnum tinus
Vinca major
Vinca minor

Drought-tolerant long-flowering perennials

Acanthus in variety
Alchemilla mollis
Anthemis in variety
Begonia grandis
Bracteantha 'Coco'
Calceolaria biflora
Centranthus ruber
Convolvulus althaeoides
Coreopsis vertticillata
Erigeron in variety
Eriophyllum lanatum
Erodium in variety
Erysimum in variety
Eucomis in variety
Gaillardia in variety
Gaura lindheimeri
Gazania in variety
Geranium in variety
Gypsophila in variety
Haplopappus glutinosus
Hypericum cerastioides
Limonium sinuatum
Linaria purpurea
Linum in variety
Lychnis in variety
Nepeta in variety
Nerine bowdenii
Oenothera in variety
Origanum laevigatum
Rehmannia elata
Rhodohypoxis baurii
Senecio doronicum
Sphaeralcea in variety
Stachys in variety

Drought-tolerant long-flowering shrubs

Anisodontea capensis
Bougainvillea glabra
Cistus in variety
Cytisus in variety
Erysimum in variety
Fremontodendron californicum
Grindelia chiloensis
Helianthemum in variety
Hypericum calycinum
Lavatera in variety
Phlomis fruticosa
Verbascum 'Letitia'

Drought-tolerant long-flowering annuals

Argemone mexicana
Brachycombe iberidifolia
Calendula officinalis
Cleome hassleriana
Dorotheanthus bellidiformis
Eschscholzia californica
Lavatera trimestris
Papaver dubium
Portulaca grandiflora

Low-allergen long-flowering perennials

Acanthus spinosus
Alcea rosea
Antirrhinum majus
Begonia in variety
Campanula persicifolia
Canna in variety
Clematis x *eriostemon*
Convolvulus sabatius
Convolvulus tricolor
Corydalis lutea
Cyrtanthus brachscyphus
Erodium in variety
Geranium in variety
Geum in variety
Hemerocallis in variety
Heuchera in variety
x *Heucherella alba*
Hypericum cerastiodes
Impatiens in variety
Lobelia x *gerardii*
Mimulus in variety
Monarda didyma
Nepeta in variety
Omphalodes cappadocica
Passiflora in variety
Penstemon in variety
Petunia x *hybrida*
Phlox 'Chattahoochee'
Potentilla in variety
Pulmonaria in variety
Roscoea purpurea
Salvia in variety
Scabiosa 'Irish perpetual-flowering'
Stachys byzantina
Symphytum x *uplandicum*
Tiarella wherryi
Tradescantia in variety
Veronica in variety
Viola in variety

APPENDICES

Low-allergen long-flowering shrubs

Antirrhinum sempervirens
Cytisus in variety
Erica in variety
Fuchsia in variety
Hebe in variety
Helianthemum in variety
Hibiscus in variety
Hydrangea in variety
Hypericum in variety
Mimulus in variety
Penstemon in variety
Potentilla in variety
Rosa in variety
Spiraea japonica

Low-allergen long-flowering annuals

Anchusa capensis
Iberis umbellulata
Papaver commutatum
Papaver dubium
Phlox drummondii

Highly allergenic long-flowering perennials

Alstroemeria in variety
Arctotis x *hybrida*
Aster in variety
Buphthalmum salicifolium
Coreopsis in variety
Dianthus in variety
Erigeron in variety
Eriophyllum lanatum
Gaillardia in variety
Gazania in variety
Helenium in variety
Helianthus in variety
Pelargonium in variety
Rudbeckia in variety
Senecio in variety

Highly allergenic long-flowering shrubs

Argyranthemum in variety
Ceanothus in variety
Euryops pectinatus
Fremontodendron californicum
Osteospermum in variety
Senecio vira-vira

Highly allergenic long-flowering annuals

Bracteantha bracteata
Calendula officinalis
Centaurea cyanus
Cleome hassleriana
Cosmos bipinnatus
Felicia bergeriana
Senecio elegans
Tagetes in variety
Zinnia elegans

Poisonous long-flowering perennials

Catharanthus roseus
Dicentra in variety
Gloriosa superba
Helenium in variety
Nerine bowdenii
Senecio in variety
Solanum in variety
Symphytum x *uplandicum*

Poisonous long-flowering shrubs

Brugmansia sanguinea
Cytisus in variety
Hydrangea in variety
Lantana camara
Lonicera in variety
Nerium oleander
Plumeria in variety
Senecio in variety
Solanum in variety
Vinca major
Vinca minor

Poisonous long-flowering annuals

Consolida ajacis
Lupinus in variety
Senecio elegans

Bibliography

Bird, R. *The Cultivation of Hardy Perennials* Batsford, London. 1994.
Brickell, C. (Editor-in-chief) *The Royal Horticultural Society Gardeners' Encyclopaedia of Plants and Flowers* Dorling Kindersley, London. 1994.
Brickell, C. (Editor-in-chief) *The Royal Horticultural Society A-Z Encyclopaedia of Plants and Flowers* Dorling Kindersley, London. 1997.
Cooke, I. *The Plantfinder's Guide to Tender Perennials* David and Charles, Newton Abbot. 1998.
Craigmyle, M. *The Illustrated Encyclopaedia of Perennials* Salamander Books, London. 1999.
Elliott, J. *The The Smaller Perennials* Batsford, London. 1997.
Griffiths, M. *The Royal Horticultural Society Index of Garden Plants* Macmillan Press, Basingstoke. 1994.
Hessayon, D.G. *The New Bedding Plant Expert* Transworld Publishers, London. 1997.
Hessayon, D.G. *The Flowering Shrub Expert* Transworld Publishers, London. 1997.
Hessayon, D.G. *The House Plant Expert* Transworld Publishers, London. 1998.
Jellito, I., Schact, W. and Fessler, A. *Hardy Herbacious Perennials* (2 volumes) Timber Press, Portland, Oregon. 1990.
Kelly, J. (Editor) *The Hillier Gardener's Guide to Trees and Shrubs* David and Charles, Newton Abbot. 1995.
Kelly, J. (Editor) *The Royal Horticultural Society Plant Guides: Annuals and Biennials* Dorling Kindersley, London. 1999.
Kohlein, F. and Menzel, P. *The Encyclopaedia of Plants for Garden Situations* Batsford, London. 1994.
Mathew, B. and Swindells, P. *The Gardener's Guide to Bulbs* Mitchell Beazley, London. 1994.
Parker, H. (Editor) *Perennials. A Royal Horticultural Society Guide*. Dorling Kindersley, London. 1996.
Philip, C. *The Plant Finder. 2000/2001 Edition. The Royal Horticultural Society*. Dorling Kindersley, London. 2000.
Phillips, R. and Rix, M. *Annuals and Biennials*. Pan Books, London. 1999.
Phillips, R. and Rix, M. *Bulbs*. Pan Books, London. 1989.
Phillips, R. and Rix, M. *Conservatory and Indoor Plants*. (2 volumes) Pan Books, London. 1997.
Phillips, R. and Rix, M. *Herbs*. Pan Books, London. 1990.
Phillips, R. and Rix, M. *Perennials*. (2 volumes) Pan Books, London. 1991.
Phillips, R. and Rix, M. *Shrubs*. Pan Books, London.
Segall, B. (Consultant) *Botanica: the Illustrated A to Z of over 10,000 Garden Plants and How to Grow Them* Mynah, N.S.W., Australia. 1997.
Thomas, G.S. *Perennial Garden Plants, or the Modern Forilegium* Dent, London. 1990.
Trehane, P. et al. *International Code of Nomenclature for Garden Plants* Quarterjack Publishing, Wimborne. 1995.

Index

A

Abelia 216
 x grandiflora 216
 schumannii 216
Abelia, glossy see
 Abelia x grandiflora
Abutilon 216–19
 'Ashford Red' 217
 'Boule de Neige' 217
 'Canary Bird' 218
 'Cannington Peter' 218
 'Kentish Belle' 219
 x suntense 'Jermyns' 219
Acanthus spinosus 16
Achillea 16–17
 'Fanal' 16
 filipendulina 'Cloth of Gold' 17
 'Hoffnung' 17
 millefolium 16
 ptarmica 16
 'Terracotta' 17
Achimenes hybrida 18
Aeonium cuneatum 18
African daisy see
 Arctotis x hybrida
African marigold see
 Tagetes erecta
Afro-French marigold see *Tagetes patula*
Ageratum houstonianum 324
Ajuga reptans 'Purple Brocade' 19
Alaska fringe-cup see
 Tellima grandiflora
Alcea rosea 'Chater's Double' 19
Alchemilla mollis 20
Alkanet see *Anchusa azurea*
Allamanda cathartica 220
Alonsoa warzcewiczii 20
Alpine wallflower see
 Erysimum linifolium
Alstroemeria 20–5
 'Apollo' 24
 aurea 21
 'Coronet' 24
 'Endless Love' 21
 'Friendship' 24
 'H.R.H. Princess Alexandra' 24
 'H.R.H. Princess Alice' 24
 ligtu hybrids 22
 'Orange Gem' 24
 'Orange Glory' 24
 'Pink Dream' 22
 'Princess Carmina' 24
 'Princess Caroline' 24
 'Princess Grace' 24
 'Princess Juliana' 24
 'Princess Mira' 24
 'Princess Paola' 24
 'Princess' strain 20
 psittacina 23

'Solent Crest' 24
'Solent Rose' 24
'Sunburst' 24
'Sunny Rebecca' 24
'Sweet Love' 25
'Yellow Friendship' 24
'Xandra' 25
Althaea officinalis 26
Althaea, shrub see
 Hibiscus syriacus
Anchusa 26–7, 324
 azurea 'Dropmore' 26
 azurea 'Feltham Pride' 26
 azurea 'Opal' 27
 capensis 324
Anemone 27–9
 hupehensis 27
 x hybrida 'Andrea Atkinson' 28
 x hybrida 'Honorine Jobert' 28
 x hybrida 'Whirlwind' 29
 multifida 29
Anemone
 dwarf Japanese see
 Anemone hupehensis
 Japanese see *Anemone x hybrida*
Angelonia gardneri 220
Angels' trumpets see
 Brugmansia aurea
Anisodontea capensis 220
Annual phlox see
 Phlox drummondii
Annuals 322–57
Anthemis 29–31
 marschalliana 30
 punctata 30
 tinctoria 31
 tinctoria 'E.C. Buxton' 31
 tinctoria 'Sauce Hollandaise' 31
Antirrhinum 32–3
 braun-blanquetii 32
 majus 'Floral Showers' 32
 majus 'Sonnet' 33
Apple-of-Peru see *Nicandra physaloides*
Arctotis x hybrida 34
Argemone mexicana 325
Argyranthemum 221–3
 'Cornish Gold' 223
 'Donington Hero' 223
 frutescens 221
 gracile 'Chelsea Girl' 223
 'Jamaica Primrose' 222
 'Levada Cream' 223
 maderense 222
 'Mary Cheek' 223
 'Petite Pink' 222
 'Quinta White' 223
 'Snowstorm' 223
 'Sugar Button' 223

'Summer Stars' 223
'Vancouver' 223
'Whiteknights' 223
Arum lily see *Zantedeschia aethiopica*
Asarina procumbens 34
Asclepias 34–5
 hallii 34
 incarnata 35
 tuberosa 35
Aster 35–7
 x frikartii 'Flora's Delight' 35
 x frikartii 'Monch' 36
 sedifolius 'Nanus' 37
Aster
 China see *Callistephus chinensis*
 Stokes' see *Stokesia laevis*
Astilbe 37–8
 x arendsii 'Brautschleir' 38
 x arendsii 'Fanal' 38
 x arendsii 'Feuer' 37
 x arendsii 'Irrlicht' 38
 'Bronce Elegans' 38
 chinensis var. *davidii* 'Jo Ophurst' 38
 chinensis var. *pumila* 38
 chinensis var. *taquetii* 'Superba' 38
 x crispa 'Perkeo' 38
 glaberrima var. *saxatilis* 38
 'Rheinland' 38
 simplicifolia 38
 'Sprite' 38
 'Straussenfeder' 38
Astrantia 39–40
 major 39
 major 'Hadspen Blood' 39
 major 'Margery Fish' see *A. major* 'Shaggy'
 major 'Rosensinfonie' 40
 major 'Shaggy' 40
 maxima 40
Avens see *Geum*
Award of Garden Merit (A.G.M.) 9

B

Banks rose see *Rosa banksiae*
Beach fleabane see
 Erigeron glaucus
Bear's-breach see
 Alchemilla mollis
Beauty bush see
 Kolkwitzia amabilis
Bee-balm see *Monarda didyma*
Beggar-ticks see *Bidens ferulifolia*
Begonia 41–2
 grandis 41
 tuberhybrida 4
 tuberhybrida 'Non-

stop' 42
 rex 41
 semperflorens
 'Cocktail' 42
Semperflorens Cultorum 41
 sutherlandii 41, 42
Begonia
 Evans see *Begoniam grandis*
 Sutherland see *B. sutherlandii*
 tuberous see *B. x tuberhybrida*
 wax see *B. semperflorens*
Bellflower see
 Campanula carpatica
 clustered see *C. glomerata*
 Carpathian see *C. carpatica*
 milky see *C. lactiflora*
 peach-leaved see *C. persicifolia*
Bellis perennis 43
 'Pomponette' 43
Bergamot see *Monarda*
Bethlehem sage see *Pulmonaria saccharata*
Betony
 common see *Stachys officinalis*
 wooly see *S. byzantina*
Beverly-bells rehmannia see *Rehmannia elata*
Bidens ferulifolia 43
Big periwinkle see
 Vinca major
Bindweed see
 Convolvulus
Bird's foot trefoil see
 Lotus corniculatus
Bistort see *Persicaria*
Black-eyed Susan see
 Rudbeckia hirta
Bladder-senna see
 Colutea arborescens
Blue blossom ceanothus see *Ceanothus thyrsiflorus repens*
Bomarea caldasii 224
Bonytip fleabane see
 Erigeron karvinskianus
Borage, common see
 Borago officinalis
Borago 44, 325
 officinalis 325
 pygmaea 44
Bougainvillea glabra 224
Bower plant see *Pandorea jasminoides*
Bowman's-root see
 Gillenia trifoliata
Brachycome iberidifolia 325
Brachyglottis
 'Sunshine' 225
Bracteantha 44, 326

362

bracteata 326
'Coco' 44
Broom see *Cytisus*; *Genista lydia*
Purple see *Chamaecytisus purpureus*
Warminster see *Cytisus praecox albus*
Brugmansia 225–6
aurea 22
sanguinea 226
Bugloss see *Echium pininiana*
Buphthalmum salicifolium 44
Bupleurum fruticosum 227
Bush cinquefoil see *Potentilla fruticosa*
Butterfly-flower see *Schizanthus pinnatus*

C

Caesalpinia pulcherrima 227
Calceolaria 45, 227, 326
biflora 45
Herbeohybrida 326
integrifolia 227
'Sunset Red' 45
Calendula officinalis 326
California lilac see *Ceanothus*
Californian poppy see *Eschscholzia californica*
Callistephus chinensis 327
Calluna vulgaris 228–9
'Allegro' 229
'Annemarie' 229
'Anthony Davis' 229
'Battle of Arnhem' 229
'Beoley Gold' 229
'County Wicklow' 228
'Dark Star' 229
'Darkness' 229
'Elsie Purnell' 229
'Finale' 229
'Firefly' 229
'Gold Haze' 229
'J.H. Hamilton' 229
'Jimmy Dyce' 229
'Joy Vanstone' 229
'Kinlochruel' 228
'Mair's Variety' 229
'Mullion' 229
'Orange Queen' 229
'Radnor' 229
'Red Star' 229
'Robert Chapman' 229
'Roland Haagen' 229
'Serlei Aurea' 229
'Silver Queen' 229
'Silver Rose' 229
'Sir John Charrington' 229
'Sister Anne' 229
'Spring Cream' 229
'Spring Torch' 228
'Sunset' 229
'Tib' 229
'Underwoodii' 229
'White Lawn' 229
'Wickwar Flame' 229
Campanula 46–9, 327

'Blue Chips' 46
carpatica 46
glomerata 'Superba' 47
lactiflora 48
latiloba 'Hidcote Amethyst' 48
medium 327
persicifolia alba 49
persicifolia 'Blue Bloomers' 49
Campsis grandiflora 229
Candytuft
evergreen see *Iberis sempervirens*
globe see *I. umbellulata*
Canna 50–2
'Assault' 50
'Champion' 50
'En Avant' 51
'Fireside' 51
'Hercule' 51
'Rosemond Coles' 52
'Taroudant' 52
Canterbury bells see *Campanula medium*
Cape colony nerine see *Nerine bowdenii*
Cape cowslip see *Lachenalia aloides lutea*
Cape-marigold, winter see *Dimorphotheca sinuata*
Cape primrose see *Streptocarpus saxorum*
Carpathian bellflower see *Campanula carpatica*
Caryopteris clandonensis 230
Catananche caerulea 52
Catharanthus roseus 53
Ceanothus 230–2
x *delileanus* 'Topaze' 232
'Italian Skies' 230
'Skylark' 231
thyrsiflorus repens 231
Celandine poppy see *Stylophorum diphyllum*
Celosia argentea 'Fairy Fountains' 53
Centaurea 54, 328
cyanus 'Diadem' 328
montana 54
Centranthus ruber 54
Cerinthe major 'Purpurascens' 329
Cestrum parqui 233
Chaerophyllum hirsutum 'Roseum' 54
Chamaecytisus purpureus 234
Chamomile, ox-eye see *Anthemis tinctoria*
Chaparral penstemon see *Penstemon heterophyllus*
Checkerbloom see *Sidalcea*
Chelone obliqua 55
Chilean cestrum see *Cestrum parqui*
Chilean gloryflower see *Eccremocarpus scaber*
China aster see *Callistephus chinensis*
Chinese forget-me-not see *Cynoglossum amabile*
Chinese hound's tongue see *Cynoglossum nervosum*
Chinese pink see *Dianthus chinensis*
Chocolate cosmos see *Cosmos atrosanguineus*
Choisya 234
'Aztec Pearl' 234
ternata 234
Chrysanthemum 329–30
carinatum 329
coronariium 330
Chrysanthemum, tricolor see *Chrysanthemum carinatum*
Chrysogonum virginianum 55
Cigarflower see *Cuphea ignea*
Cinquefoil see *Potentilla*
Cirsium 56
helenioides 56
rivulare 'Atropurpureum' 56
Cistus 235–8
x *dansereaui* 235
'Elma' 235
ladanifer 236
x *laxus* 'Snow White' 236
x *pulverulentus* 'Sunset' 236
x *purpureus* 237
x *skanbergii* 238
Clarkia amoena 330
Claytonia megarhiza 56
Clematis 57–61, 238
'Countess of Lovelace' 58
'Etoile Violette' 58
'Fireworks' 58
florida 'Sieboldii' 59
Group 1, 2, 3 57
'Minuet' 59
'Multi Blue' 59
'Nelly Moser' 60
'Sir Trevor Lawrence' 60
viticella 'Purpurea Plena Elegans' 60
'Vyvyan Pennell' 61
Cleome hassleriana 331
Clianthus puniceus 238
Clockvine see *Thumbergia alata*
Clustered bellflower see *Campanula glomerata*
Cobaea scandens 61
Colutea arborescens 239
Commelina tuberosa 61
Common betony see *Stachys officinalis*
Common borage see *Borago officinalis*
Common cosmos see *Cosmos bipinnatus*
Common daisy see *Bellis perennis*
Common evening primrose see *Oenothera biennis*
Common four-o'clock see *Mirabilis jalapa*
Common goats-rue see *Galega officinalis*
Common hydrangea see *Hydrangea macrophylla*
Common lantana see *Lantana camara*
Common nasturtium see *Tropaeolum majus*
Common portulaca see *Portulaca grandiflora*
Common snapdragon see *Antirrhinum majus*
Common stock see *Matthiola incana*
Common sundrops see *Oenothera fruticosa*
Common sunflower see *Helianthus annuus*
Common viper's bugloss see *Echium vulgare*
Common zinnia see *Zinnia elegans*
Coneflower see *Echinacea purpurea*
great see *Rudbeckia maxima*
showy see *R. fulgida*
sweet see *R. subtomentosa*
Consolida ajacis 331
Convolvulus 62–3, 239
althaeoides 62
cneorum 239
sabatius 62
tricolor 62
tricolor 'Royal Ensign' 63
Coreopsis 64–6
grandiflora 'Early Sunrise' 64
grandiflora 'Sunray' 64
rosea 'American Dream' 65
verticillata 'Moonbeam' 65
verticillata 'Zagreb' 66
Coreopsis
rose see *Coreopsis rosea*
threadleaf see *C. verticillata*
Cormous see *rocosmia*
Cornflower see *Centaurea cyanus*
Coronilla valentina 239
Corydalis 66
lutea 66
ochroleuca 66
Corydalis, yellow see *Corydalis lutea*
Cosmos 67, 332
atrosanguineus 67

INDEX

bipinnatus 332
Cosmos
  chocolate see *Cosmos atrosanguineus*
  common see *C. bipinnatus*
Cotton lavender see *Santolina rosmarinifolia*
Cowslip, Cape see *Lachenalia aloides lutea*
Cranesbill see *Geranium*
Creeping gypsophila see *Gypsophila repens*
Crepis 67–8
  incana 67
  rubra 68
Crocosmia 68–70
  x *crocosmiiflora* 68
  'Lucifer' 69
  masoniorum 69
  'Severn Sunrise' 70
  'Solfatare' 70
Cup-and-saucer vine see *Cobaea scandens*
Cupflower see *Nierembergia*
Cuphea 240
  cyanea 240
  ignea 240
Cupid's bower see *Achimenes hybrida*
Cupid's dart see *Catananche caerulea*
Cynoglossum 70, 333
  amabile 333
  nervosum 70
Cypella herbertii 71
Cyrtanthus brachyscyphus 71
Cytisus 241–4
  'Goldfinch' 241
  'La Coquette' 242
  'Lena' 242
  nigricans 244
  praecox albus 244

D

Daboecia 245
  cantabrica 'Silverwells' 245
  cantabrica 'William Buchanan' 245
Dactylorhiza elata 72
Dahlia 72–5
  'Bishop of Llandaff' 73
  'David Howard' 73
  Dwarf Border Mixed 74
  merckii 74
  'Moonfire' 75
Daisy
  African see *Arctotis* x *hybrida*
  common see *Bellis perennis*
  fleabane see *Erigeron aurantiacus*
  kingfisher see *Felicia bergeriana*
  Swan River see *Brachycome iberidifolia*
  Transvaal see *Gerbera jamesonii*
Daisy bush see *Olearia* 'Henry Travers'

Dandelion, pink see *Crepis incana*
Darley heath see *Erica* x *darleyensis*
Day flower see *Commelina tuberosa*
Day-lily see *Hemerocallis*
Deutzia 246
  'Mont Rose' 246
  pulchra 246
Dianthus 75–6
  barbatus 75
  chinensis 'Carpet' 76
  chinensis 'Strawberry Parfait' 76
Diascia 76–8
  'Eclat' 76
  'Elizabeth' 77
  integerrima 78
  rigescens 78
  'Ruby Field' 78
Dicentra 79
  'Pearl Drops' 79
  scandens 79
  'Spring Morning' 79
Digitalis 80–1
  grandiflora 80
  lanata 80
  lutea 81
  x *mertonensis* 81
Dimorphotheca sinuata 334
Dog fennel see *Anthemis punctata*
Doronicum 82
  orientale 'Finesse' 82
  pardalianches 82
Dorotheanthus bellidiformis 334
Drummond phlox see *Phlox drummondii*
Dwarf glorybind see *Convolvulus tricolor*
Dwarf Japanese anemone see *Anemone hupehensis*

E

Eccremocarpus scaber 82
Echinacea purpurea 83
Echium 83, 334
  pininiana 83
  vulgare 'Dwarf Bedder' 334
Edging lobelia see *Lobelia erinus*
Epilobium 83–4
  angustifolium 'Album' 83
  dodonaei 84
Eremurus 84–5
  himalaicus 84
  robustus 85
Erica 247–50
  carnea 'Winter Snow' 247
  cinerea 'C.D. Eason' 247
  cinerea 'Domino' 248
  cinerea 'Pink Ice' 248
  cinerea 'Stephen Davis' 249
  x *darleyensis* 'Darley Dale' 249
  x *darleyensis* 'George

Rendall' 250
  erigena 'Irish Dusk' 250
  gracilis 250
  vagans 247
Erigeron 85–8
  aurantiacus 85
  'Dignity' 86
  'Four Winds' 86
  glaucus 85, 86
  karvinskianus 85, 87
  'Quakeress' 87
  'Serenity' 88
Eriogonum umbellatum 251
Eriophyllum lanatum 88
Eriophyllum, wooly see *Eriophyllum lanatum*
Erodium 88–90
  'Fran's Choice' 88
  manescaui 89
  'Merstham Pink' 89
  pelargoniiflorum 90
Erysimum 90–2, 251
  'Bowles' Mauve' 251
  'Bredon' 90
  cheiri 91
  'Constant Cheer' 91
  linifolium 'Variegatum' 91
  'Orange Flame' 92
  'Sprite' 92
Escallonia 252
  'Apple Blossom' 252
  'Donard Radiance' 252
  'Edinensis' 252
  'Iveyi' 252
  'Langleyensis' 252
  'Peach Blossom' 252
  'Pride of Donard' 252
  rubra 'Crimson Spire' 252
Eschscholzia californica 335
Eucomis 92–3
  autumnalis 92
  bicolor 93
Euphorbia 93–4
  polychroma 93
  schillingii 94
  sikkimensis 94
Euryops pectinatus 253
Eustoma grandiflorum 335
Evans begonia see *Begonia grandis*
Evening primrose see *Oenothera fruticosa*
  common see *O. biennis*
  showy see *O. speciosa*
Evergreen candytuft see *Iberis sempervirens*
Everlasting pea see *Lathyrus latifolius*

F

False mallow see *Malvastrum lateritium*
Felicia bergeriana 335
Fennel, dog see *Anthemis punctata*
Feverfew see *Tanacetum*
Filipendula 95
  purpurea 95
  ulmaria 95
Fire lily see *Cyrtanthus

brachyscyphus*
Flannel-bush see *Fremontodendron californicum*
Flax see *Linum arboreum*
  perennial see *L. perenne*
Fleabane see *Erigeron*
Flower shapes 10–11
Flowering-maple see *Abutilon*
Flower-of-love see *Lynchis flos-jovis*
Forget-me-not, Chinese see *Cynoglossum amabile*
Formosa-honeysuckle see *Leycesteria formosa*
Four-o'clock, common see *Mirabilis jalapa*
Foxglove see *Digitalis*
Foxtail lily see *Eremurus himalaicus*
Fragaria 'Lipstick' 95
Fremontodendron californicum 253
French lavender see *Lavandula stoechas*
French marigold see *Tagetes patula*
Fringe-cup, Alaska see *Tellima grandiflora*
Fuchsia 254–8
  'Bicentennial' 254
  'Coralle' 254
  'Happy Wedding' 255
  'Love's Reward' 255
  'Lye's Unique' 255
  'Madame Cornelissen' 256
  'Phenomenal' 257
  'Reading Show' 257
  'Thalia' 258

G

Gaillardia x *grandiflora* 96–7, 336
  x *grandiflora* 'Burgunder' 96
  x *grandiflora* 'Kobold' 96
  x *grandiflora* 'Red Plume' 97
  pulchella 336
Gaillardia, painted see *Gaillardia pulchella*
Galega 98
  x *hartlandii* 'Alba' 98
  'Lady Wilson' 98
  officinalis 98
Galium odoratum 99
Garrya elliptica 258
Gaura lindheimeri 99
  'Siskyou Pink' 99
Gaura, white see *Gaura lindheimeri*
Garden petunia see *Petunia* x *hybrida*
Gazania 100
  'Christopher Lloyd' 100
  'Daybreak' 100
Genista 258–9
  hispanica 258
  lydia 259
Gentian salvia see

INDEX

Salvia patens
Geranium 101–5
  'Ann Folkard' 101
  himalayense 'Plenum' 102
  maderense 102
  x *oxonianum* 'Rose Clair' 103
  psilostemon 103
  pyrenaicum 'Bill Wallis' 103
  riversleianum 'Mavis Simpson' 104
  riversleianum 'Russell Pritchard' 104
  sylvaticum 'Album' 105
  wallichianum 'Buxton's variety' 105
Geranium see *Erodium pelargoniiflorum*
Gerbera jamesonii 'Pandora' 43
Geum 106–7
  'Borisii' 106
  'Lady Stratheden' 106
  'Mrs J. Bradshaw' 106
  'Tangerine' 107
Giant desert candle see *Eremurus robustus*
Gillenia trifoliata 107
Glaucium grandiflorum 107
Globe candytuft see *Iberis umbellulata*
Gloriosa superba 108
Glorybind, dwarf see *Convolvulus tricolor*
Glossy abelia see *Abelia* x *grandiflora*
Gloxinia see *Sinningia speciosa*
Goats-rue see *Galega* x *hartlandii*
  common see *G. officinalis*
Golden marguerite see *Anthemis tinctoria*
Golden monkey-flower see *Mimulus luteus*
Goldenstar see *Chrysogonum virginianum*
Gorse, Spanish see *Genista hispanica*
Great coneflower see *Rudbeckia maxima*
Grevillea 259
  'Canberra Gem' 259
  rosmarinifolia 259
Grindelia chiloensis 260
Groundsel, silver see *Senecio cineraria*
Gum rock rose see *Cistus ladanifer*
Gypsophila 108
  paniculata 'Rosenschleier' 108
  repens 'Dorothy Teacher' 108

H

x *Halimiocistus sahucii* 260
Halimium ocymoides 260
Haplopappus glutinosus 109
hardiness zones 12–13
Harebell phacelia see *Phacelia campanularia*
Hawk's beard see *Crepis*
Heartleaf maskflower see *Alonsoa warzcewiczii*
Heath see *Erica*
  Darley see *E.* x *darleyensis*
  Irish see *Daboecia cantabrica*
  spring see *E. carnea*
Heather see *Calluna vulgaris*
Hebe 261–3
  albicans 261
  x *franciscana* 'Blue Gem' 261
  'Great Orme' 262
  hulkeana 262
  ochracea 'James Stirling' 262
  'Youngii' 263
Hedysarum coronarium 110
Helenium 111
  'Pumilum magnificum' 111
  'Rubinzwerg' 111
Helianthemum 264–5
  'Ben Hope' 264
  'Coppernob' 264
  'Fireball' 265
  'Raspberry Ripple' 265
Helianthus 111–12, 336
  annuus 336
  decapetalus 111
  'Lemon Queen' 112
  multiflorus 'Loddon Gold' 112
  salicifolius 112
Heliopsis 113–14
  helianthoides 'Bressingham Dublon' 113
  helianthoides 'Mars' 114
Heliotrope see *Heliotropium arborescens*
Heliotropium arborescens 'Marine' 266
Hemerocallis 114–17
  'Chicago Royal Robe' 114
  'Corky' 115
  'Frans Hals' 115
  'Green Flutter' 116
  'Silver Veil' 116
  'Stafford' 117
  'Tutunkhamun' 117
Herb tree-mallow see *Lavatera*
Heronbill see *Erodium pelargoniiflorum*
Heuchera 'Red Spangles' 117
x *Heucherella alba* 'Bridget Bloom' 118
Hibiscus 266–8
  rosa-sinensis hybridus 266, 267
  syriacus 'Blue Bird' 267
  syriacus 'Hamabo' 268
Hollyhock see *Alcea rosea*
Honeysuckle, Late Dutch see *Lonicera periclymenum*
Honeywort see *Cerinthe major*
Horned poppy see *Glaucium grandiflorum*
Hosta sieboldii 118
Hot water plant see *Achimenes hybrida*
Houttuynia cordata 'Flore Pleno' 119
Hydrangea 269–73
  macrophylla 'Blaumeise' 269
  macrophylla 'Lady Nobuko' 270
  macrophylla 'Leuchtfeuer' 270
  paniculata 272
  'Preziosa' 272
  quercifolia 273
  'Sabrina' 271
  'Sandra' 271
  serrata 'Bluebird' 273
Hydrangea common see *Hydrangea macrophylla*
  oak-leaved see *H. quercifolia*
  panicle see *H. paniculata*
Hylomecon japonica 119
Hypericum 120, 274–5
  calycinum 274
  cerastioides 120
  'Hidcote' 274
  x *inodorum* 'Elstead' 275
  olympicum 'Citrinum' 275
  'Rowallane' 275
Hyssop see *Hyssopus*
Hyssopus officinalis 120

I

Iberis 276, 337
  sempervirens 276
  umbellulata 'Fantasia' 337
Icelandic poppy see *Papaver croceum*
Impatiens 120–2, 338
  balfourii 338
  glandulifera 338
  'New Guinea' 121
  niamniamensis 'Congo Cockatoo' 121
  walleriana 'Accent' 122
Ipomoea 122, 338
  lobata 122
  purpurea 338
Iris japonica 122
Irish heath see *Daboecia cantabrica*
Ixora coccinea 277

J

Japanese anemone see *Anemone* x *hybrida*
  dwarf see *Anemone hupehensis*
Japanese iris see *Iris japonica*
Japanese meadowsweet see *Filipendula purpurea*
Japanese spirea see *Spiraea japonica*
Justicia carnea 277

K

Kaffir lily see *Schizostylis coccinea*
Kerria see *Kerria japonica*
Kerria japonica 'Pleniflora' 278
Kingfisher-daisy see *Felicia bergeriana*
Kirengeshoma palmata 123
Knautia macedonica 123
Kolkwitzia amabilis 'Pink Cloud' 278

L

Lachenalia aloides lutea 124
Lamb's ears see *Stachys byzantina*
Lantana camara 'Radiation' 279
Lantana, common see *Lantana camara*
Larkspur see *Consolida ajacis*
Late Dutch honeysuckle see *Lonicera periclymenum*
Lathyrus 124, 339
  latifolius 124
  odoratus 'Winston Churchill' 339
  vernus 124
Laurentia axillaris 'Blue Stars' 125
Laurestinus viburnum see *Viburnum tinus*
Lavandula stoechas 279
Lavatera 125, 280–1, 340
  'Barnsley' 280
  'Bredon Springs' 280
  'Burgundy Wine' 281
  'Candy Floss' 281
  thuringiaca 'Ice Cool' 125
  trimestris 340
Lavender, French see *Lavandula stoechas*
leaf shapes 10–11
Leopard's bane see *Doronicum*
Leptospermum 282
  scoparium 'Nicholsii Nanum' 282
  scoparium 'Red Damask' 282
Leucanthemum 126–7
  x *superbum* 'Beaute Nivelloise' 126
  x *superbum* 'Phyllis

INDEX

Smith' 126
x *superbum*
  'Sonnenschein' 126
x *superbum* 'Wirral
  Supreme' 127
Lewisia cotyledon 127
Leycesteria formosa
  283
Libertia formosa 127
Lilac, California see
  Ceanothus
Lily
  arum see *Zantedeschia aethiopica*
  fire see *Cyrtanthus brachyscyphus*
  foxtail see *Eremurus himalaicus*
  Kaffir see *Schizostylis coccinea*
  pineapple see *Eucomis*
Lilyturf see *Liriope muscari*
Limnanthes douglasii 340
Limonium sinuatum 128
Linaria 128
  purpurea 128
  purpurea 'Winifred's Delight' 128
Lindley mentzelia see
  Mentzelia lindleyi
Ling see *Calluna vulgaris* 'Tib'
Linum 129–30, 283
  arboreum 283
  Gemmell's hybrid 129
  narbonense 130
  perenne 130
Liriope muscari 130
Lobelia 131–2
  erinus 131
  erinus pendula 131
  x *geradii*
    'Vedrariensis' 132
  'Kompliment
    Scharlach' 132
  tupa 132
Lobelia, edging see
  Lobelia erinus
Lobster claw see
  Clianthus puniceus
Lobularia maritima
  'Easter Bonnet' 133
Lonicera 283–4
  x *brownii* 'Dropmore Scarlet' 283
  periclymenum
    'Serotina' 284
Loosestrife pink see
  Lythrum salicaria
  purple see *L. salicaria*
  yellow see *Lysimachia punctata*
Lotus corniculatus 133
Love-in-a-mist see
  Nigella damascena
Lupinus texensis 341
Lychnis 134–5
  coronaria 134
  coronaria 'Oculata' 135
  flos-jovis 'Hort's Variety' 135
Lysimachia punctata 136
Lythrum 136

salicaria 136
salicaria 'Robert' 136

M

Mallow see *Lavatera thuringiaca*
  false see *Malvastrum lateritium*
  musk see *Malva moschata*
  prairie see *Sidalcea* 'Party Girl'
Malva 137–8
  moschata 137
  sylvestris 'Primley Blue' 137
  sylvestris 'Zebrina' 138
Malvastrum lateritium 138
Maple, flowering- see
  Abutilon
Marguerite see *Argyranthemum frutescens*
  golden see *Anthemis tinctoria*
Marigold see *Tagetes*
  African see *T. erecta*
  Afro-French see *T. patula*
  French see *T. patula*
  pot see *Calendula officinalis*
  winter Cape see *Dimorphotheca sinuata*
Marsh orchid see
  Dactylorhiza elata
Marshmallow see
  Althaea officinalis
Maskflower, heartleaf
  see *Alonsoa warzcewiczii*
Masterwort see
  Astrantia
Matilija-poppy see
  Romneya coulteri
Matthiola 138–9
  incana 'Brompton' 138
  incana 'Ten Week' 139
Meadow-foam see
  Limnanthes douglasii
Meadowsweet,
  Japanese see *Filipendula purpurea*
Meconopsis 139–40
  cambrica 139
  cambrica 'Flore Pleno' 140
Mentzelia lindleyi 341
Mertensia simplicissima 140
Mexican hat see
  Ratibida pinnata
Mexican-orange see
  Choisya ternata
Mexican prickle-poppy
  see *Argemone mexicana*
Microseris ringens 141
Milkweed see *Asclepias tuberosa*
  swamp see *A. incarnata*
Milky bellflower see
  Campanula lactiflora
Mimulus 141–3, 284

'Andean Nymph' 141
aurantiacus 284
cardinalis 142
lewisii 142
luteus 142
moschatus 143
puniceus 284
Mirabilis jalapa 143
Mock orange see
  Philadelphus
Monarda 144–5
  'Cambridge Scarlet' 144
  'Croftway Pink' 144
  didyma 145
  'Loddon Crown' 145
Monkey-flower see
  Mimulus
  golden see *M. luteus*
Montbretia see
  Crocosmia
Mullein see *Verbascum*
Musk mallow see
  Malva moschata
Myrtle see *Vinca minor*

N

Narbonne flax see
  Linum narbonense
Nasturtium see
  Tropaeolum
  common see *T. majus*
  vermilion see *T. speciosum*
  wreath see *T. polyphyllum*
Nemesia 146, 342–3
  denticulata 146
  strumosa 'Carnival' 342
  strumosa 'K.L.M.' 342
  strumosa 'National Ensign' 343
Nemesia, pouch see
  Nemesia strumosa
Nepal cinquefoil see
  Potentilla nepalensis
Nepeta 146–8
  longipes 146
  'Six Hills Giant' 147
  subsessilis 147
  tuberosa 148
Nerine bowdenii 148
Nerium oleander 285
Nicandra physaloides
  'Violacea' 343
Nicotiana 148–50, 286, 343–4
  'Domino Lime Green' 344
  glauca 286
  langsdorfii 343
  'Roulette' 150
  x *sanderae* 'Havana Appleblossom' 149
  sylvestria 150
Nierembergia 150–1
  repens 150
  scoparia 'Mont Blanc' 151
Nigella 344–5
  damascena 'Miss Jekyll' 344
  hispanica 'Curiosity' 345
Nightshade, Paraguay
  see *Solanum rantonnetti*

Nolana paradoxa 'Blue Bird' 151
Notch-leaf sea-lavender
  see *Limonium sinuatum*

O

Oak-leaved hydrangea
  see *Hydrangea quercifolia*
Oenothera 152–3, 346
  biennis 346
  fructicosa 152
  glazioviana 152
  macrocarpa 153
  speciosa 'Siskyou' 153
Old man's beard see
  Clematis
Oleander see *Nerium oleander*
Olearia 'Henry Travers' 286
Omphalodes cappadocica 'Starry Eyes' 153
Onopordum acanthium 347
Orange streptosolen
  see *Streptosolen jamesonii*
Orange Welsh-poppy
  see *Meconopsis cambrica* var. *aurantiaca*
Orchid, marsh see
  Dactylorhiza elata
Origanum 154
  'Buckland' 154
  laevigatum
    'Herrenhausen' 154
Osteospermum 154, 286–8
  'Buttermilk' 287
  caulescens 287
  jucundum 154
  'Nairobi Purple' 288
  'Whirligig' 288
  'White Pim' see *O. caulescens*
Ox eye see *Heliopsis*
  chamomile see
  Anthemis tinctoria
Ox-eye see *Anthemis tinctoria*
  willowleaf see
  Buphthalmum salicifolium

P

Pachystachys lutea 288
Painted gaillardia see
  Gaillardia pulchella
Painted-tongue see
  Salpiglossis sinuata
Pandorea jasminoides 'Rosea' 155
Panicle hydrangea see
  Hydrangea paniculata
Papaver 155–6, 347
  commutatum 347
  croceum 155
  'Fireball' 155
  dubium 347
  spicatum 156
Paraguay nightshade
  see *Solanum rantonnetti*

INDEX

Passiflora 156
　caerulea 156
　quadrangularis 156
Passion-flower see
　Passiflora
Peach-leaved bellflower
　see Campanula
　persicifolia
Pelargonium 157–9
　endlicherianum 157
　peltatum 158
　regale hybridus 158
　'Splendide' 158
　tricolor 158
　zonale hybridus 159
Penstemon 160–2, 289
　'Flamingo' 160
　heterophyllus 'Blue
　　Springs' 161
　isophyllus 289
　'Osprey' 161
　'Rosy Blush' 161
　'Sour Grapes' 162
Pentas lanceolata 289
Perennial flax see
　Linum perenne
Perennials 14–213
Pericallis lanata 'Kew'
　290
Periwinkle see Vinca
　minor
　big see V. major
Perovskia 'Blue Spire'
　291
Persicaria 162–3
　affinis 'Superba' 162
　amplexicaulis
　　'Firetail' 162
　bistorta 'Superba' 163
Petrea volubilis 163
Petunia 164–5
　x hybrida 'Prism
　　Sunshine' 164
　x hybrida 'Summer
　　Morn' 164
　x hybrida 'Surfinia'
　　164
　x hybrida 'Ultra' 165
Petunia, garden see P. x
　hybrida
Phacelia campanularia
　348
Philadelphus 291–2
　'Belle Etoile' 291
　'Voie Lactee' 292
Phlomis fruticosa 292
Phlox 165, 348–9
　'Chattahoochee' 165
　drummondii 'Beauty'
　　348
　drummondii 'Dolly'
　　349
Phlox
　annual see Phlox
　　drummondii
　Drummond see P.
　　drummondii
Phuopsis stylosa 166
Phygelius 293–4
　aequalis 293
　aequalis 'Sensation'
　　293
　aequalis 'Yellow
　　Trumpet' 294
　x rectus 294
　x rectus 'Moonraker'
　　294
Pieris formosa 295

Pineapple flower/lily
　see Eucomis
Pink, Chinese see
　Dianthus chinensis
Pink dandelion see
　Crepis incana
Pink loosestrife see
　Lythrum salicaria
Plumbago auriculata
　295
Plumeria 296
　alba 296
　rubra 296
Podranea ricasoliana
　166
Polygala myrtifolia 297
Poppy see Papaver
　Californian see Esch-
　　scholzia californica
　celandine see Stylo-
　　phorum diphyllum
　horned see Glaucium
　　grandiflorum
　Icelandic see P.
　　croceum
　Matilija see Romneya
　　coulteri
　Welsh see Meconopsis
　　cambrica
Portulaca, common see
　Portulaca
　grandiflora
Portulaca grandiflora
　349
Pot marigold see Cal-
　endula officinalis
Potato vine see
　Solanum laxum
Potentilla 167–9, 297–8
　aurea 167
　'Flamenco' 167
　fruticosa
　　'Abbotswood' 297
　fruticosa 'Goldfinger'
　　297
　fruticosa 'Pretty Polly'
　　298
　'Gloire de Nancy' 168
　nepalensis 'Miss
　　Willmott' 168
　recta 'Alba' 168
　'William Rollison' 169
Pouch nemesia see
　Nemesia strumosa
Prairie-gentian, Russell
　see Eustoma
　grandiflorum
Prairie mallow see
　Sidalcea 'Party Girl'
Pratia pedunculata 169
Prickle-poppy, Mexican
　see Argemone
　mexicana
Primrose, Cape see
　Streptocarpus
　saxorum
Primula obconica 170
Pulmonaria 170–1
　rubra 'Bowles Red'
　　170
　saccharata 171
Punica granatum flore
　plena 298
Purple broom see
　Chamaecytisus
　purpureus
Purple loosestrife see
　Lythrum salicaria

Purple toadflax see
　Linaria purpurea
Pyrenees heronbill see
　Erodium manescaui

Q

Queen of the meadow
　see Filipendula
　ulmaria

R

Ratibida pinnata 171
Red valerian see
　Centranthus ruber
Rehmannia elata 172
Rhodanthemum
　hosmariense 298
Rhodochiton
　atrosanguineus 172
Rhodohypoxis baurii
　173
Rock rose, gum see
　Cistus ladanifer
Romneya coulteri 299
Rosa 300–15
　'Ballerina' 300
　banksiae 'Lutea' 301
　'Blue Moon' 301
　'Charles de Mills' 302
　'Compassion' 303
　'De Rescht' 303
　'Double Delight' 303
　'Elina' 304
　'Ena Harkness' 304
　'Flower Carpet' 305
　'Fragrant Cloud' 306
　'Fred Loads' 306
　'Fulton Mackay' 306
　'Gertrude Jekyll' 307
　'Golden Wedding' 307
　'Gordon's College' 308
　'Happy Times' 309
　'Joseph's Coat' 309
　'Lady MacRobert'
　　310
　'Lavender Lassie' 310
　'Mme. Isaac Pereire'
　　311
　'National Trust' 311
　'Oranges and Lemons'
　　311
　'Paul Ricault' 312
　'Pink Grootendorst'
　　313
　'Queen Mother' 313
　'Samaritan' 314
　'Warm Wishes' 314
　'William Quarrier' 315
Roscoea purpurea 173
Rose see Rosa
Rose campion see
　Lychnis coronaria
Rose coreopsis see
　Coreopsis rosea
Rose of Sharon see
　Hypericum
　calycinum
Rudbeckia 173–6
　fulgida 174
　'Herbstonne' 174
　hirta 173
　hirta 'Rustic Dwarf'
　　174
　laciniata 'Goldquelle'
　　175
　maxima 176
　subtomentosa 176
Russell prairie-gentian

　see Eustoma
　grandiflorum

S

Sage see Salvia
　Bethlehem see Pul-
　　monaria saccharata
　scarlet see S. splendens
St John's wort see
　Hypericum
　cerastioides
Saintpaulia ionantha
　176
Salpiglossis sinuata 350
Salvia 177–83
　africana-lutea 177
　coccinea 178
　farinacea 'Snowball'
　　178
　farinacea 'Victoria' 178
　involucrata 'Berhellii'
　　179
　microphyla 180
　nemorosa
　　'Pusztaflamme' 180
　patens 181
　pratensis 181
　sclarea 181
　splendens 'Scarlet
　　King' 182
　splendens 'Sizzler' 182
　uliginosa 183
Salvia, gentian see
　Salvia patens
Sandersonia aurantiaca
　183
Santolina
　rosmarinifolia 316
Sanvitalia procumbens
　350
Sanvitalia, trailing see
　Sanvitalia
　procumbens
Scabiosa 184
　caucasica 'Clive
　　Greaves' 184
　columbaria 184
　'Irish Perpetual-
　　flowering' 184
Scabious see Scabiosa
　small see S. columbaria
Scarlet sage see Salvia
　splendens
Schizanthus pinnatus
　351
Schizostylis 185
　coccinea 185
　coccinea 'Sunrise' 185
Sea-lavender, notch-leaf
　see Limonium
　sinuatum
Senecio 186–7, 316, 351
　cineraria 316
　doronicum 186
　elegans 351
　smithii 186
　vira-vira 316
Senna didymobotrya
　317
Serratula seoanei 187
Showy coneflower see
　Rudbeckia fulgida
Showy evening
　primrose see
　Oenothera speciosa
Shrub althea see
　Hibiscus syriacus
Shrubby hare's ear see

367

INDEX

Bupleurum fruticosum
Shrubs 214–321
Sidalcea 187–9
  'Croftway Red' 187
  'Party Girl' 188
  'William Smith' 189
Silk tassel bush see *Garrya elliptica*
Silkweed see *Asclepias tuberosa*
Silver groundsel see *Senecio cineraria*
Silybum marianum 351
Sinningia speciosa 189
Slipperflower see *Calceolaria biflora; C. integrifolia*
Slipperwort see *Calceolaria biflora; C. integrifolia*
Small scabious see *Scabiosa columbaria*
Snapdragon see *Antirrhinum braunblanquetti*
  common see *A. majus*
Snapweed, Sultan see *Impatiens walleriana*
Solanum 189–90, 318
  crispum 'Glasnevin' 190
  laciniatum 318
  laxum 'Album' 190
  rantonnetti 318
Spanish gorse see *Genista hispanica*
Speedwell, wooly see *Veronica spicata*
Sphaeralcea 191
  fendleri 191
  munroana 191
Spiderflower see *Cleome hassleriana*
Spiraea 318–19
  japonica 'Goldflame' 318
  japonica 'Shirobana' 319
Spirea, Japanese see *Spiraea japonica*
Spring beauty see *Claytonia megarhiza*
Spring heath see *Erica carnea*
Spring vetchling see *Lathyrus vernus*
Spurge see *Euphorbia*
Stachys 192
  byzantina 192
  macarantha 'Superba' 192
  officinalis 'Rosea Superba' 192
Stock, common see *Matthiola incana*
Stokes' aster see *Stokesia laevis*
Stokesia laevis 193
Strawberry see *Fragaria*
Streptocarpus 194
  'Crystal Ice' 194
  hybridus 194
  saxorum 194
Streptosolen jamesonii 319
Stylophorum
  diphyllum 195
Sulla sweetvetch see *Hedysarum coronarium*
Sulphur flower see *Eriogonum umbellatum*
Sultan snapweed see *Impatiens walleriana*
Sundrops, common see *Oenothera fruticosa*
Sunflower see *Helianthus*
  common see *H. annuus*
  thinleaf see *H. decapetalus*
  willow-leaved see *H. salicifolius*
Sunplant see *Portulaca grandiflora*
Sunrose see *Helianthemum*
Sutherland begonia see *Begonia sutherlandii*
Swamp milkweed see *Asclepias incarnata*
Swan River daisy see *Brachycome iberidifolia*
Sweet coneflower see *Rudbeckia subtomentosa*
Sweet pea see *Lathyrus odoratus*
Sweet William see *Dianthus barbatus*
Symphytum x *uplandicum* 195

T

Tagetes 352–4
  erecta 'Antigua' series 352
  patula 'Beaux' series 353
  patula 'Boy' series 353
  patula 'Orange Boy' 353
  tenuifolia 'Lemon Gem' 354
  tenuifolia 'Tangerine Gem' 354
Tanacetum
  parthenium 'Aureum' 196
  parthenium 'Rowallane' 196
Tea-of-heaven see *Hydrangea serrata*
Tellima grandiflora 197
Thalicrum kiusianum 198
Thinleaf sunflower see *Helianthus decapetalus*
Threadleaf coreopsis see *Coreopsis verticillata*
Thunbergia alata 198
Tiarella wherryi 198
Tickseed see *Coreopsis grandiflora*
Toadflax, purple see *Linaria purpurea*
Tobacco, tree see *Nicotiana glauca*
Torenia 355
  fournieri 'Clown' series 355
  fournieri 'Panda' series 355
Tradescantia 199
  x *andersoniana* 'Iris' 199
  x *andersoniana* 'Osprey' 199
Trailing sanvitalia see *Sanvitalia procumbens*
Transvaal daisy see *Gerbera jamesonii*
Travellers' joy see *Clematis*
Treasure flower see *Gazania*
Tree tobacco see *Nicotiana glauca*
Tricolor chrysanthemum see *Chrysanthemum carinatum*
Tropaeolum 200–1, 356–7
  'Alaska' 356
  'Empress of India' 356
  majus 357
  polyphyllum 200
  speciosum 201
  tuberosum 'Ken Aslet' 201
Trumpetvine see *Campsis grandiflora*
Tuberous begonia see *Begonia* x *tuberhybrida*
Tulbaghia 201–2
  cepacea 201
  violacea 202
Turtlehead see *Chelone obliqua*
Tweedia caerulea 319
Twinspur see *Diascia*

V

Valerian, red see *Centranthus ruber*
Verbascum 202–4, 320
  chaixii 'Album' 202
  dumulosum 203
  'Helen Johnson' 203
  'Jackie' 203
  'Letitia' 320
  phoenicum 204
Verbena 204–8
  bonariensis 204
  hastata 205
  x *hybrida* 'Imagination' 205
  x *hybrida* 'Loveliness' 206
  x *hybrida* 'Peaches and Cream' 206
  x *hybrida* 'Quartz Burgundy' 206
  x *hybrida* 'Red Cascade' 207
  x *hybrida* 'Sissinghurst' 208
Vermilion nasturtium see *Tropaeolum speciosum*
Veronica 208–9
  spicata 208
  spicata 'Rotfuchs' 209
Viburnum tinus 320
Vinca 320–1
  major 'Variegata' 320
  minor 'Alba Variegata' 321
Vine, potato see *Solanum laxum*
Viola 209–12
  'Columbine' 209
  cornuta 'Alba' 210
  'Etain' 211
  'Jackanapes' 212
Viper's bugloss, common see *Echium vulgare*
Virgin bower see *Clematis texensis hybridus*

W

Wallflower see *Erysimum*
Warminster broom see *Cytisus praecox albus*
Wax begonia see *Begonia semperflorens*
Welsh-poppy see *Meconopsis cambrica*
White cupflower see *Nierembergia repens*
White gaura see *Gaura lindheimeri*
White Kaffir lily see *Schizostylis coccinea*
Widow's tears see *Commelina tuberosa*
Willow herb see *Epilobium*
Willowleaf-oxeye see *Buphthalmum salicifolium*
Willow-leaved sunflower see *Helianthus salicifolius*
Winter Cape-marigold see *Dimorphotheca sinuata*
Wooly betony see *Stachys byzantina*
Wooly eriophyllum see *Eriophyllum lanatum*
Wooly speedwell see *Veronica spicata*
Wreath nasturtium see *Tropaeolum polyphyllum*

Y

Yarrow see *Achillea*
Yellow corydalis see *Corydalis lutea*
Yellow loosestrife see *Lysimachia punctata*

Z

Zatedeschia aethiopica 213
Zauschneria californica 213
Zephyranthes candida 213
Zinnia, common see *Zinnia elegans*
Zinnia elegans 35